Bernard Shaw

LAST PLAYS

'IN GOOD KING CHARLES'S GOLDEN DAYS'
BUOYANT BILLIONS
FARFETCHED FABLES
SHAKES VERSUS SHAV
WHY SHE WOULD NOT

DEFINITIVE TEXT
under the editorial
supervision of
DAN H. LAURENCE

PENGUIN BOOKS

Penguin Books Ltd, Harmondsworth, Middlesex, England
Viking Penguin Inc., 40 West 23rd Street, New York, New York 10010, U.S.A.
Penguin Books Australia Ltd, Ringwood, Victoria, Australia
Penguin Books Canada Ltd, 2801 John Street, Markham, Ontario, Canada L3R 1B4
Penguin Books (N.Z.) Ltd, 182–190 Wairau Road, Auckland 10, New Zealand

'In Good King Charles's Golden Days' first published 1939;
first produced in Malvern 1939
Buoyant Billions first published in a German translation 1948;
first published in English 1949; first produced in German in Zurich 1948
Farfetched Fables first published 1951;
first produced in London 1950
Shakes versus Shav first published 1949;
first produced in Malvern 1949
Why She Would Not first published 1956;
first produced in New York 1957
First published in one volume as Last Plays in Penguin Books 1985

Made and printed in Great Britain by
Richard Clay (The Chaucer Press) Ltd, Bungay, Suffolk
Set in Monophoto Photina

In Great Britain, all business connected with Bernard Shaw's plays
is in the hands of THE SOCIETY OF AUTHORS, 84 Drayton Gardens,
London SW10 9SD (Telephone: 01–373 6642), to which all inquiries
and applications for licences should be addressed and fees paid.
Dates and places of contemplated performances must be precisely
stated in all applications.

In the United States of America and Canada, applications for
permission to give stock and amateur performances of Bernard Shaw's
plays should be made to Samuel French, Inc., 25 West 45th Street,
New York, New York 10036. In all other cases, whether for stage,
radio, or television, application should be made to the Society of
Authors, 84 Drayton Gardens, London SW10 9SD, England.

Contents

'In Good King Charles's Golden Days':

A True History
That Never Happened

with

Preface

Preface

In providing a historical play for the Malvern Festival of 1939 I departed from the established practice sufficiently to require a word of explanation. The 'histories' of Shakespear are chronicles dramatized; and my own chief historical plays, Caesar and Cleopatra and St Joan, are fully documented chronicle plays of this type. Familiarity with them would get a student safely through examination papers on their periods.

Stage Chapters of History

A much commoner theatrical product is the historical romance, mostly fiction with historical names attached to the stock characters of the stage. Many of these plays have introduced their heroines as Nell Gwynn, and Nell's principal lover as Charles II. As Nell was a lively and lovable actress, it was easy to reproduce her by casting a lively and lovable actress for the part; but the stage Charles, though his costume and wig were always unmistakeable, never had any other resemblance to the real Charles, nor to anything else on earth except what he was not: a stage walking gentleman with nothing particular to say for himself.

Now the facts of Charles's reign have been chronicled so often by modern historians of all parties, from the Whig Macaulay to the Jacobite Hilaire Belloc, that there is no novelty left for the chronicler to put on the stage. As to the romance, it is intolerably stale: the spectacle of a Charles sitting with his arm round Nell Gwynn's waist, or with Moll Davis seated on his knee, with the voluptuous termagant Castlemaine raging in the background, has no interest for me, if it ever had for any grown-up person.

But when we turn from the sordid facts of Charles's reign, and from his Solomonic polygamy, to what might have happened to him but did not, the situation becomes interesting and fresh. For instance, Charles might have met that human prodigy Isaac Newton. And Newton might have met that prodigy of another sort, George Fox, the founder of the morally mighty Society of Friends, vulgarly called the Quakers. Better again, all three might have met. Now anyone who considers a hundred and fiftieth edition of Sweet Nell of Old Drury more attractive than Isaac Newton had better avoid my plays: they are not meant for such. And anyone who is more interested in Lady Castlemaine's hips than in Fox's foundation of the great Cult of Friendship should keep away from theatres and frequent worse places. Still, though the interest of my play lies mainly in the clash of Charles, George, and Isaac, there is some fun in the clash between all three and Nelly, Castlemaine, and the Frenchwoman Louise de Kéroualle, whom we called Madame Carwell. So I bring the three on the stage to relieve the intellectual tension.

Newton's Rectilinear Universe

There is another clash which is important and topical in view of the hold that professional science has gained on popular credulity since the middle of the nineteenth century. I mean the eternal clash between the artist and the physicist. I have therefore invented a collision between Newton and a personage whom I should like to have called Hogarth; for it was Hogarth who said 'the line of beauty is a curve', and Newton whose first dogma it was that the universe is in principle rectilinear. He called straight lines right lines; and they were still so called in my school Euclid eighty years ago. But Hogarth could not by any magic be fitted into the year 1680, my chosen date; so I had to fall back on Godfrey Kneller. Kneller had not Hogarth's brains; but I have had to endow him with them to provide Newton with a victorious antagonist. In point of date Kneller just fitted in.

But I must make an exception to this general invitation. If by any chance you are a great mathematician or astronomer you had perhaps better stay away. I have made Newton aware of something wrong with the perihelion of Mercury. Not since Shakespear made Hector of Troy quote Aristotle has the stage perpetrated a more staggering anachronism. But I find the perihelion of Mercury so irresistible as a laugh catcher (like Weston-super-Mare) that I cannot bring myself to sacrifice it. I am actually prepared to defend it as a possibility. Newton was not only a lightning calculator with a monstrous memory: he was also a most ingenious and dexterous maker of apparatus. He made his own telescope; and when he wanted to look at Mercury without being dazzled by the sun he was quite clever enough to produce an artificial eclipse by putting an obturator into the telescope, though nobody else hit on that simple device until long after. My ignorance in these matters is stupendous; but I refuse to believe that Newton's system did not enable him to locate Mercury theoretically at its nearest point to the sun, and then to find out with his telescope that it was apparently somewhere else.

For the flash of prevision in which Newton foresees Einstein's curvilinear universe I make no apology. Newton's first law of motion is pure dogma. So is Hogarth's first law of design. The modern astronomers have proved, so far, that Hogarth was right and Newton wrong. But as the march of science during my long lifetime has played skittles with all the theories in turn I dare not say how the case will stand by the time this play of mine reaches its thousandth performance (if it ever does). Meanwhile let me admit that Newton in my play is a stage astronomer: that is, an astronomer not for an age but for all time. Newton as a man was the queerest of the prodigies; and I have chapter and verse for all his contradictions.

Charles's Golden Days

As to Charles, he adolesced as a princely cosmopolitan vagabond of curiously mixed blood, and ended as the first king of England whose kingship was purely symbolic, and who was clever enough to know that the work of the regicides could not be undone, and that he had to reign by his wits and not by the little real power they had left him. Unfortunately the vulgarity of his reputation as a Solomonic polygamist has not only obscured his political ability, but eclipsed the fact that he was the best of husbands. Catherine of Braganza, his wife, has been made to appear a nobody, and Castlemaine, his concubine, almost a great historical figure. When you have seen my play you will not make that mistake, and may therefore congratulate yourself on assisting at an act of historical justice.

Let us therefore drop the popular subject of The Merry Monarch and his women. On the stage, and indeed off it, he is represented as having practically no other interest, and being a disgracefully unfaithful husband. It is inferred that he was politically influenced by women, especially by Louise de Kéroualle, who, as an agent of Louis XIV, kept him under the thumb of that Sun of Monarchs as his secret pensioner. The truth is that Charles, like most English kings, was continually in money difficulties because the English people, having an insuperable dislike of being governed at all, would not pay taxes enough to finance an efficient civil and military public service. In Charles's day especially they objected furiously to a standing army, having had enough of that under Cromwell, and grudged their king even the lifeguards which were the nucleus of such an army. Charles, to carry on, had to raise the necessary money somewhere; and as he could not get it from the Protestant people of England he was clever enough to get it from the Catholic king of France; for, though head of the Church of England, he privately ranked Protestants as an upstart vulgar middle-class sect, and the Catholic Church as the authentic original Church of Christ, and the only possible faith for a gentleman. In achieving this he made use of Louise: there is no evidence that she made use of him. To the Whig historians the transaction makes Charles a Quisling in the service of Louis and a traitor to his own country. This is mere Protestant scurrility: the only shady part of it is that Charles, spending the money in the service of England, gave *le Roi Soleil* no value for it.

The other mistresses could make him do nothing that his good nature did not dispose him to do, whether it was building Greenwich Hospital or making dukes of his bastards. As a husband he took his marriage very seriously, and his sex adventures as calls of nature on an entirely different footing. In this he was in the line of evolution, which leads to an increasing separation of the unique and intensely personal and permanent marriage relation from the carnal intercourse described in Shakespear's sonnet. This, being a response to the biological decree that the world must be peopled, may arise irresistibly between persons who could not live together endurably for a week but can produce excellent children. Historians who confuse Charles's feelings for his wife with his appetite for Barbara Villiers do not know chalk from cheese biologically.

The Future of Women in Politics

The establishment of representative government in England is assumed to have been completed by the enfranchisement of women in 1928. The enormous hiatus left by their previous disenfranchisement is supposed to have been filled up and finished with. As a matter of fact it has only reduced Votes for Women to absurdity; for the women immediately used their vote to keep women out of Parliament. After seventeen years of it the nation, consisting of men and women in virtually equal numbers, is misrepresented at Westminster by 24 women and 616 men. During the Suffragette revolt of 1913 I gave great offence to the agitators by forecasting this result, and urging that what was needed was not the vote, but a constitutional amendment enacting that all representative bodies shall consist of women and men in equal numbers, whether elected or nominated or co-opted or registered or picked up in the street like a coroner's jury.

The Coupled Vote

In the case of elected bodies the only way of effecting this is by the Coupled Vote. The representative unit must be not a man *or* a woman but a man *and* a woman. Every vote, to be valid, must be for a human pair, with the result that the elected body must consist of men and women in equal numbers. Until this is achieved it is idle to prate about political democracy as existing, or ever having existed, at any known period of English history.

It is to be noted that the half-and-half proportion is valid no matter what the proportion of women to men is in the population. It never varies considerably; but even if it did the natural unit would still be the complete couple and not its better (or worse) half.

The wisdom or expediency of this reform is questioned on various grounds. There are the people who believe that the soul is a masculine organ lacking in women, as certain physical organs are, and is the seat of male political faculty. But, so far, dissection, spectrum analysis, the electronic microscope, have failed to discover in either sex any specific organ or hormone that a biologist can label as the soul. So we christen it The Holy Ghost or The Lord of Hosts and dechristen it as a Life Force or *Élan Vital*. As this is shared by women and men, and, when it quits the individual, produces in both alike the dissolution we call death, democratic representation cannot be said to exist where women are not as fully enfranchised and qualified as men. So far no great harm has been done by their legal disabilities because men and women are so alike that for the purposes of our crude legislation it matters little whether juries and parliaments are packed with men or women; but now that the activities of government have been greatly extended, detailed criticism by women has become indispensable in Cabinets. For instance, the House of Lords is more representative than the House of Commons because its members are there as the sons of their fathers, which is the reason for all of us being in the world; but it would be a much more human body if it were half-and-half sons and daughters.

All this went on with the approval of the women, who formed half the community, and yet were excluded not only from the franchise but from the professions and public services, except the thrones. Up to a point this also did not matter much; for in oligarchies women exercise so much influence privately and irresponsibly that the cleverest of them are for giving all power to the men, knowing that they can get round them without being hampered by the female majority whose world is the kitchen, the nursery, and the drawingroom if such a luxury is within their reach.

But representation on merely plangent Parliamentary bodies is not sufficient. Anybody can complain of a grievance; but its remedy demands constructive political capacity. Now political capacity is rare; but it is not rarer in women than in men. Nature's supply of five per cent or so of born political thinkers and administrators are all urgently needed in modern civilization; and if half of that natural supply is cut off by the exclusion of women from Parliament and Cabinets the social machinery will fall short and perhaps break down for lack of sufficient direction. Competent women, of whom enough are available, have their proper places filled by incompetent men: there is no Cabinet in Europe that would not be vitally improved by having its male tail cut off and female heads substituted.

But how is this to be done? Giving all women the vote makes it impossible because it only doubles the resistance to any change. When it was introduced in England not a single woman was returned at the ensuing General Election, though there were women of proved ability in the field. They were all defeated by male candidates who were comparative noodles and nobodies.

Therefore I suggest and advocate The Coupled Vote, making all votes invalid except those for a bi-sexed couple, and thus ensuring the return of a body in which men and women are present in equal numbers. Until this is done, adult suffrage will remain the least democratic of all political systems. I leave it to our old parliamentary hands to devise a plan by which our electorate can be side-tracked, humbugged, cheated, lied to, or frightened into tolerating such a change. If it has to wait for their enlightenment it will wait too long.

Malvern, 1939
Ayot Saint Lawrence, 1945

Act I

The library in the house of Isaac Newton in Cambridge in the year 1680. It is a cheerful room overlooking the garden from the first floor through a large window which has an iron balcony outside, with an iron staircase down to the garden level. The division of the window to the left as you look out through it is a glass door leading to these stairs, making the room accessible from the garden. Inside the room the walls are lined with cupboards below and book-shelves above. To the right of the window is a stand-up writing desk. The cupboards are further obstructed by six chairs ranged tidily along them, three to the right of the window and three to the left (as you look out). Between them a table belonging to the set of chairs stands out in the middle with writing materials on it and a prodigious open Bible, made for a church lectern. A comfortable chair for the reader faces away from the window. On the reader's left is a handsome armchair, apparently for the accommodation of distinguished visitors to the philosopher.

Newton's housekeeper, a middle aged woman of very respectable appearance, is standing at the desk working at her accounts.

A serving maid in morning deshabille comes in through the interior door, which is in the side wall to the left of the window (again as you look out through it).

THE MAID. Please, Mrs Basham, a Mr Rowley wants to know when the master will be at home to receive him.

MRS BASHAM. Rowley? I dont know him. This is no hour to call on Mr Newton.

THE MAID. No indeed, maam. And look at me! not dressed to open the door to gentlefolk.

MRS BASHAM. Is he a gentleman? Rowley is not much of a name.

THE MAID. Dressed like a nobleman, maam. Very tall and very dark. And a lot of dogs with him, and a lackey. Not a person you could shut the door in the face of, maam. But very condescending, I must say.

MRS BASHAM. Well, tell him to come back at half past eleven; but I cant promise that Mr Newton will be in. Still, if he likes to come on the chance. And without his dogs, mind. Our Diamond would fight with them.

THE MAID. Yes, maam: I'll tell him [*going*].

15

MRS BASHAM. Oh, Sally, can you tell me how much is three times seven. You were at school, werent you?

SALLY. Yes, maam; but they taught the boys to read, write, and cipher. Us girls were only taught to sew.

MRS BASHAM. Well, never mind. I will ask Mr Newton. He'll know, if anybody will. Or stop. Ask Jack the fish hawker. He's paunching the rabbit in the kitchen.

SALLY. Yes, maam. [*She goes*].

MRS BASHAM. Three sixpences make one and sixpence and three eight-pences make two shillings: they always do. But three sevenpences! I give it up.

Sally returns.

SALLY. Please, maam, another gentleman wants Mr Newton.

MRS BASHAM. Another nobleman?

SALLY. No, maam. He wears leather clothes. Quite out of the common.

MRS BASHAM. Did he give his name?

SALLY. George Fox, he said, maam.

MRS BASHAM. Why, thats the Quaker, the Man in Leather Breeches. He's been in prison. How dare he come here wanting to see Mr Newton? Go and tell him that Mr Newton is not at home to the like of him.

SALLY. Oh, he's not a person I could talk to like that, maam. I dursnt.

MRS BASHAM. Are you frightened of a man that would call a church a steeple house and walk into it without taking off his hat? Go this instant and tell him you will raise the street against him if he doesnt go away. Do you hear. Go and do as I tell you.

SALLY. I'd be afraid he'd raise the street against us. I will do my best to get rid of him without offence. [*She goes*].

MRS BASHAM [*calling after her*] And mind you ask Jack how much three times seven is.

SALLY [*outside*] Yes'm.

Newton, aged 38, comes in from the garden, hatless, deep in calculation, his fists clenched, tapping his knuckles together to tick off the stages of the equation. He stumbles over the mat.

MRS BASHAM. Oh, do look where youre going, Mr Newton. Someday youll walk into the river and drown yourself. I thought you were out at the university.

NEWTON. Now dont scold, Mrs Basham, dont scold. I forgot to go out. I thought of a way of making a calculation that has been puzzling me.

MRS BASHAM. And you have been sitting out there forgetting everything else since breakfast. However, since you have one of your calculating fits on I wonder would you mind doing a little sum for me to check the washing bill. How much is three times seven?

NEWTON. Three times seven? Oh, that is quite easy.

MRS BASHAM. I suppose it is to you, sir; but it beats me. At school I got as far as addition and subtraction; but I never could do multiplication or division.

NEWTON. Why, neither could I: I was too lazy. But they are quite unnecessary: addition and subtraction are quite sufficient. You add the logarithms of the numbers; and the antilogarithm of the sum of the two is the answer. Let me see: three times seven? The logarithm of three must be decimal four seven seven or thereabouts. The logarithm of seven is, say, decimal eight four five. That makes one decimal three two two, doesnt it? What's the antilogarithm of one decimal three two two? Well, it must be less than twentytwo and more than twenty. You will be safe if you put it down as –

Sally returns.

SALLY. Please, maam, Jack says it's twentyone.

NEWTON. Extraordinary! Here was I blundering over this simple problem for a whole minute; and this uneducated fish hawker solves it in a flash! He is a better mathematician than I.

MRS BASHAM. This is our new maid from Woolsthorp, Mr Newton. You havnt seen her before.

NEWTON. Havnt I? I didnt notice it. [*To Sally*] Youre from Woolsthorp, are you? So am I. How old are you?

SALLY. Twentyfour, sir.

NEWTON. Twentyfour years. Eight thousand seven hundred and sixty days. Two hundred and ten thousand two hundred and forty hours. Twelve million six hundred and fourteen thousand, four hundred minutes. Seven hundred and fiftysix million eight hundred and sixtyfour thousand seconds. A long long life.

MRS BASHAM. Come now, Mr Newton: you will turn the child's head with your figures. What can one do in a second?

NEWTON. You can do, quite deliberately and intentionally, seven distinct actions in a second. How do you count seconds? Hackertybackertyone, hackertybackertytwo, hackertybackertythree and so on. You pronounce seven syllables in every second. Think of it! This young woman has had time to perform more than five thousand millions of considered and intentional actions in her lifetime. How many of them can you remember, Sally?

SALLY. Oh sir, the only one I can remember was on my sixth birthday. My father gave me sixpence: a penny for every year.

NEWTON. Six from twentyfour is eighteen. He owes you one and six-pence. Remind me to give you one and sevenpence on your next birthday if you are a good girl. Now be off.

SALLY. Oh, thank you, sir. [*She goes out*].

NEWTON. My father, who died before I was born, was a wild, extrava-gant, weak man: so they tell me. I inherit his wildness, his extrava-gance, his weakness, in the shape of a craze for figures of which I am most heartily ashamed. There are so many more important things to be worked at: the transmutations of matter, the elixir of life, the magic of light and color, above all, the secret meaning of the Scriptures. And when I should be concentrating my mind on these I find myself wandering off into idle games of speculation about numbers in infinite series, and dividing curves into indivisibly short triangle bases. How silly! What a waste of time, priceless time!

MRS BASHAM. There is a Mr Rowley going to call on you at half past eleven.

NEWTON. Can I never be left alone? Who is Mr Rowley? What is Mr Rowley?

MRS BASHAM. Dressed like a nobleman. Very tall. Very dark. Keeps a lackey. Has a pack of dogs with him.

NEWTON. Oho! So that is who he is! They told me he wanted to see my telescope. Well, Mrs Basham, he is a person whose visit will be counted a great honor to us. But I must warn you that just as I have my terrible weakness for figures Mr Rowley has a very similar weakness for women; so you must keep Sally out of his way.

MRS BASHAM. Indeed! If he tries any of his tricks on Sally I shall see that he marries her.

NEWTON. He is married already. [*He sits at the table*].

MRS BASHAM. Oh! That sort of man! The beast!

NEWTON. Shshsh! Not a word against him, on your life. He is privileged.

MRS BASHAM. He is a beast all the same!

NEWTON [*opening the Bible*] One of the beasts in the Book of Revelation, perhaps. But not a common beast.

MRS BASHAM. Fox the Quaker, in his leather breeches had the impu-dence to call.

NEWTON [*interested*] George Fox? If he calls again I will see him. Those two men ought to meet.

MRS BASHAM. Those two men indeed! The honor of meeting you ought to be enough for them, I should think.

NEWTON. The honor of meeting me! Dont talk nonsense. They are great men in their very different ranks. I am nobody.

MRS BASHAM. You are the greatest man alive, sir. Mr Halley told me so.

NEWTON. It was very wrong of Mr Halley to tell you anything of the sort. You must not mind what he says. He is always pestering me to publish my methods of calculation and to abandon my serious studies. Numbers! Numbers! Numbers! Sines, cosines, hypotenuses, fluxions, curves small enough to count as straight lines, distances between two points that are in the same place! Are these philosophy? Can they make a man great?

He is interrupted by Sally, who throws open the door and announces visitors.

SALLY. Mr Rowley and Mr Fox.

King Charles the Second, aged 50, appears at the door, but makes way for George Fox the Quaker, a big man with bright eyes and a powerful voice in reserve, aged 56. He is decently dressed; but his garments are made of leather.

CHARLES. After you, Mr Fox. The spiritual powers before the temporal.

FOX. You are very civil, sir; and you speak very justly. I thank you [*he passes in*].

Sally, intensely impressed by Mr Rowley, goes out.

FOX. Am I addressing the philosopher Isaac Newton?

NEWTON You are, sir. [*Rising*] Will your noble friend do me the honor to be seated in my humble dwelling?

Charles bows and takes the armchair with easy grace.

FOX. I must not impose on you by claiming the gentleman as my friend. We met by chance at your door; and his favorite dog was kind enough to take a fancy to me.

CHARLES. She is never mistaken, sir. Her friends are my friends, if so damaged a character as mine can claim any friends.

NEWTON [*taking a chair from the wall and placing it near his table to his left*] Be seated, Mr Fox, pray.

FOX. George Fox at your service, not Mister. But I am very sensible of your civility. [*He sits*].

NEWTON [*resuming his seat at the table*] It seems that it is I who am at your service. In what way can I oblige you?

FOX. As you remind me, I have come here uninvited. My business will keep while you discharge yours with this nobleman – so called.

CHARLES. I also am uninvited, Pastor. I may address you so both truthfully and civilly, may I not?

FOX. You have found the right word. I tended my father's sheep when I was a child. Now I am a pastor of men's souls.

CHARLES. Good. Well, Pastor, I must inform you I have no business here except to waste our host's invaluable time and to improve my own, if

19

he will be good enough to allow me such a liberty. Proceed then with your business; and take no notice of me. Unless, that is, you would prefer me to withdraw.

FOX. I have no business in this world that all men may not hear: the more the better.

CHARLES. I guessed as much; and confess to an unbounded curiosity to hear what George Fox can have to say to Isaac Newton. It is not altogether an impertinent curiosity. My trade, which is a very unusual one, requires that I should know what Tom, Dick and Harry have to say to oneanother. I find you two gentlemen much more interesting and infinitely more important.

MRS BASHAM [*posted behind Newton's chair*] What is your business, Mr Rowley? Mr Newton has much to do this morning. He has no time for idle conversation.

NEWTON. I had forgotten to make this lady known to you, gentlemen. Mrs Basham: my housekeeper, and the faithful guardian of my hours.

CHARLES. Your servant, Mistress Basham.

FOX. God be with you, woman.

NEWTON. Mr Rowley is a gentleman of great consequence, Mrs Basham. He must not be questioned as if he were Jack the fish hawker. His business is his father's business.

CHARLES. No, no. My father's business is abolished in England: he was executed for practising it. But we keep the old signboard up over the door of the old shop. And I stand at the shop door in my father's apron. Mrs Basham may ask me as many questions as she pleases; for I am far less important now in England than Jack the fish hawker.

MRS BASHAM. But how do you live, sir? That is all I meant to ask.

CHARLES. By my wits, Mistress Basham: by my wits. Come, Pastor: enough of me. You are face to face with Isaac Newton. I long to hear what you have to say to him.

FOX. Isaac Newton: I have friends who belong to the new so-called Royal Society which the King has established, to enquire, it seems, into the nature of the universe. They tell me things that my mind cannot reconcile with the word of God as revealed to us in the Holy Scriptures.

NEWTON. What is your warrant for supposing that revelation ceased when King James's printers finished with the Bible?

FOX. I do not suppose so. I am not one of those priestridden churchmen who believe that God went out of business six thousand years ago when he had called the world into existence and written his book about it. We three sitting here together may have a revelation if we open our hearts and minds to it. Yes: even to you, Charles Stuart.

CHARLES. The mind of Charles Stuart is only too open, Pastor.

MRS BASHAM. What did you call the gentleman, Mr Fox?

CHARLES. A slip of the tongue, Mistress Basham. Nowhere in Holy writ, Pastor, will you find any disapproval of Paul when he changed his name from Saul. Need you be more scrupulous than the apostles?

FOX. It is against my sinful nature to disoblige any man; so Mr Rowley you shall be if you so desire. But I owed it to you to let you know that I was not deceived by your new name.

CHARLES. I thank you, Pastor. Your sinful nature makes you the best mannered man in the kingdom. And now, what about the revelations?

FOX. I am troubled. I cannot conceive that God should contradict himself. How must the revelation of today be received if it be contrary to the revelation of yesterday? If what has been revealed to you, Isaac Newton, be true, there is no heaven above us and no hell beneath us. The sun which stood still upon Gibeon and the moon in the Valley of Ajalon had stood still since the creation of the world.

NEWTON. Do not let that trouble you, Pastor. Nothing has ever stood still for an instant since the creation of the world: neither the sun, the moon, the stars, nor the smallest particle of matter, except on two occasions.

CHARLES. Two! I remember only one.

NEWTON. Yes, sir: two. The first was when the sun stood still on Gibeon to give Joshua time to slaughter the Amorites. The second was when the shadow on the dial of Ahaz went ten degrees backward as a sign from God to good King Hezekiah who was dying of a boil until the prophet Isaiah made them put a lump of figs on it.

MRS BASHAM. There is nothing like a poultice of roasted figs to cure a gumboil. And to think that is because it is in the Holy Bible! I never knew it.

NEWTON. On reflection, the sun has stopped three times; for it must have stopped for an infinitesimal moment when it turned back, and again when it resumed its course.

FOX. I thank God that you are not an unbeliever and would not make me one.

NEWTON. My good friend, there is nothing so wonderful that a philosopher cannot believe it. The philosopher sees a hundred miracles a day where the ignorant and thoughtless see nothing but the daily round, the common task. Joshua was an ignorant soldier. Had he been a philosopher he would have known that to stop the nearest speck of dust would have served his turn as well as to stop the sun and moon; for it could not have stopped without stopping the whole machinery of the heavens. By the way, Mrs Basham, the fact that the sun and moon were visible at the same time may help me to fix the day on which the miracle occurred. [*To the others*] Excuse me, gentlemen: I have written a chronological history of the world; and the dates give me some trouble.

CHARLES. Did not the late Archbishop Ussher fix the dates of everything that ever happened?

NEWTON. Unfortunately he did not allow for the precession of the equinoxes. I had to correct some of his results accordingly.

CHARLES. And, saving the pastor's presence, what the divvle is the precession of the equinoxes?

FOX. I am sinful enough to be glad that you are as ignorant as myself. I suffer greatly from shame at my ignorance.

NEWTON. Shame will not help you, Pastor. I spend my life contemplating the ocean of my ignorance. I once boasted of having picked up a pebble on the endless beach of that ocean. I should have said a grain of sand.

CHARLES. I can well believe it. No man confronted with the enormity of what he does not know can think much of what he does know. But what is the precession of the equinoxes? If I fire off those words at court the entire peerage will be prostrate before the profundity of my learning.

MRS BASHAM. Oh, tell the gentlemen, Mr Newton; or they will be here all day.

NEWTON. It is quite simple: a child can understand it. The two days in the year on which the day and night are of equal duration are the equinoxes. In each successive sidereal year they occur earlier. You will see at once that this involves a retrograde motion of the equinoctial points along the ecliptic. We call that the precession of the equinoxes.

FOX. I thank you, Isaac Newton. I am as wise as I was before.

MRS BASHAM. You ought to be ashamed of yourself, Mr Newton, injuring the poor gentlemen's brains with such outlandish words. You must remember that everybody is not as learned as you are.

NEWTON. But surely it is plain to everybody –

MRS BASHAM. No: it isnt plain to anybody, Mr Newton.

SALLY [*bursting in*] Mr Rowley: theres a lady in a coach at the door wants to know are you ready to take a drive with her.

CHARLES. Any name?

SALLY. No, sir. She said youd know.

CHARLES. A duchess, would you say?

SALLY. Oh no, sir. Spoke to me quite familiar.

CHARLES. Nelly! Mr Newton: would you like to be introduced to Mistress Gwynn, the famous Drury Lane actress?

MRS BASHAM [*turning imperatively to Charles*] Oh, I couldnt allow that, Mr Rowley. I am surprised at you mentioning such a person in my presence.

CHARLES. I apologize. I did not know that you disapproved of the playhouse, Mrs Basham.

MRS BASHAM. I do not disapprove of the playhouse, sir. My grandfather, who is still alive and hearty, was befriended in his youth by Mr William Shakespear, a wellknown player and writer of comedies, tragedies, and the like. Mr Shakespear would have died of shame to see a woman on the stage. It is unnatural and wrong. Only the most abandoned females would do such a thing.

CHARLES. Still, the plays are more natural with real women in them, are they not?

MRS BASHAM. Indeed they are not, Mr Rowley. They are not like women at all. They are just like what they are; and they spoil the play for anyone who can remember the old actors in the women's parts. They c o u l d make you believe you were listening to real women.

CHARLES. Pastor Fox: have you ever spoken with a female player?

FOX [*shuddering*] I! No, sir: I do not frequent such company.

CHARLES. Why not, Pastor? Is your charity so narrow? Nell is no worse than Mary Magdalen.

MRS BASHAM. I hope Mary Magdalen made a good end and was forgiven; though we are nowhere told so. But I should not have asked her into my house. And at least she was not on the stage. [*She retires behind Newton's chair*].

CHARLES. What do you say, Pastor? Is Nelly not good enough for you?

FOX. Sir: there is nobody who is not good enough for me. Have I not warned our Christian friends who are now captives in Barbary not to forget that the life of God and the power of God are in their heathen masters the Turks and the Moors as well as in themselves? Is it any the less in this player woman than in a Turk or a Moor? I am not afraid of her.

CHARLES. And you, Mr Newton?

NEWTON. Women enter a philosopher's life only to disturb it. They expect too much attention. However, Mistress Gwynn has called to take you away, not to interrupt my work on fluxions. And if you will condescend to go down to her she need not come up to us. [*He rises in dismissal of the King*].

CHARLES [*rising*] I see I must take my leave.

23

Nelly dashes in. Sally withdraws.

NELLY. Rowley darling: how long more are you going to keep me waiting in the street?

CHARLES. You are known to everyone present, Mistress Gwynn, I think. May I make our host known to you? The eminent philosopher, Mr Newton.

NELLY [*going past Charles to Newton*] I dont know what a philosopher is, Mr Newton; but you look one, every inch. Your servant, sir. [*She curtsies to him*].

NEWTON. Yours, madam. I am ashamed that you should have been kept waiting at the wrong side of my door.

NELLY. It is an honor to be seen at your door, Mr Newton. [*Looking round her*] And who keeps your house so beautifully? I thought philosophers were like Romish priests, not allowed to marry.

NEWTON. Is my house beautifully kept? I have never noticed it. This is Mrs Basham, my housekeeper. [*He sits resignedly*].

NELLY. You never noticed it! You dont deserve such a housekeeper. Your servant, Mrs Basham.

Mrs Basham bows stiffly, trying not to be flattered.

CHARLES. The other gentleman is the famous founder of the sect of Quakers.

FOX. Of Friends, Friend Rowley.

NELLY [*running to Fox*] I know. I know. The man in the leather breeches.

FOX [*stubbornly seated*] I am also known as George Fox.

NELLY [*clapping him on the shoulder*] What of that? Anybody might be George Fox; but there is only one man in the leather breeches. Your servant, George.

FOX. Yours, Nelly.

NELLY. There! Nelly! [*She goes to the wall for a chair and plants it at Fox's left, quite close*]. If I may add you to the list of my beaus I shall be the proudest woman in London.

FOX. I did not found the order of beaus. I founded that of Friends.

NELLY. Ten times better. Our beaus are our foes: they care for nothing but to steal our honor. Pray for me, Friend Fox: I think you have God by the ear closer than the bishops.

FOX. He is closer to you than you have placed yourself to me. Let no priest come between you.

CHARLES. We must not waste any more of Mr Newton's time, Mistress Gwynn. He is at work on fluxions.

NELLY. On what?

CHARLES. Fluxions I think you said, Mr Newton.

NELLY. What are fluxions?

CHARLES. Mr Newton will tell you. I should be glad to know, myself.

NEWTON. Fluxions, madam, are the rates of change of continuously varying quantities.

NELLY. I must go home and think about that, Mr Philosopher.

NEWTON [*very seriously*] I shall be much indebted to you, madam, if you will communicate to me the result of your reflections. The truth is, I am not quite satisfied that my method – or perhaps I had better say the notation of my method – is the easiest that can be devised. On that account I have never cared to publish it.

NELLY. You really think I could teach you something, Mr Newton? What a compliment! Did you hear that, Rowley darling?

NEWTON. In these very simple matters one may learn from anyone. And you, madam, must have very remarkable mental powers. You repeat long parts from memory in the theatre. I could not do that.

NELLY. Bless me, so I do, Mr Newton. You are the first man I ever met who did not think an actress must be an ignorant ninny – except schoolboys, who think she is a goddess. I declare you are the wisest man in England, and the kindest.

CHARLES. And the busiest, Nelly. Come. He has given us as much of his time as we have any right to ask for.

NELLY. Yes, I know. I am coming. [*She rises and goes to Charles, whose left arm she takes*]. May I come again, Mr Newton?

NEWTON [*rising*] No no no no no, madam, I cannot entertain ladies. They do not fit into my way of life. Mr Rowley: you are well known to be as interested in ladies as I am interested in the Scriptures; and I thank you for bringing this very attractive sample for my diversion –

NELLY [*as if tasting a sweet*] Oh!

NEWTON [*continuing*] – but sufficient unto the day is the evil thereof –

NELLY [*in violent protest*] Oh!!!

NEWTON. – and I beg you will bring no more ladies here until I have time to set aside a day of relaxation for their reception.

NELLY. We must go, Rowley darling. He doesnt want us.

CHARLES. You are fortunate, Mr Newton, in suffering nothing worse than Nell. But I promise you your house shall be a monastery henceforth.

As Charles and Nell turn to the door to go out, the Duchess of Cleveland, 39, formerly Lady Castlemaine, and born Barbara Villiers, bursts into the room and confronts them in a tearing rage.

BARBARA. Ah! I have caught you, have I, with your trull. This is the scientific business which made it impossible for you to see me this morning.

CHARLES. Be silent for a moment, Barbara, whilst I present you to Mr

Newton, the eminent philosopher, in whose house you are an uninvited guest.

BARBARA. A pretty house. A pretty philosopher. A house kept for you to meet your women in.

MRS BASHAM [*coming indignantly to the middle of the room*] Oh! Mr Newton: either this female leaves the house this instant or I do.

BARBARA. Do you know, woman, that you are speaking of the Duchess of Cleveland?

MRS BASHAM. I do not care who I am speaking of. If you are the Duchess of Cleveland and this house were what you said it was you would be only too much at home in it. The house being what it is you are out of place in it. You go or I go.

BARBARA. You insolent slut, I will have you taken to the Bridewell and whipped.

CHARLES. You shall not, Barbara. If you do not come down with me to your carriage without another word, I will throw you downstairs.

BARBARA. Do. Kill me; and be happy with that low stage player. You have been unfaithful to me with her a thousand times.

NEWTON. Patience, patience, patience. Mrs Basham: the lady is not in a state of reason: I will prove to you that what she says has no sense and need not distress us. [*To Barbara*] Your Grace alleges that Mr Rowley has been unfaithful to you a thousand times.

BARBARA. A hundred thousand times.

NEWTON. For each unfaithfulness allow a day – or shall I say a night? Now one hundred thousand nights are almost two hundred and seventyfour years. To be precise, 273 years 287 days, allowing 68 days for Leap Year every four years. Now Mr Rowley is not 300 years old: he is only fifty, from which you must deduct at least fifteen years for his childhood.

BARBARA. Fourteen.

NEWTON. Let us say fourteen. Probably your Grace was also precocious. How many years shall we strike off your age for the days of your innocence?

NELL. Five at most.

BARBARA. Be silent, you.

NEWTON. Say twelve. That makes you in effect about twentyeight.

BARBARA. Have I denied it?

NELL. Flatterer!

NEWTON. Twentyeight to Mr Rowley's thirtysix. Your grace has been available since, say, the year 1652, twentyeight years ago. My calculation is therefore correct.

BARBARA. May I ask what you mean by available?

NEWTON. I mean that the number of occasions on which Mr Rowley could possibly be unfaithful to you is ten thousand two hundred and twenty plus seven for leap years. Yet you allege one hundred thousand occasions, and claim to have lived for nearly three centuries. As that is impossible, it is clear that you have been misinformed about Mistress Gwynn.

Nell claps vigorously.

BARBARA [*to Newton*] Are you mocking me, sir?

NEWTON. Figures cannot mock, because they cannot feel. That is their great quality, and their great fault. [*He goes to the door*]. And now may I have the honor of conducting your Grace to your coach – or is it one of those new fangled sedan chairs? Or would your Grace prefer to be thrown down my humble staircase by Mr Rowley? It has twentyfour steps, in two flights.

BARBARA. I will not leave this house until that player woman has gone first. [*She strides past them and plants herself in Newton's chair*].

NELL. After all, dear, it's Mr Newton's house and not ours. He was in the act of putting me out when you burst in. I stayed only because I wanted to see you in one of those tantrums of yours that Rowley so often tells me about. I might copy them on the stage.

BARBARA. He dares talk to you about me!!

NELL. He talks to me about everything, dear, because I let him get in a word occasionally, which is more than you do.

BARBARA [*to Charles*] Will you stand there and let me be insulted by this woman?

CHARLES [*with conviction*] Barbara: I am tired of your tantrums. I made you a duchess: you behave like a streetwalker. I pensioned you and packed you off to Paris; you have no business to be here. Pastor: what have you to say to all this? You are the oldest and wisest person present, are you not?

FOX. Fiftysix. And still a child in wisdom.

BARBARA [*contemptuously, noticing Fox for the first time*] What does this person know about women?

FOX. Only what the woman in myself teaches me.

NELL. Good for leather breeches! What do you think of her, George?

FOX. She prates overmuch about unfaithfulness. The man Rowley cannot be unfaithful to her because he has pledged no faith to her. To his wife only can he be unfaithful.

CHARLES. Wrong, Pastor. You do not know my wife. To her only I can never be unfaithful.

NELL. Yes: you are kind to us; but we are nothing to you. [*Sighing*] I would change places with her.

BARBARA. Will you order this common player to be silent in my presence?

NELL. It is not fair of her to keep mentioning my profession when I cannot decently mention hers.

With a scream of rage the duchess rises to fly at Nell, but is seized by Fox, who drags down her raised fists and throws her back into the chair.

FOX [*sternly*] Woman: behave yourself. In any decent English village you would go to the ducking stool to teach you good manners and gentle speech. You must control yourself –

He is interrupted by the clangor of a church bell, which has a terrible effect on him.

FOX [*in a thundering voice, forgetting all about the duchess*] Ha! I am called: I must go.

He makes for the door but is stopped by Charles, who, releasing Nell, shuts it quickly and posts himself with his back to it.

CHARLES. Stop. You are going to brawl in church. You will be thrown into prison; and I shall not be able to save you.

FOX. The bell, the bell. It strikes upon my life. I am called. Earthly kings cannot stay me. Let me pass.

CHARLES. Stand back, Mr Fox. My person is sacred.

NEWTON. What is the matter?

CHARLES. The church bell: it drives him mad. Someone send and stop it.
The bell stops.

FOX. God has stopped it. [*He falls on his knees and collapses, shivering like a man recovering from a fit*].

Charles and Newton help him to his feet and lead him back to his chair.

FOX [*to Charles*] Another stroke, and I should not have answered for your life.

BARBARA. You must control yourself, preacher. In any decent English village you would be put in the stocks to teach you good manners.

FOX. Woman: I h a v e been put in the stocks; and I shall be put there again. But I will continue to testify against the steeple house and the brazen clangor of its belfries.

MRS BASHAM. Now Mr Fox. You must not say such things here.

FOX. I tell you that from the moment you allow this manmade monster called a Church to enter your mind your inner light is like an extinguished candle; and your soul is plunged in darkness and damned. There is no atheist like the Church atheist. I have converted many a poor atheist who would have been burnt or hanged if God had not sent him into my hands; but I have never converted a churchman: his answer to everything is not his God, but the Church, the Church, the Church. They burn each other, these churchmen: they persecute: they do wickednesses of which no friend of God would be capable.

MRS BASHAM. The Popish Church, not the Protestant one, Mr Fox.

FOX. All, all, all of them. They are all snares of the devil. They stand between Man and his Maker, and take on themselves divine powers when they lack divine attributes. Am I to hold my peace in the face of this iniquity? When the bell rings to announce some pitiful rascal twaddling in his pulpit, or some fellow in a cassock pretending to bind and loose, I hear an Almighty Voice call 'George Fox, George Fox: rise up: testify: unmask these impostors: drag them down from their pulpits and their altars; and let it be known that what the world needs to bring it back to God is not Churchmen but Friends, Friends of God, Friends of man, friendliness and sincerity everywhere, superstition and pulpit playacting nowhere.'

CHARLES. Pastor: it is not given to every man as it has been to you to make a religion for himself. A ready-made Church is an indispensable convenience for most of us. The inner light must express itself in music, in noble architecture, in eloquence: in a word, in beauty, before it can pass into the minds of common men. I grant you the clergy are mostly dull dogs; but with a little disguise and ritual they will pass as holy men with the ignorant. And there are great mysteries that must be symbolized, because though we feel them we do not know them, Mr Newton having not yet discovered their nature, in spite of all his mathematics. And this reminds me that we are making a most unwarrantable intrusion on our host's valuable time. Mr Newton: on my honor I had no part in bringing upon you this invasion of womanhood. I hasten to take them away, and will wait upon you at some happier moment. Come, ladies: we must leave Mr Newton to his mathematics. [He is about to go to the door. Barbara rises to accompany him].

NEWTON [stopping him] I must correct that misunderstanding, sir. I would not have you believe that I could be so inhospitable as to drive away my guests merely to indulge in the trifling pursuit of mathematical calculation, which leads finally nowhere. But I have more serious business in hand this morning. I am engaged in a study of the prophecies in the book of Daniel. [He indicates the Bible]. It may prove of the greatest importance to the world. I beg you to allow me to proceed with it in the necessary solitude. The ladies have not wasted my time: I have to thank her Grace of Cleveland for some lights on the Book of

Revelation suggested to me by her proceedings. But solitude – solitude absolutely free from the pleasant disturbance of ladies' society – is now necessary to me; and I must beg you to withdraw.

Sally, now dressed in her best, throws the door open from without, and proudly announces –

SALLY. Her Grace the Duchess of Portsmouth.

Louise de Kéroualle, a Frenchwoman who at 30 retains her famous babyish beauty, appears on the threshold.

NEWTON [*beside himself*] Another woman! Take her away. Take them all away. [*He flings himself into his chair at the table and buries his face in his hands*].

CHARLES. Louise: it is unlike you to pursue me. We are unwelcome here.

LOUISE [*coming over to him*] Pursue you! But I have never been so surprised in my life as to find you here. And Nelly! And her Grace of Cleveland back from Paris! What are you all doing here? I came to consult Mr Newton, the alchemist. [*Newton straightens up and stares*]. My business with him is private: it is with him, not with you, chéri. I did not know he was holding a reception.

CHARLES. Mr Newton is not an alchemist.

LOUISE. Pardon me: he is.

CHARLES. Mr Newton: are you an alchemist?

NEWTON. My meditations on the ultimate constitution of matter have convinced me that the transmutation of metals, and indeed of all substances, must be possible. It is occurring every day. I understand that you, Mr Rowley, have a private laboratory at Whitehall, in which you are attempting the fixation of mercury.

CHARLES. Without success, Mr Newton. I shall give it up and try for the philosopher's stone instead.

FOX. Would you endanger your souls by dabbling in magic? The scripture says 'Thou shalt not suffer a witch to live.' Do you think that God is fonder of sorcerers and wizards than of witches? If you count the wrath of God as nothing, and are above the law by your rank, are you not ashamed to believe such old wives' tales as the changing of lead into gold by the philosopher's stone?

NEWTON. Pastor Fox: I thank you for your well-meant warning. Now let me warn you. The man who begins by doubting the possibility of the philosopher's stone soon finds himself beginning to doubt the immortality of the soul. He ends by doubting the existence of the soul. There is no witchcraft about these things. I am as certain of them as I am of the fact that the world was created four thousand and four years before the birth of our Lord.

FOX. And what warrant have you for that? The Holy Bible says nothing of your four thousand and four. It tells us that the world was created 'in the beginning': a mighty word. 'In the beginning'! Think of it if you have any imagination. And because some fool in a steeplehouse, dressed up like a stage player in robes and mitre, dares to measure the days of the Almighty by his kitchen clock, you take his word before the word of God! Shame on you, Isaac Newton, for making an idol of an archbishop! There is no credulity like the credulity of philosophers.

NEWTON. But the archbishop has counted the years! My own chronology of the world has been founded on his calculation. Do you mean to tell me that all the labor I have bestowed on that book has been wasted?

FOX. Sinfully wasted.

NEWTON. George Fox: you are an infidel. Leave my house.

FOX [*rising*] Your philosophy has led you to the conclusion that George Fox is an infidel. So much the worse for your philosophy! The Lord does not love men that count numbers. Read second Samuel, chapter twentyfour: the book is before you. Good morning; and God bless you and enlighten you. [*He turns to go*].

CHARLES. Stay, Pastor. [*He makes Fox sit down again and goes to Newton, laying a hand on his shoulder*]. Mr Newton: the word infidel is not one to be used hastily between us three. Old Tom Hobbes, my tutor, who was to me what Aristotle was to Alexander the Great, was called an infidel. You yourself, in spite of your interest in the book of Daniel, have been suspected of doubting whether the apple falls from the tree by the act of God or by a purely physical attraction. Even I, the head of the Church, the Defender of the Faith, stand between the Whigs who suspect me of being a Papist and the Tories who suspect me of being an atheist. Now the one thing that is true of all three of us is that if the common people knew our real minds they would hang us and bury us in unconsecrated ground. We must stand together, gentlemen. What does it matter to us whether the world is four thousand years old, or, as I should guess, ten thousand?

NEWTON. The world ten thousand years old! Sir: you are mad.

NELL [*shocked*] Rowley darling: you mustnt say such things.

BARBARA. What business is it of yours, pray? He has always defied God and betrayed women. He does not know the meaning of the word religion. He laughed at it in France. He hated it in Scotland. In England he believes nothing. He loves nothing. He fears nothing except having to go on his travels again, as he calls it. What are ten thousand years to him, or ten million?

FOX. Are ten million years beyond the competence of Almighty God?

They are but a moment in His eyes. Four thousand years seem an eternity to a mayfly, or a mouse, or a mitred fool called an archbishop. Are we mayflies? Are we mice? Are we archbishops?

MRS BASHAM. Mr Fox: I have listened to too much blasphemy this morning. But to call an archbishop a mitred fool and compare him to a mouse is beyond endurance. I cannot believe that God will ever pardon you for that. Have you no fear of hell?

FOX. How shall I root out the sin of idolatry from this land? Worship your God, woman, not a dressed-up priest.

MRS BASHAM. The archbishop is not a graven image. And when he is officiating he is not in the likeness of anything in the heavens above or on the earth beneath. I am afraid you do not know your catechism, Mr Fox.

CHARLES [*laughing*] Excellent, Mrs Basham. Pastor: she has gravelled you with the second commandment. And she has put us to shame for quarrelling over a matter of which we know nothing. By the way, where were we when we began to quarrel? I have clean forgotten.

LOUISE. It was my business with Mr Newton, I think. Nellie: will you take our sovereign lord away and leave me to speak with the alchemist in private?

CHARLES. Mr Newton: not for worlds would I deprive you of a *tête-à-tête* with her Grace of Portsmouth. Pastor: you will accompany us. Nellie: you will come with the pastor. But first I must throw the Duchess of Cleveland downstairs [*moving towards her*].

BARBARA [*screaming and making for the door*] Coward! Help! Murder! [*She rushes out*].

CHARLES. Your servant, Mrs Basham.

Mrs Basham curtsies. Charles salutes her and goes out.

NELL [*beckoning to Fox*] Come on, leather breeches.

FOX [*rising and going towards the door*] Well, what you are, God made you. I am bound to be your friend.

NELL [*taking his arm as he passes*] I am proud of your friendship, George.

They go out arm in arm.

Louise, being now the person of highest rank present, follows them as far as the armchair, in which she seats herself with distinguished elegance.

LOUISE [*to Mrs Basham*] Madam: may I have a moment alone with the alchemist?

NEWTON. You certainly may not, your Grace. I will not have Mr Locke and his friends accuse me of having relations with women. If your business cannot be discussed before Mrs Basham it cannot be discussed with me. And you will please not speak of me as 'the alchemist' as you might speak of the apothecary or the chimney sweep. I am by profession – if it can be called a profession – a philosopher.

LOUISE. Pardon: I am not habituated to your English manners. It is strange to me that a philosopher should need a chaperon. In France it is I who should need one.

NEWTON. You are quite safe with me and Mrs Basham, madam. What is your business?

LOUISE. I want a love charm.

NEWTON. A what?

LOUISE. A love charm. Something that will make my lover faithful to me if I drop it into his tay. And mind! it must make him love me, and not love everybody. He is far too amorous already of every pretty woman he meets. I make no secret of who he is: all the world knows it. The love charm must not do him any harm; for if we poison the king we shall be executed in the most horrible manner. It must be something that will be good for him.

NEWTON. And peculiar to yourself? Not to Mistress Gwynn?

LOUISE. I do not mind Nellie: she is a dear, and so helpful when there is any trouble or illness. He picked her up out of the gutter; but the good God sometimes drops a jewel there: my nurse, a peasant woman, was worth a thousand duchesses. Yes: he may have Nellie: a change is sometimes good for men.

MRS BASHAM [*fearfully shocked*] Oh! Mr Newton: I must go. I cannot stay and listen to this French lady's talk. [*She goes out with dignity*].

LOUISE. I shall never understand the things that Englishwomen are prudish about. And they are so extraordinarily coarse in other things. May I stay, now that your chaperon has gone?

NEWTON. You will not want to stay when I tell you that I do not deal in love potions. Ask the nearest apothecary for an aphrodisiac.

LOUISE. But I cannot trust a common apothecary: it would be all over the town tomorrow. Nobody will suspect you. I will pay any price you like.

NEWTON. I tell you, madam, I know nothing about such things. If I wished to make you fall in love with me – which God forbid! – I should not know how to set about it. I should learn to play some musical instrument, or buy a new wig.

LOUISE. But you are an alchemist: you must know.

NEWTON. Then I am not an alchemist. But the changing of Bodies into Light and Light into Bodies is very conformable to the Course of Nature, which seems delighted with Transmutations.

LOUISE. I do not understand. What are transmutations?

NEWTON. Never mind, madam. I have other things to do than to peddle love charms to the King's ladies.

LOUISE [*ironically*] Yes: to entertain the Duchess of Cleveland and Mistress Gwynn, and hire a mad preacher to amuse them! What else have you to do that is more important than my business with you?

NEWTON. Many other things. For instance, to ascertain the exact distance of the sun from the earth.

LOUISE. But what a waste of time! What can it possibly matter whether the sun is twenty miles away or twentyfive?

NEWTON. Twenty or twentyfive!!! The sun is millions and millions of miles from the earth.

LOUISE. Oh! Oh!! Oh!!! You are quite mad, Monsieur Nieuton. At such a distance you could not see it. You could not feel its heat. Well, you cannot see it so plainly here as in France, nor so often; but you can see it quite plainly sometimes. And you can feel its heat. It burns your skin, and freckles you if you are sandyhaired. And then comes a little cloud over it and you shiver with cold. Could that happen if it were a thousand miles away?

NEWTON. It is very very large, madam. It is one million three hundred thousand times heavier than the earth.

LOUISE. My good Monsieur Nieuton: do not be so fanciful. [*Indicating the window*] Look at it. Look at it. It is much smaller than the earth. If I hold up a sou – what you call a ha-pen-ny – before my eye, it covers the sun and blots it out. Let me teach you something, Monsieur Nieuton. A great French philosopher, Blaise Pascal, teached me this. You must never let your imagination run away with you. When you think of grandiose things – hundreds of millions and things like that – you must continually come down to earth to keep sane. You must see: you must feel: you must measure.

NEWTON. That is very true, madam. Above all, you must measure. And when you measure you find that many things are bigger than they look. The sun is one of them.

LOUISE [*rising and going to the table to coax him*] Ah! You are impossible. But you will make me a love potion, will you not?

NEWTON. I will write you a prescription, madam.

He takes a sheet of paper and writes the prescription. Louise watches as he writes.

LOUISE. Aqua? But aqua is only water, monsieur.

NEWTON. Water with a cabalistic sign after it, madam.

LOUISE. Ah, parfaitement. And this long magical word, what is it? Mee-kah-pah-nees. What is that?

NEWTON. Micapanis, madam. A very powerful lifegiving substance.

LOUISE. It sounds wonderful. Is it harmless?

NEWTON. The most harmless substance in the world, madam, and the most precious.

LOUISE. Truly you are a great man, Monsieur Nieuton, in spite of your millions of miles. And this last word here?

NEWTON. Only sugar, to sweeten the micapanis, but with the cabalistic sign after it. Here is your love charm, madam. But it is not a potion: the apothecary will make it into pills for you.

LOUISE [*taking the paper and tucking it into the bosom of her dress*] Good. That is better, much better. It is so much easier to make men take pills than drink potions. And now, one thing more. You must swear to give this prescription to no other woman of the court. It is for me alone.

NEWTON. You have my word of honor, madam.

LOUISE. But a word of honor must be a gentleman's word of honor. You, monsieur, are a bourgeois. You must swear on your Bible.

NEWTON. My word is my word, madam. And the Bible must not be mixed up with the magic of micapanis.

LOUISE. Not black magic, is it? I could not touch that.

NEWTON. Neither black nor white, madam. Shall we say grey? But quite harmless, I assure you.

LOUISE. Good. And now I must make you a little present for your pills. How much shall it be?

NEWTON. Keep your money for the apothecary, madam: he will be amply satisfied with five shillings. I am sufficiently rewarded by the sound scientific advice you have given me from your friend Blaise Pascal. He was anticipated by an Englishman named Bacon, who was, however, no mathematician. You owe me nothing.

LOUISE. Shall I give one of the new golden guineas to the lady I shocked if I meet her on the stairs?

NEWTON. No. She would not take it.

LOUISE. How little you know the world, Monsieur! Nobody refuses a golden guinea.

NEWTON. You can try the experiment, madam. That would be the advice of your friend Pascal. [*He goes to the door, and opens it for her*].

LOUISE. Perhaps I had better make it two guineas. She will never refuse that.

NEWTON [*at the door, calling*] Sally!

LOUISE [*with a gracious inclination of her head*] Monsieur –

NEWTON. I wish your Grace good morning.

SALLY [*at the door*] Yes, sir?

NEWTON. Shew her Grace the Duchess of Portsmouth to her chair or whatever it is.

LOUISE. Au plaisir de vous revoir, Monsieur le philosophe.

The Duchess goes out, Sally making her a rustic curtsey as she passes, and following her out, leaving Newton alone.

NEWTON [*greatly relieved*] Ouf!

He returns to his place at the table and to his Bible, which, helped by a marker, he opens at the last two chapters of the book of Daniel. He props his head on his elbows.

NEWTON. Twelve hundred and ninety days. And in the very next verse thirteen hundred and thirtyfive days. Five months difference! And the king's daughter of the south: who was she? And the king of the south? And he that cometh against him? And the vile person who obtains the kingdom by flatteries? And Michael? Who was Michael? [*He considers this a moment; then suddenly snatches a sheet of paper and writes furiously*].

SALLY [*throwing open the door, bursting with pride*] His Royal Highness the Duke of York.

The Duke, afterwards James II, comes in precipitately.

JAMES [*imperiously*] Where is his Majesty the King?

NEWTON [*rising in ungovernable wrath*] Sir: I neither know nor care where the King is. This is my house; and I demand to be left in peace in it. I am engaged in researches of the most sacred importance; and for them I require solitude. Do you hear, sir? solitude!

JAMES. Sir: I am the Duke of York, the King's brother.

NEWTON. I am Isaac Newton, the philosopher. I am also an Englishman; and my house is my castle. At least it was until this morning, when the whole court came here uninvited. Are there not palaces for you and the court to resort to? Go away.

JAMES. I know you. You are a follower of the arch infidel Galileo!

NEWTON. Take care, sir. In my house the great Galileo shall not be called an infidel by any Popish blockhead, prince or no prince. Galileo had more brains in his boots than you have in your whole body.

JAMES. Had he more brains in his boots than the Catholic Church? Than the Pope and all his cardinals, the greatest scholars of his day? Is there more learning in your head than in the libraries of the Vatican?

NEWTON. Popes and cardinals are abolished in the Church of England. Only a fool would set up these superstitious idolaters against the Royal Society, founded by your royal brother for the advancement of British science.

JAMES. A club of damnable heretics. I shall know how to deal with them.

NEWTON [*rising in a fury and facing him menacingly*] Will you leave my house, or shall I throw you out through the window?

JAMES. You throw me out! Come on, you scum of a grammar school.
They rush at one another, and in the scuffle fall on the floor, Newton uppermost. Charles comes in at this moment.

CHARLES. Odsfish, Mr Newton, whats this? A wrestling match?
Newton hastily rolls off James. The two combatants remain sitting on the floor, staring up at Charles.

CHARLES. And what the divvle are you doing here, Jamie? Why arnt you in Holland?

JAMES. I am here where I have been thrown by your friend and protégé, the infidel philosopher Newton.

CHARLES. Get up, man: dont play the fool. Mr Newton: your privilege with me does not run to the length of knocking my brother down. It is a serious matter to lay hands on a royal personage.

NEWTON. Sir: I had no intention of knocking your royal brother down. He fell and dragged me down. My intention was only to throw him out of the window.

CHARLES. He could have left by the door, Mr Newton.

NEWTON. He could; but he would not, in spite of my repeated requests. He stayed here to heap insults on the immortal Galileo, whose shoe latchet he is unworthy to unloose.
He rises and confronts the King with dignity.

CHARLES. Will you get up, Jamie, and not sit on the floor grinning like a Jackanapes. Get up, I tell you.

JAMES [*rising*] You see what comes of frequenting the houses of your inferiors. They forget themselves and take liberties. And you encourage heretics. I do not.

CHARLES. Mr Newton: we are in your house and at your orders. Will you allow my brother and myself to have this room to ourselves awhile?

NEWTON. My house is yours, sir. I am a resolute supporter of the Exclusion Bill because I hope to prove that the Romish Church is the little horn of the fourth beast mentioned by the prophet Daniel. But the great day of wrath is not yet come. Your brother is welcome here as long as you desire it.
Newton goes out. Charles takes the armchair. When he is seated James takes Newton's chair at the table.

JAMES. That fellow is crazy. He called me a Popish blockhead. You see what comes of encouraging these Protestants. If you had a pennorth of spunk in you you would burn the lot.

CHARLES. What I want to know is what you are doing here when you should be in Holland. I am doing what I can to stop this Exclusion Bill and secure the crown for you when I die. I sent you to Holland so that your talent for making yourself unpopular might be exercised there and not here. Your life is in danger in London. You had no business to come back. Why have you done it?

JAMES. Charles: I am a prince.

CHARLES. Oh, do I not know it, God help you!

JAMES. Our father lost his head by compromising with Protestants, Republicans, Levellers and Atheists. What did he gain by it? They beheaded him. I am not going to share his fate by repeating that mistake. I am a Catholic; and I am civil to none but Catholics, however unpopular it may make me. When I am king – as I shall be, in my own right, and not by the leave of any Protestant parliamentary gang – I shall restore the Church and restore the monarchy: yes, the monarchy, Charles; for there has been no real Restoration: you are no king, cleverly as you play with these Whigs and Tories. That is because you have no faith, no principles: you dont believe in anything; and a man who doesnt believe in anything is afraid of everything. Youre a damned coward, Charles. I am not. When I am king I shall reign: these fellows shall find what a king's will is when he reigns by divine right. They will get it straight in the teeth then; and Europe will see them crumble up like moths in a candle flame.

CHARLES. It is a funny thing, Jamie, that you, who are clever enough to see that the monarchy is gone and that I keep the crown by my wits, are foolish enough to believe that you have only to stretch out your clenched fist and take it back again. I sometimes ask myself whether it would not be far kinder of me to push the Exclusion Bill through and save you from the fate of our father. They will have your head off inside of five years unless you jump into the nearest fishing smack and land in France.

JAMES. And leave themselves without a king again! Not they: they had enough of that under old Noll's Major-Generals. Noll knew how to rule: I will say that for him; and I thank him for the lesson. But when he died they had to send for us. When they bully you you give in to them and say that you dont want to go on your travels again. But by God, if they try to bully me I will threaten to go on my travels and leave them without a king. That is the way to bring them down on their marrowbones.

CHARLES. You could not leave them without a king. Protestant kings – Stuart kings – are six a penny in Europe today. The Dutch lad's grand-

38

father-in-law was our grandfather. Your daughter Mary is married to him. The Elector of Hanover has the same hook on to grandfather James. Both of them are rank Protestants and hardened soldiers, caring for nothing but fighting the French. Besides Mary there is her sister Anne, Church of England to the backbone. With the Protestants you do not succeed by divine right: they take their choice and send for you, just as they sent for me.

JAMES. Yes, if you look at it in that way and let them do it, Charles: you havnt the spirit of a king: that is what is the matter with you. As long as they let you have your women, and your dogs, and your pictures, and your music, and your chemical laboratory, you let them do as they like. The merry monarch: thats what you are.

CHARLES. Something new in monarchs, eh?

JAMES. Psha! A merry monarch is no monarch at all.

CHARLES. All the same, I must pack you off to Scotland. I cannot have you here until I prorogue parliament to get rid of the Exclusion Bill. And you will have to find a Protestant husband for Anne: remember that.

JAMES. You pretend you are packing me off to save me from my Catholic unpopularity. The truth is you are jealous of my popularity.

CHARLES. No, Jamie: I can beat you at that game. I am an agreeable sort of fellow: old Newcastle knocked that into me when I was a boy. Living at the Hague on two hundred and forty pounds a year finished my education in that respect. Now you, Jamie, became that very disagreeable character a man of principle. The people, who have all sorts of principles which they havnt gathered out of your basket, will never take to you until you go about shouting No Popery. And you will die rather than do that: wont you?

JAMES. Certainly I shall; and so, I trust, would you. Promise me you will die a Catholic, Charles.

CHARLES. I shall take care not to die in an upstart sect like the Church of England, and perhaps lose my place in Westminster Abbey when you are king. Your principles might oblige you to throw my carcase to the dogs. Meanwhile, however popular you may think yourself, you must go and be popular in Scotland.

JAMES. I am popular everywhere: thats what you dont understand because you are not a fighting man; and I am. In the British Isles, Charles, nothing is more popular than the navy; and nobody is more popular than the admiral who has won a great naval victory. Thats what I have done, and you havnt. And that puts me ahead of you with the British people every time.

CHARLES. No doubt; but the British people do not make kings in England. The crown is in the hands of the damned Whig squirearchy who got rich by robbing the Church, and chopped off father's head, crown and all. They care no more for your naval victory than for a bunch of groundsel. They would not pay for the navy if we called it ship money, and let them know what they are paying for.

JAMES. I shall make them pay. I shall not be their puppet as you are. Do you think I will be in the pay of the king of France, whose bitter bread we had to eat in our childhood, and who left our mother without firewood in the freezing winter? And all this because these rebellious dogs will not disgorge enough of their stolen wealth to cover the cost of governing them! If you will not teach them their lesson they shall learn it from me.

CHARLES. You will have to take your money where you can get it, Jamie, as I do. French money is as good as English. King Louis gets little enough for it: I take care of that.

JAMES. Then you cheat him. How can you stoop?

CHARLES. I must. And I know that I must. To play the king as you would have me I should need old Noll's army; and they took good care I should not have that. They grudge me even the guards.

JAMES. Well, what old Noll could do I can do; and so could you if you had the pluck. I will have an army too.

CHARLES. Of Protestants?

JAMES. The officers will be Catholics. The rank and file will be what they are ordered to be.

CHARLES. Where will you get the money to pay them? Old Noll had the city of London and its money at his back.

JAMES. The army will collect the taxes. How does King Louis do it? He keeps the biggest army in Europe; and he keeps you into the bargain. He hardly knows what a parliament is. He dragoons the Protestants out of France into Spitalfields. I shall dragoon them out of Spitalfields.

CHARLES. Where to?

JAMES. To hell, or to the American plantations, whichever they prefer.

CHARLES. So you are going to be the English Louis, the British Roi Soleil, the sun king. This is a deuced foggy climate for sun kings, Jamie.

JAMES. So you think, Charles. But the British climate has nothing to do with it. What is it that nerves Louis to do all these things? The climate of the Catholic Church. His foot is on the rock of Saint Peter; and that makes him a rock himself.

CHARLES. Your son-in-law Dutch Billy is not afraid of him. And Billy's house is built, not on a rock, not even on the sands, but in the mud of the North Sea. Keep your eye on the Orangeman, Jamie.

JAMES. I shall keep my eye on your Protestant bastard Monmouth. Why do you make a pet of that worthless fellow? Know you not he is longing for your death so that he may have a try for the crown while this rascally Popish plot is setting the people against me?

CHARLES. For my death! What a thought! I grant you he has not the makings of a king in him: I am not blind to his weaknesses. But surely he is not heartless.

JAMES. Psha! there is not a plot in the kingdom to murder either of us that he is not at the bottom of.

CHARLES. He is not deep enough to be at the bottom of anything, Jamie.

JAMES. Then he is at the top. I forgive him for wanting to make an end of me: I am no friend of his. But to plot against you, his father! you, who have petted him and spoilt him and forgiven him treason after treason! for that I shall not forgive him, as he shall find if ever he falls into my hand.

CHARLES. Jamie: this is a dreadful suspicion to put into my mind. I thought the lad had abused my affection until it was exhausted; but it still can hurt. Heaven keep him out of your hand! that is all I can say. Absalom! O Absalom: my son, my son!

JAMES. I am sorry, Charles; but this is what comes of bringing up your bastards as Protestants and making dukes of them.

CHARLES. Let me tell you a secret, Jamie: a king's secret. Peter the fisherman did not know everything. Neither did Martin Luther.

JAMES. Neither do you.

CHARLES. No; but I must do the best I can with what I know, and not with what Peter and Martin knew. Anyhow, the long and the short of it is that you must start for Scotland this very day, and stay there until I send you word that it is safe for you to come back.

JAMES. Safe! What are you afraid of, man? If you darent face these Protestant blackguards, is that any reason why I should run away from them?

CHARLES. You were talking just now about your popularity. Do you know who is the most popular man in England at present?

JAMES. Shaftesbury, I suppose. He is the Protestant hero just as Nelly is the Protestant whoor. I tell you Shaftesbury will turn his coat as often as you crack your whip. Why dont you crack it?

CHARLES. I am not thinking of Shaftesbury.

JAMES. Then who?

CHARLES. Oates.

JAMES. Titus Oates! A navy chaplain kicked out of the service for the sins of Sodom and Gomorrah! Are you afraid of him?

CHARLES. Yes. At present he is the most popular man in the kingdom. He is lodged in my palace at Whitehall with a pension of four hundred pounds a year.

JAMES. What!!!

CHARLES. And I, who am called a king, cannot get rid of him. This house is Isaac Newton's; and he can order you out and throw you out of the window if you dont go. But my house must harbor the vilest scoundrel in Europe while he parades in lawn sleeves through the street with his No Popery mob at his heels, and murders our best Catholic families with his brazen perjuries and his silly Popish plot that should not impose on a rabbit. No man with eyes in his head could look at the creature for an instant without seeing that he is only half human.

JAMES. Flog him through the town. Flog him to death. They can if they lay on hard enough and long enough. The same mob that now takes him for a saint will crowd to see the spectacle and revel in his roarings.

CHARLES. That will come, Jamie. I am hunting out his record; and your man Jeffries will see to it that the poor divvle shall have no mercy. But just now it is not Oates that we have to kill: the people would say that he was murdered by the Catholics and run madder than ever. They blame the Catholics now for the Great Fire of London and the plague. We must kill the Popish Plot first. When we have done that, God help Titus Oates! Meanwhile, away with you to Scotland and try your cat-o-ninetails on the Covenanters there.

JAMES. Well, I suppose I must, since England is governed by its mob instead of by its king. But I tell you, Charles, when I am king there shall be no such nonsense. You jeer at me and say that I am the protector of your life, because nobody will kill you to make me king; but I take that as the highest compliment you could pay me. This mob that your Protestant Republicans and Presbyterians and Levellers call the people of England will have to choose between King James the Second and King Titus Oates. And James and the Church – and there is only one real Church of God – will see to it that their choice will be Hobson's choice.

CHARLES. The people of England will have nothing to do with it. The real Levellers today, Jamie, are the lords and the rich squires – Cromwell's sort – and the moneyed men of the city. They will keep the people's noses to the grindstone no matter what happens. And their choice will be not between you and Titus Oates, but between your daughter Mary's Protestant husband and you.

JAMES. He will have to cross the seas to get here. And I, as Lord High

Admiral of England, will meet him on the seas and sink him there. He is no great general on land: on water he is nothing. I have never been beaten at sea.

CHARLES. Jamie, Jamie: nothing frightens me so much as your simple stupid pluck, and your faith in Rome. You think you will have the Pope at your back because you are a Catholic. You are wrong: in politics the Pope is always a Whig, because every earthly monarch's court is a rival to the Vatican.

JAMES. Do you suppose that if Orange Billy, the head of the Protestant heresy in Europe, the anti-Pope you might call him, dared to interfere with me, a Catholic king, the Pope could take his part against me in the face of all Europe! How can you talk such nonsense? Do you think Mary would share the crown if he tore it from her father's head? Rochester called you the king that never said a foolish thing and never did a wise one; but it seems to me that you talk silly-clever nonsense all day, though you are too wise: that is, too big a coward, ever to risk a fight with the squirearchy. What are they in France? Lackeys round the throne at Versailles: not one of them dare look King Louis straight in the face. But in France there is a real king.

CHARLES. He has a real army and real generals. And taxes galore. Old Noll went one better than Louis: he was a general himself. And what a general! Preston, Dunbar, Worcester: we could do nothing against him though we had everything on our side, except him. I have been looking for his like ever since we came back. I sometimes wonder whether Jack Churchill has any military stuff in him.

JAMES. What! That henpecked booby! I suppose you know that he got his start in life as your Barbara's kept man?

CHARLES. I know that the poor lad risked breaking his bones by jumping out of Barbara's window when she was seducing him and I came along unexpectedly. I have always liked him for that.

JAMES. It was worth his while. She gave him five thousand pounds for it.

CHARLES. Yes: I had to find the money. I was tremendously flattered when I heard of it. I had no idea that Barbara put so high a price on my belief in her faithfulness, in which, by the way, I did not believe. Poor Barbara was never alone with a pretty fellow for five minutes without finding out how much of a man he was. I threw Churchill in her way purposely to keep her in good humor. What struck me most in the affair was that Jack bought an annuity with the money instead of squandering it as any other man of his age would have done. That was a sign of solid ability. He may be henpecked: what married man is not? But he is no booby.

43

JAMES. Meanness. Pure meanness. The Churchills never had a penny to bless themselves with. Jack got no more education than my groom.

CHARLES. Latin grammar is not much use on the battlefield, as we found out. Turenne found Jack useful enough in Spain; and Turenne was supposed to be France's greatest general. Your crown may depend on Jack: by the time I die he will be as old a soldier as Oliver was at Dunbar.

JAMES. Never fear. I shall buy him if he's worth it.

CHARLES. Or if you are worth it. Jack is a good judge of a winner.

JAMES. He has his price all the same.

CHARLES. All intelligent men have, Jamie.

JAMES. Pshal Dont waste your witticisms on me: they butter no parsnips. If he can pick a winner he had better pick me.

CHARLES. There are only two horses in the race now: the Protestant and the Catholic. I have to ride both at once.

JAMES. That was what Father tried to do. See what he got by it!

CHARLES. See what I get by it! Not much, perhaps; but I keep my head on my shoulders. It takes a man of brains to do that. Our father unfortunately tried his hand at being also a man of blood, as Noll called him. We Stuarts are no good at that game: Noll beat us at it every time. I hate blood and battles: I have seen too much of them to have any dreams of glory about them. I am, as you say, no king. To be what you call a king I lack military ambition; and I lack cruelty. I have to manage Protestants who are so frightfully cruel that I dare not interfere with Protestant judges who are merciless. The penalty for high treason is so abominable that only a divvle could have invented it, and a nation of divvles crowd to see it done. The only time I risked my crown was when I stopped them after they had butchered ten of the regicides: I could bear no more. They were not satisfied: they dug up the body of old Noll, and butchered it rather than have their horrible sport cut short.

JAMES. Serve the rascals right! A good lesson for them and their like. Dont be such a mollycoddle, Charles. What you need is a bit of my sea training to knock the nonsense out of you.

CHARLES. So you will try your luck as a man of blood, will you?

JAMES. I will do what is necessary. I will fight my enemies if they put me to it. I will take care that those who put me to it shall not die easy deaths.

CHARLES. Well, that will seem very natural to the mob. You will find plenty of willing tools. But I would not light the fires of Smithfield again if I were you. Your pet Jeffries would do it for you and enjoy it; but Protestants do not like being burnt alive.

JAMES. They will have to lump it if they fly in the face of God.

44

CHARLES. Oh, go to Scotland: go to Jericho. You sicken me. Go.

JAMES. Charles! We must not part like this. You know you always stand
by me as far as you dare. I ought not to talk to you about government
and kingcraft: you dont understand these matters and never will; and
I do understand them. I have resolved again and again not to mention
them to you; for after all we are brothers; and I love you in spite of all
the times you have let me down with the Protestants. It is not your
fault that you have no head for politics and no knowledge of human
nature. You need not be anxious about me. I will leave for Scotland
tomorrow. But I have business in London tonight that I will not post-
pone for fifty thousand Titus Oateses.

CHARLES. Business in London tonight! The one redeeming point in your
character, Jamie, is that you are not a man of principle in the matter of
women.

JAMES. You are quite wrong there: I am in all things a man of principle
and a good Catholic, thank God. But being human I am also a man of
sin. I confess it; and I do my penances!

CHARLES. The women themselves are worse penances than any priest
dare inflict on you. Try Barbara: a week with her is worse than a
month in hell. But I have given up all that now. Nelly is a good little
soul who amuses me. Louise manages my French affairs. She has French
brains and manners, and is always a lady. But they are now my friends
only: affectionate friends, family friends, nothing else. And they alone
are faithful to the elderly king. I am fifty, Jamie, fifty: dont forget that.
And women got hold of me when I was fourteen, thirtysix years ago. Do
you suppose I have learnt nothing about women and what you call love
in that time? You still have love affairs: I have none. However, I am
not reproaching you: I am congratulating you on being still young and
green enough to come all the way from Holland for a night in London.

Mrs Basham returns, much perturbed.

MRS BASHAM. Mr Rowley: I must tell you that I cannot receive any
more of your guests. I have not knives nor plates nor glasses enough. I
have had to borrow chairs from next door. Your valet, Mr Chiffinch,
tells who ever has any business with you this morning to come on
here. Mr Godfrey Kneller, the new Dutch painter, with a load of imple-
ments connected with his trade, had got in in spite of me: he heard the
noise your people were making. There are the two ladies and the
player woman, and yourself and your royal brother and Mr Fox and
the painter. That makes seven; and Mr Newton makes eight and I
make nine. I have nothing to offer them but half a decanter of sherry
that was opened last Easter, and the remains of a mouldy cake. I have

sent Sally out with orders that will run away with a fortnight's house-keeping money; and that wont be half what theyll expect. I thought they were all going away when they came downstairs; but the French lady wanted to look through Mr Newton's telescope; and the jealous lady wouldnt leave until the French lady left; and the player woman is as curious as a magpie and makes herself as much at home as if she lived here. It has ended in their all staying. And now Mr Newton is explaining everything and shewing off his telescope and never thinking what I am to do with them! How am I to feed them?

CHARLES. Dont feed them, Mrs Basham. Starve them out.

MRS BASHAM. Oh no: I cant do that. What would they think of us? Mr Newton has his position to keep up.

CHARLES. It is the judgment of heaven on you for turning away my pretty spaniels from your door this morning.

MRS BASHAM. There were twelve of them, sir.

CHARLES. You would have found them much better company than nine human beings. But never mind. Sally will tell all the tradesmen that Mr Newton is entertaining me and my brother. They will call themselves Purveyors to his Majesty the King. Credit will be unlimited.

JAMES. Remember that this is Friday: a fast day. All I need is three or four different kinds of fish.

MRS BASHAM. No, sir: in this house you will have to be content with a Protestant dinner. Jack the fish hawker is gone. But he left us a nice piece of cod; and thats all youll get, sir.

CHARLES. Jamie: we must clear out and take the others with us. It seems we cannot visit anyone without ruining them.

JAMES. Pooh! What can a few pounds more or less matter to anybody?

CHARLES. I can remember when they meant a divvle of a lot to me, and to you too. Let us get back to Newmarket.

MRS BASHAM. No, sir: Mr Newton would not like that: he knows his duties as your host. And if you will excuse me saying so, sir: you all look as if a plain wholesome dinner would do you no harm for once in a way. By your leave I will go to look after it. I must turn them all out of the laboratory and send them up here while I lay the table there.

She goes out.

JAMES. 'A nice piece of cod!' Among nine people!

CHARLES. 'Isnt that a dainty dish to set before a king?' Your fast will be a real fast, Jamie, for the first time in your life.

JAMES. You lie. My penances are all real.

CHARLES. Well, a hunk of bread, a lump of cheese, and a bottle of ale are enough for me or for any man at this hour.

46

All the rest come back except Mrs Basham, Barbara, and Newton. Fox comes first.

FOX. I have made eight new friends. But has the Lord sent them to me? Such friends! [*He takes his old seat much perplexed*].

NELL [*coming in*] Oh, Rowley darling, they want me to recite my big speech from The Indian Emperor. But I cant do that without proper drapery: its classical. [*Going to the Duke*] And what is my Jamie doing here?

LOUISE [*taking a chair from the wall and planting it at Charles's right, familiarly close*] Why not give us a prologue? Your prologues are your best things. [*She sits*].

CHARLES and JAMES. Yes, yes: a prologue.

All are now seated, except Nell.

NELL. But I cant do a prologue unless I am in breeches.

FOX [*rising*] No. Eleanor Gwyn: how much more must I endure from you? I will not listen to a prologue that can be spoken only by a woman in breeches. And I warn you that when I raise my voice to heaven against mummery, whether in playhouse or steeplehouse, I can drown and dumb the loudest ribald ranter.

CHARLES. Pastor: Mistress Gwyn is neither a ribald nor a ranter. The plays and prologues in which she is famous are the works of the greatest poet of the age: the poet Laureate, John Dryden.

FOX. If he has given to the playhouse talents that were given to him for the service of God, his guilt is the deeper.

CHARLES. Have you considered, Pastor, that the playhouse is a place where two or three are gathered together?

NELL. Not when I am playing, Rowley darling. Two or three hundred, more likely.

FOX [*resuming his seat in the deepest perplexity*] Sir: you are upsetting my mind. You have forced me to make friends with this player woman; and now you would persuade me that the playhouse is as divine as my meeting house. I find your company agreeable to me, but very unsettling.

CHARLES. The settled mind stagnates, Pastor. Come! Shall I give you a sample of Mr Dryden at his best?

NELL. Oh yes, Rowley darling: give us your pet speech from Aurengzebe.

LOUISE. Yes yes. He speaks it beautifully. He is almost as good an actor as King Louis; and he has really more of the grand air.

CHARLES. Thank you, Louise. Next time leave out the almost. My part is more difficult than that of Louis.

JAMES. Pray silence for his Majesty the King, who is going to make a fool of himself to please the Quaker.

CHARLES. Forgive Jamie, ladies and gentlemen. He will give you his own favorite recitation presently; but the King comes first. Now listen. [*He rises. They all rise, except Fox*]. No, pray. My audience must be seated. [*They sit down again*].

Charles recites the pessimistic speech from Aurengzebe as follows:

> When I consider life, 'tis all a cheat;
> Yet, fooled with hope, men favor the deceit;
> Trust on, and think tomorrow will repay:
> Tomorrow's falser than the former day;
> Lies worse; and, while it says we shall be blest
> With some new choice, cuts off what we possessed.
> Strange cozenage! None would live past years again;
> Yet all hope pleasure in what yet remain;
> And from the dregs of life think to receive
> What the first sprightly running could not give.
> I'm tired of waiting for this chemic gold
> Which fools us young, and beggars us when old.

Nell and Louise applaud vigorously.

CHARLES. What do you think of that, Pastor? [*He sits*].

FOX. It is the cry of a lost soul from the bottomless blackness of its despair. Never have I heard anything so terrible. This man has never lived. I must seek him out and shew him the light and the truth.

NELL. Tut tut, George! The man in the play is going to be killed. To console himself he cries Sour Grapes: that is all. And now what shall I give you?

JAMES. Something oldfashioned. Give him a bit of Shakespear.

NELL. What! That author the old actors used to talk about. Kynaston played women in his plays. I dont know any. We cannot afford them nowadays. They require several actors of the first quality; and – would you believe it, George? – those laddies will not play now for less than fifteen shillings a week.

FOX [*starting up again*] Fifteen shillings a week to a player when the servants of God can scarce maintain themselves alive by working at mechanical trades! Such wickedness will bring a black judgment on the nation. Charles Stuart: have you no regard for your soul that you suffer such things to be done?

CHARLES. You would not grudge these poor fellows their fifteen shillings if you knew what women cost.

FOX. What manner of world is this that I have come into? Is virtue unknown here, or is it despised? [*He gives it up, and relapses into his seat*].

JAMES. Mr Dryden has an answer for that. [*He recites, seated*].

> How vain is virtue which directs our ways
> Through certain danger to uncertain praise!
> The world is made for the bold impious man
> Who stops at nothing, seizes all he can.
> Justice to merit does weak aid afford;
> She trusts her balance, and ignores her sword.
> Virtue is slow to take whats not her own,
> And, while she long consults, the prize is gone.

FOX. I take no exception to this. I have too good reason to know that it is true. But beware how you let these bold impious fellows extinguish hope in you. Their day is short; but the inner light is eternal.

JAMES. I am safe in the bosom of my Church, Pastor.

LOUISE. Take the gentleman's mind off his inner light, Nell. Give us a speech.

NELL. They dont want a speech from me. Rowley began talking about speeches because he wanted to do one himself. And now His Highness the Duke of York must have his turn.

JAMES. Are we poor devils of princes not to have any of the good things, nor do any of the pleasant things, because we are Royal Highnesses? Were you not freer and happier when you sold oranges in Drury Lane than you are now as a court lady?

FOX. Did you sell oranges in Drury Lane?

NELL. They say I did. The people like to believe I did. They love me for it. I say nothing.

CHARLES. Come! Give us one of Cydara's speeches from The Indian Emperor. It was in that that you burst on the world as the ambitious orange girl.

NELL. A wretched part: I had to stand mum on the stage for hours while the others were spouting. Mr Dryden does not understand how hard that is. Just listen to this, the longest speech I had.

> May I believe my eyes! What do I see?
> Is this her hate to him? her love to me?
> 'Tis in my breast she sheathes her dagger now.
> False man: is this thy faith? Is this thy vow?

Then somebody says something.

CHARLES.

> What words, dear saint, are these I hear you use?
> What faith? what voice? are those which you accuse?

NELL. 'Those which you accuse': thats my cue.

> More cruel than the tiger o'er his spile
> And falser than the weeping crocodile
> Can you add vanity to guilt, and take
> A pride to hear the conquests which you make?
> Go: publish your renown: let it be said
> The woman that you love you have betrayed –

Rowley darling: I cannot go on if you keep laughing at me. If only Mr Dryden had given me some really great lines, like the ones he gave to Montezuma. Listen.

> Still less and less my boiling spirits flow
> And I grow stiff, as cooling metals do.
> Farewell, Almira.

FOX. Now do you tell me that living men and women, created by God in His likeness and not in that of gibbering apes, can be bribed to utter such trash, and that others will pay to hear them do it when they will not enter a meeting house for a penny in the plate to hear the words of God Himself? What society is this I am in? I must be dreaming that I am in hell.

NELL. George: you are forgetting yourself. You should have applauded me. I will recite no more for you. [*She takes a chair from the wall and seats herself beside Louise, on her right*].

CHARLES. He does not understand, Nell. Tell him the story of the play, and why Montezuma says such extravagant things.

NELL. But how can I, Rowley darling? I dont know what it is all about: I know only my part and my cue. All I can say is that when Montezuma speaks those lines he drops dead.

FOX. Can you wonder that he does so? I should drop dead myself if I heard such fustian pass my lips.

JAMES. Is it worse than the fustian that passes the lips of the ranters in your conventicles?

FOX. I cannot deny it: the preachers are a greater danger than the players. I had not thought of this before. Again you unsettle my mind.

There is one Jeremy Collier who swears he will write such a book on the profaneness and immorality of the stage as will either kill the theatre or shame it into decency; but these lines just uttered by Eleanor Gwyn are not profane and immoral: they are mad and foolish.

LOUISE. All the less harmful, monsieur. They are not meant to be taken seriously; and no one takes them so. But your Huguenot ranters pretend to be inspired; and foolish people are deluded by them. And what sort of world would they make for us if they got the upper hand? Can you name a single pleasure that they would leave us to make life worth living?

FOX. It is not pleasure that makes life worth living. It is life that makes pleasure worth having. And what pleasure is better than the pleasure of holy living?

JAMES. I have been in Geneva, blasphemously called the City of God under that detestable Frenchman Calvin, who, thank God, has by now spent a century in hell. And I can testify that he left the wretched citizens only one worldly pleasure.

CHARLES. Which one was that?

JAMES. Moneymaking.

CHARLES. Odsfish! That was clever of him. It is a very satisfying pleasure, and one that lasts til death.

LOUISE. It does not satisfy me.

CHARLES. You have never experienced it, Louise. You spend money: you do not make it. You spend ten times as much as Nelly; but you are not ten times as happy. If you made ten times as much as she, you would never tire of it and never ask for anything better.

LOUISE. Charles: if I spent one week making money or even thinking about it instead of throwing it away with both hands all my charm would be gone. I should become that dull thing, a plain woman. My face would be full of brains instead of beauty. And you would send me back to France by the next ship, as you sent Barbara.

CHARLES. What if I did? You will soon be tired of me; for I am an ugly old fellow. But you would never tire of moneymaking.

NELL. Now the Lord be praised, my trade is one in which I can make money without losing my good looks!

LOUISE [to Charles] If you believe what you say, why do you not make money yourself instead of running after women?

CHARLES. Because there is a more amusing occupation for me.

LOUISE. I have not seen you practise it, Charles. What is it?

CHARLES. Kingcraft.

JAMES. Of which you have not the faintest conception.

51

CHARLES. Like Louise, you have not seen me practise it. But I am King of England; and my head is still on my shoulders.

NELL. Rowley darling: you must learn to keep King Charles's head out of your conversation. You talk too much of him.

CHARLES. Why is it that we always talk of my father's head and never of my great grandmother's? She was by all accounts a pretty woman; but the Protestants chopped her head off in spite of Elizabeth. They had Strafford's head off in spite of my father. And then they had his own off. I am not a bit like him; but I have more than a touch in me of my famous grandfather Henry the Fourth of France. And he died with a Protestant's dagger in his heart: the deadliest sort of Protestant: a Catholic Protestant. There are such living paradoxes. They burnt the poor wretch's hand off with the dagger in it, and then tore him to pieces with galloping horses. But Henry lay dead all the same. The Protestants will have you, Jamie, by hook or crook: I foresee that: they are the real men of blood. But they shall not have me. I shall die in my bed, and die King of England in spite of them.

FOX. This is not kingcraft: it is chicanery. Protestantism gives the lie to itself: it overthrows the Roman Church and immediately builds itself another nearer home and makes you the head of it, though it is now plain to me that your cleverness acknowledges no Church at all. You are right there: Churches are snares of the divvle. But why not follow the inner light that has saved you from the Churches? Be neither Catholic nor Protestant, Whig nor Tory: throw your crown into the gutter and be a Friend: then all the rest shall be added to you.

They all laugh at him except Charles.

CHARLES. A crown is not so easy to get rid of as you think, Pastor. Besides, I have had enough of the gutter: I prefer Whitehall.

JAMES [*to Fox*] You would like to have a king for your follower, eh?

FOX. I desire Friends, not followers. I am simple in my tastes. I am not schooled and learned as you two princes are.

CHARLES. Thank your stars for that, Pastor: you have nothing to unlearn.

FOX. That is well said. Too often have I found that a scholar is one whose mind is choked with rubbish that should never have been put there. But how do you come to know this? Things come to my knowledge by the Grace of God; yet the same things have come to you who live a most profane life and have no sign of grace at all.

CHARLES. You and I are mortal men, Pastor. It is not possible for us to differ very greatly. You have to wear leather breeches lest you be mistaken for me.

Barbara storms in with a sheet of drawing paper in her hand.

BARBARA [*thrusting the paper under Charles's nose*] Do you see this?

CHARLES [*scrutinizing it admiringly*] Splendid! Has Mr Kneller done this? Nobody can catch a likeness as he can.

BARBARA. Likeness! You have bribed him to insult me. It makes me look a hundred.

CHARLES. Nonsense, dear. It is you to the life. What do you say, Jamie? [*He hands the drawing to James*].

JAMES. It's you, duchess. He has got you, wrinkle for wrinkle.

BARBARA. You say this to my face! You, who have seen my portrait by Lilly!

NELL. You were younger then, darling.

BARBARA. Who asked you for your opinion, you jealous cat?

CHARLES. Sit down; and dont be silly, Barbara. A woman's face does not begin to be interesting until she is our age.

BARBARA. Our age! You old wreck, do you dare pretend that you are as young as I am?

CHARLES. I am only fifty, Barbara. But we are both getting on.

BARBARA. Oh! [*With a scream of rage she tears the drawing to fragments and stamps on them*].

CHARLES. Ah, that was wicked of you: you have destroyed a fine piece of work. Go back to France. I tell you I am tired of your tantrums.

Barbara, intimidated, but with a defiant final stamp on the drawing, flings away behind James to one of the chairs against the cupboards, and sits there sulking.

Newton comes in from the garden, followed by Godfrey Kneller, a Dutchman of 34, well dressed and arrogant. They are both almost as angry as Barbara.

NEWTON. Mr Kneller: I will dispute with you no more. You do not understand what you are talking about.

KNELLER. Sir: I must tell you in the presence of His Majesty you are a most overweening, a most audacious man. You presume to teach me my profession.

CHARLES. What is the matter, Mr Newton?

NEWTON. Let it pass, Mr Rowley. This painter has one kind of under-standing: I have another. There is only one course open to us both; and that is silence. [*Finding his chair occupied by the Duke of York he takes another from beside Barbara and seats himself at the side of the table on the Duke's left*].

CHARLES. Mr Newton is our host, Mr Kneller; and he is a very eminent philosopher. Will you not paint his picture for me? That can be done in silence.

KNELLER. I will paint his picture if your Majesty so desires. He has an interesting head: I should have drawn it this morning had not Her Grace of Cleveland insisted on my drawing her instead. But how can an interesting head contain no brain: that is the question.

CHARLES. Odsfish, man, he has the greatest brain in England.

KNELLER. Then he is blinded by his monstrous conceit. You shall judge between us, sir. Am I or am I not the greatest draughtsman in Europe?

CHARLES. You are certainly a very skilful draughtsman, Mr Kneller.

KNELLER. Can anyone here draw a line better than I?

CHARLES. Nobody here can draw a line at all, except the Duchess of Cleveland, who draws a line at nothing.

BARBARA. Charles —

CHARLES. Be quiet, Barbara. Do not presume to contradict your King.

KNELLER. If there is a science of lines, do I not understand it better than anyone?

CHARLES. Granted, Mr Kneller. What then?

KNELLER. This man here, this crazy and conceited philosopher, dares to assert in contradiction of me, of ME! that a right line is a straight line, and that everything that moves moves in a straight line unless some almighty force bends it from its path. This, he says, is the first law of motion. He lies.

CHARLES. And what do you say, Mr Kneller?

KNELLER. Sir: I do not say: I k n o w. The right line, the line of beauty, is a curve. My hand will not draw a straight line: I have to stretch a chalked string on my canvas and pluck it. Will you deny that your duchess here is as famous for her beauty as the Psyche of the divine Raphael? Well, there is not a straight line in her body: she is all curves.

BARBARA [outraged, rising] Decency, fellow! How dare you?

CHARLES. It is true, Barbara. I can testify to it.

BARBARA. Charles: you are obscene. The impudence! [She sits].

KNELLER. The beauty, madam. Clear your mind of filth. There is not a line drawn by the hand of the Almighty, from the rainbow in the skies to the house the snail carries on his back, that is not a curve, and a curve of beauty. Your apple fell in a curve.

NEWTON. I explained that.

KNELLER. You mistake explanations for facts: all you sciencemongers do. The path of the world curves, as you yourself have shewn; and as it whirls on its way it would leave your apple behind if the apple fell in a straight line. Motion in a curve is the law of nature; and the law of nature is the law of God. Go out into your garden and throw a stone straight if you can. Shoot an arrow from a bow, a bullet from a pistol, a cannon ball from the mightiest cannon the King can lend you, and though you had the strength of Hercules, and gunpowder more powerful than the steam which hurls the stones from Etna in eruption, yet cannot you make your arrow or your bullet fly straight to its mark.

NEWTON [*terribly perturbed*] This man does not know what he is saying. Take him away; and leave me in peace.

CHARLES. What he says calls for an answer, Mr Newton.

JAMES. The painter is right. A cannon ball flies across the sea in curves like the arches of a bridge, hop, hop, hop. But what does it matter whether it flies straight or crooked provided it hits between wind and water?

NEWTON. To you, admiral, it matters nothing. To me it makes the difference between reason and madness.

JAMES. How so?

NEWTON. Sir: if what this man believes be true, then not only is the path of the cannon ball curved, but space is curved; time is curved; the universe is curved.

KNELLER. Of course it is. Why not?

NEWTON. Why not! Only my life's work turned to waste, vanity, folly. This comes of admitting strangers to break into my holy solitude with their diabolical suggestions. But I am rightly rebuked for this vice of mine that led me to believe that I could construct a universe with empty figures. In future I shall do nothing but my proper work of interpreting the scriptures. Leave me to that work and to my solitude. [*Desperately, clutching his temples*] Begone, all of you. You have done mischief enough for one morning.

CHARLES. But, Mr Newton, may we not know what we have done to move you thus? What diabolical suggestions have we made? What mischief have we done?

NEWTON. Sir: you began it, you and this infidel quaker. I have devoted months of my life to the writing of a book – a chronology of the world – which would have cost any other man than Isaac Newton twenty years hard labor.

CHARLES. I have seen that book, and been astounded at the mental power displayed in every page of it.

NEWTON. You may well have been, Mr Rowley. And now what have you and Mr Fox done to that book? Reduced it to a monument of the folly of Archbishop Ussher, who dated the creation of the world at four thousand and four, B.C., and of my stupidity in assuming that he had proved his case. My book is nonsense from beginning to end. How could I, who have calculated that God deals in millions of miles of infinite space, be such an utter fool as to limit eternity, which has neither beginning nor end, to a few thousand years? But this man Fox, without education, without calculation, without even a schoolboy's algebra, knew this when I, who was born one of the greatest mathematicians in the world, drudged over my silly book for months, and could not see what was staring me in the face.

JAMES. Well, why howl about it? Bring out another edition and confess that your Protestant mathematics are a delusion and a snare, and your Protestant archbishops impostors.

NEWTON. You do not know the worst, sir. I have another book in hand: one which should place me in line with Kepler, Copernicus, and Galileo as a master astronomer, and as the completer of their celestial systems. Can you tell me why the heavenly bodies in their eternal motion do not move in straight lines, but always in ellipses?

CHARLES. I understand that this is an unsolved problem of science. I certainly cannot solve it.

NEWTON. I have solved it by the discovery of a force in nature which I call gravitation. I have accounted for all the celestial movements by it. And now comes this painter, this ignorant dauber who, were it to save his soul – if he has a soul – could not work out the simplest equation, or as much as conceive an infinite series of numbers! this fellow substitutes for my first law of motion – straight line motion – motion in a curve.

JAMES. So bang goes your second volume of Protestant philosophy! Squashed under Barbara's outlines.

BARBARA. I will not have my outlines discussed by men. I am not a heathen goddess: I am a Christian lady. Charles always encourages infidels and libertines to blaspheme. And now he encourages them to insult me. I will not bear it.

CHARLES. Do not be an idiot, Barbara: Mr Kneller is paying you the greatest compliment in taking you for a model of the universe. The choice would seem to be between a universe of Barbara's curves and a universe of straight lines seduced from their straightness by some purely mathematical attraction. The facts seem to be on the side of the painter. But in a matter of this kind can I, as founder of the Royal Society, rank the painter as a higher authority than the philosopher?

KNELLER. Your Majesty: the world must learn from its artists because God made the world as an artist. Your philosophers steal all their boasted discoveries from the artists; and then pretend they have deduced them from figures which they call equations, invented for that dishonest purpose. This man talks of Copernicus, who pretended to discover that the earth goes round the sun instead of the sun going round the earth. Sir: Copernicus was a painter before he became an astronomer. He found astronomy easier. But his discovery was made by the great Italian painter Leonardo, born twentyone years before him, who told all his intimates that the earth is a moon of the sun.

NEWTON. Did he prove it?

KNELLER. Man: artists do not prove things. They do not need to. They KNOW them.

NEWTON. This is false. Your notion of a spherical universe is borrowed from the heathen Ptolemy, from all the magicians who believed that the only perfect figure is the circle.

KNELLER. Just what such blockheads would believe. The circle is a dead thing like a straight line: no living hand can draw it: you make it by twirling a pair of dividers. Take a sugar loaf and cut it slantwise, and you will get hyperbolas and parabolas, ellipses and ovals, which Leonardo himself could not draw, but which any fool can make with a knife and a lump of sugar. I believe in none of these mechanical forms. The line drawn by the artist's hand, the line that flows, that strikes, that speaks, that reveals! that is the line that shews the divine handiwork.

CHARLES. So you, too, are a philosopher, Mr Kneller!

KNELLER. Sir: when a man has the gift of a painter, that qualification is so magical that you cannot think of him as anything else. Who thinks of Leonardo as an engineer? of Michael Angelo as an inventor or a sonneteer? of me as a scholar and a philosopher? These things are all in our day's work: they come to us without thinking. They are trifles beside our great labor of creation and interpretation.

JAMES. I had a boatswain once in my flagship who thought he knew everything.

FOX. Perhaps he did. Divine grace takes many strange forms. I smell it in this painter. I have met it in common sailors like your boatswain. The cobbler thinks there is nothing like leather—

NELL. Not when you make it into breeches instead of boots, George.

BARBARA. Be decent, woman. One does not mention such garments in well-bred society.

NELL. Orange girls and players and such like poor folk think nothing of mentioning them. They have to mend them, and sometimes to make them; so they have an honest knowledge of them, and are not ashamed like fine ladies who have only a dishonest knowledge of them.

CHARLES. Be quiet, Nelly; you are making Barbara blush.

NELL. Thats more than you have ever been able to do, Rowley darling.

BARBARA. It is well for you that you have all these men to protect you, mistress. Someday when I catch you alone I'll make you wish you had ten pairs of leather breeches on you.

CHARLES. Come come! no quarrelling.

NELL. She began it, Rowley darling.

CHARLES. No matter who began it, no quarrelling, I command.

LOUISE. Charles: the men have been quarrelling all the morning. Does your command apply to them too?

CHARLES. Their quarrels are interesting, Louise.

NELL. Are they? They bore me to distraction.

CHARLES. Much blood has been shed for them; and much more will be after we are gone.

BARBARA. Oh, do not preach, Charles. Leave that to this person who is dressed partly in leather. It is his profession: it is not yours.

CHARLES. The Protestants will not let me do anything else, my dear. But come! Mr Newton has asked us to leave his house many times. And we must not forget that he never asked us to come into it. But I have a duty to fulfil before we go. I must reconcile him with Mr Kneller, who must paint his portrait to hang in the rooms of the Royal Society.

KNELLER. It is natural that your Majesty should desire a work of mine for the Society. And this man's head is unusual, as one would expect from his being a philosopher: that is, half an idiot. I trust your Majesty was pleased with my sketch of Her Grace of Cleveland.

BARBARA. Your filthy caricature of Her Grace of Cleveland is under your feet. You are walking on it.

KNELLER [*picking up a fragment and turning it over to identify it*] Has the King torn up a work of mine? I leave the country this afternoon.

CHARLES. I would much sooner have torn up Magna Carta. Her Grace tore it up herself.

KNELLER. It is a strange fact, your Majesty, that no living man or woman can endure his or her portrait if it tells all the truth about them.

BARBARA. You lie, you miserable dauber. When our dear Peter Lilly, who has just died, painted me as I really am, did I destroy his portrait? But he was a great painter; and you are fit only to whitewash unmentionable places.

CHARLES. Her Grace's beauty is still so famous that we are all tired of it. She is the handsomest woman in England. She is also the stupidest. Nelly is the wittiest: she is also the kindest. Louise is the loveliest and cleverest. She is also a lady. I should like to have portraits of all three of them as they are now, not as Lilly painted them.

LOUISE. No, Charles: I do not want to have the whole truth about me handed down to posterity.

NELL. Same here. I prefer the orange girl.

KNELLER. I see I shall not succeed in England as a painter. My master Rembrandt did not think a woman worth painting until she was seventy.

NELL. Well, you shall paint me when I am seventy. In the theatre the young ones are beginning to call me Auntie! When they call me Old Mar Gwyn I shall be ready for you; and I shall look my very best then.

CHARLES. What about your portrait, Mr Fox? You have been silent too long.

FOX. I am dumbfounded by this strange and ungodly talk. To you it may seem mere gossip; but to me it is plain that this painter claims that his hand is the hand of God.

KNELLER. And whose hand is it if not the hand of God? You need hands to scratch your heads and carry food to your mouths. That is all your hands mean to you. But the hand that can draw the images of God and reveal the soul in them, and is inspired to do this and nothing else even if he starves and is cast off by his father and all his family for it: is not his hand the hand used by God, who, being a spirit without body, parts or passions, has no hands?

FOX. So the men of the steeplehouse say; but they lie. Has not God a passion for Creation? Is He not all passion of that divine nature?

KNELLER. Sir: I do not know who you are; but I will paint your portrait.

CHARLES. Bravo! We are getting on. How about your portrait, Mr Newton?

NEWTON. Not by a man who lives in a curved universe. He would distort my features.

LOUISE. Perhaps gravitation would distort them equally, Mr Newton.

CHARLES. That is very intelligent of you, Louise.

BARBARA. It takes some intelligence to be both a French spy and a bluestocking. I thank heaven for my stupidity, as you call it.

CHARLES. Barbara: must I throw you downstairs?

LOUISE. In France they call me the English spy. But this is the first time I have been called a bluestocking. All I meant was that Mr Kneller and Mr Newton seem to mean exactly the same thing; only one calls it beauty and the other gravitation; so they need not quarrel. The portrait will be the same both ways.

NEWTON. Can he measure beauty?

KNELLER. No. I can paint a woman's beauty; but I cannot measure it in a pint pot. Beauty is immeasurable.

NEWTON. I can measure gravitation. Nothing exists until it is measured. Fine words are nothing. Do you expect me to go to the Royal Society and tell them that the orbits of a planet are curved because painters think them prettier so? How much are they curved? This man cannot tell you. I can. Where will they be six months hence? He cannot tell you. I can. All he has to say is that the earth is a moon of the sun and that the line of beauty is a curve. Can he measure the path of the moon? Can he draw the curve?

KNELLER. I can draw your portrait. Can you draw mine?

NEWTON. Yes, with a camera obscura; and if I could find a chemical salt sensitive to light I could fix it. Some day portraits will be made at the street corners for sixpence apiece.

KNELLER. A looking glass will make your portrait for nothing. It makes the duchess's portrait fifty times a day.

BARBARA. It does not. I dont look at myself in the glass fifty times a day. Charles never passes one without looking at himself. I have watched him.

CHARLES. It rebukes my vanity every time, Barbara. I am an ugly fellow; yet I always think of myself as an Adonis.

LOUISE. You are not so ugly as you think, Charles. You were an ugly baby; and your wicked mother told you so. You have never got over it. But when I was sent to England to captivate you with my baby face, it was you who captivated me with your seventy inches and your good looks.

BARBARA. Ay, flatter him, flatter him: he loves it.

CHARLES. I cannot bear this. The subject is to be dropped.

LOUISE. But, Charles –

CHARLES. No, no, No. Not a word more. The King commands it.

Dead silence. They sit as if in church, except Fox, who chafes at the silence.

FOX. In the presence of this earthly king all you great nobles become dumb flunkeys. What will you be when the King of Kings calls you from your graves to answer for your lives?

NELL. Trust you, George, to put in a cheerful word. Rowley darling: may we all stop being dumb flunkeys and be human beings again?

CHARLES. Mr Rowley apologizes for his lapse into royalty. Only, the King's person is not to be discussed.

LOUISE. But, Charles, I love you when you put on your royalty. My king, Louis Quatorze, le grand monarque, le roi soleil, never puts off his royalty for a moment even in the most ridiculous circumstances.

BARBARA. Yes; and he looks like a well-to-do grocer, and will never look like anything else.

LOUISE. You would not dare to say so at Versailles, or even to think so. He is always great; and his greatness makes us great also. But it is true that he is not six feet high, and that the grand manner is not quite natural to him. Charles can do it so much better when he chooses. Charles: why dont you choose?

CHARLES. I prefer to keep the crown and the grand manner up my sleeve until I need them. Louis and I played together when we were boys. We know each other too well to be pleasant company; so I take care to keep out of his way. Besides, Louise, when I make you all great you become terrible bores. I like Nelly because nothing can make a courtier of her. Do you know why?

BARBARA. Because the orange girl has the gutter in her blood.

CHARLES. Not at all. Tell her the reason, Nell.

NELL. I dont know it, Rowley darling. I never was an orange girl; but I have the gutter in my blood all right. I think I have everything in my blood; for when I am on the stage I can be anything you please, orange girl or queen. Or even a man. But I dont know the reason why. So you can tell it to her, Rowley darling, if you know it.

CHARLES. It is because in the theatre you are a queen. I tell you the world is full of kings and queens and their little courts. Here is Pastor Fox, a king in his meeting house, though his meetings are against the law. Here is Mr Newton, a king in the new Royal Society. Here is Godfrey Kneller: a king among painters. I can make you duchesses and your sons dukes; but who would be mere dukes or duchesses if they could be kings and queens?

NELL. Dukes will be six a penny if you make all Barbara's sons dukes.

BARBARA. Oh! My sons have gentle blood in their veins, not gutter dirt.

CHARLES. For shame, Nelly! It was illbred of you to reproach her Grace for the most amiable side of her character.

NELL. I beg pardon. God forgive me, I am no better myself.

BARBARA. No better! You impudent slut.

NELL. Well, no worse, if you like. One little duke is enough for me.

LOUISE. Change the subject, Charles. What you were saying about little kings and queens being everywhere was very true. You are very spiritual.

BARBARA. Ha ha! Ha ha ha! He spiritual!

LOUISE. Clever, you call it. I am always in trouble with my English. And Charles is too lazy to learn French properly, though he lived in France so long.

BARBARA. If you mean clever, he is as clever as fifty foxes.

FOX. He may be fifty times as clever as I; but so are many of the blackest villains. Value him rather for his flashes of the inner light? Did he not stop the butchering of the regicides on the ground that if he punished them they could never punish themselves? That was what made me his loyal subject.

BARBARA. I did not mean fifty of you: I meant real foxes. He is so clever that he can always make me seem stupid when it suits him: that is, when I want anything he wont give me. He is as stingy as a miser.

CHARLES. You are like a dairymaid: you think there is no end to a king's money. Here is my Nelly, who is more careful of my money than she is of her own. Well, when I am dying, and all the rest of you are forgotten, my last thought will be of Nelly.

NELL. Rowley darling: dont make me cry. I am not the only one. Louise is very thoughtful about money.

BARBARA. Yes: she knows exactly how much he has: she gets it for him from the King of France.

LOUISE. This subject of conversation is in the worst possible taste. Charles: be a king again; and forbid it.

CHARLES. Nobody but Barbara would have introduced it. I forbid it absolutely.

Mrs Basham returns.

MRS BASHAM. Mr Newton: dinner is served.

BARBARA. You should address yourself to His Majesty. Where are your manners, woman?

MRS BASHAM. In this house Mr Newton comes first. Come along quick, all of you; or your victuals will be cold.

NEWTON [*rising*] Mr Kneller: will you take her Grace of Cleveland, as you are interested in her curves?

BARBARA [*violently*] No. I am the senior duchess: it is my right to be taken in by the King.

CHARLES [*rising and resignedly giving her his arm*] The Duke of York will follow with the junior duchess. Happy man!

All rise, except Fox.

BARBARA. Brute! [*She tries to disengage herself*].

CHARLES [*holding her fast*] You are on the King's arm. Behave yourself. [*He takes her out forcibly*].

MRS BASHAM. Now, your Highness. Now, Madam Carwell.

JAMES [*taking Louise*] You have remembered, I hope, that Madam Carwell is a Catholic?

MRS BASHAM. Yes: there will be enough cod for the two of you.

LOUISE. Provided Charles does not get at it first. Let us hurry. [*She hurries James out*].

MRS BASHAM. Will you take the player woman, Mr Kneller?

NELL. No no. The player woman goes with her dear old Fox. [*She swoops on the Quaker and drags him along*] George: today you will dine with publicans and sinners. You will say grace for them.

FOX. You remind me that where my Master went I must follow. [*They go out*].

MRS BASHAM. There is no one left for you to take in, Mr Kneller. Mr Newton must take me in and come last.

KNELLER. I will go home. I cannot eat in this house of straight lines.

MRS BASHAM. You will do nothing of the sort, Mr Kneller. There is a cover laid for you; and the King expects you.

NEWTON. The lines are not straight, Mr Kneller. Gravitation bends them. And at bottom I know no more about gravitation than you do about beauty.

KNELLER. To you the universe is nothing but a clock that an almighty clockmaker has wound up and set going for all eternity.

NEWTON. Shall I tell you a secret, Mr Beautymonger? The clock does not keep time. If it did there would be no further need for the Clockmaker. He is wiser than to leave us to our foolish selves in that fashion. When He made a confusion of tongues to prevent the Tower of Babel from reaching to heaven He also contrived a confusion of time to prevent us from doing wholly without Him. The sidereal clock, the clock of the universe, goes wrong. He has to correct it from time to time. Can you, who know everything because you and God are both artists, tell me what is amiss with the perihelion of Mercury?

KNELLER. The what?

NEWTON. The perihelion of Mercury.

KNELLER. I do not know what it is.

NEWTON. I do. But I do not know what is amiss with it. Not until the world finds this out can it do without the Clockmaker in the heavens who can set the hands back or forward, and move the stars with a touch of His almighty finger as He watches over us in the heavens.

KNELLER. In the heavens! In your universe there is no heaven. You have abolished the sky.

NEWTON. Ignoramus: there may be stars beyond our vision bigger than the whole solar system. When I have perfected my telescope it will give you your choice of a hundred heavens.

MRS BASHAM. Mr Kneller: your dinner will be cold; and you will be late for grace. I cannot have any more of this ungodly talk. Down with you to your dinner at once.

KNELLER. In this house, you said, Mr Newton comes first. But you take good care that he comes last. The mistress of this and every other house is she who cooks the dinner. [*He goes out*].

MRS BASHAM [*taking Newton out*] Thats a funny fellow, sir. But you really should not begin talking about the stars to people just as they are going away quietly. It is a habit that is growing on you. What do they know or care about the perry healing of Mercury that interests you so much? We shall never get these people out of the house if – [*They pass out of hearing*].

There is peace in the deserted room.

Act II

The boudoir of Catherine of Braganza, Charles's queen, in his not too palatial quarters in Newmarket late in the afternoon on the same day. A prie-dieu, and the pictures, which are all devotional, are signs of the queen's piety. Charles, in slippers and breeches, shirt and cravat, wrapped in an Indian silk dressing gown, is asleep on a couch. His coat and boots are on the carpet where he has thrown them. His hat and wig are on a chair with his tall walking stick. The door, opening on a staircase landing, is near the head of the couch, between it and the prie-dieu. There is a clock in the room.

Catherine, aged 42, enters. She contemplates her husband and the untidiness he has made. With a Portuguese shake of the head (about six times) she sets to work to put the room in order by taking up the boots and putting them tidily at the foot of the couch. She then takes out the coat and hangs it on the rail of the landing. Returning, she purposely closes the door with a bang sufficient to wake Charles.

CHARLES. How long have I been asleep?

CATHERINE. I not know. Why leave you your things about all over my room? I have to put them away like a chambermaid.

CHARLES. Why not send for Chiffinch? It is his business to look after my clothes.

CATHERINE. I not wish to be troubled with Chiffinch when we are alone.

CHARLES [*rising*] Belovéd: you should make me put away my clothes myself. Why should you do chambermaid's work for me? [*His 'beloved' always has three syllables*].

CATHERINE. I not like to see you without your wig. But I am your wife and must put up with it.

CHARLES [*getting up*] I am your husband; and I count it a great privilege. [*He kisses her*].

CATHERINE. Yes yes; but why choose you my boudoir for your siesta?

CHARLES. Here in our Newmarket lodging it is the only place where the women cannot come after me.

CATHERINE. A wife is some use then, after all.

CHARLES. There is nobody like a wife.

CATHERINE. I hear that Cleveland has come back from Paris. Did you send for her?

65

CHARLES. Send for her! I had as soon send for the divvle. I finished with Barbara long ago.

CATHERINE. How often have you told me that you are finished with all women! Yet Portsmouth keeps her hold on you, and Nelly the player. And now Cleveland comes back.

CHARLES. Beloved: you do not understand. These women do not keep their hold on me: I keep my hold on them. I have a bit of news for you about Louise. What do you think I caught her at this morning?

CATHERINE. I had rather not guess.

CHARLES. Buying a love potion. That was for me. I do not make love to her enough, it seems. I hold her because she is intelligent and ladylike and keeps me in touch with France and the French court, to say nothing of the money I have to extract from Louis through her.

CATHERINE. And Nelly? She can play the fine lady; but is she one?

CHARLES. Nelly is a good creature; and she amuses me. You know, beloved, one gets tired of court ladies and their conversation, always the same.

CATHERINE. And you really did not send for Cleveland to come back?

CHARLES. Beloved: when I was young I thought that there was only one unbearable sort of woman: the one that could think of nothing but her soul and its salvation. But in Barbara I found something worse: a woman who thought of nothing but her body and its satisfaction, which meant men and money. For both, Barbara is insatiable. Grab, grab, grab. When one is done with Barbara's body – a very fine body, I admit – what is there left?

CATHERINE. And you are done with Barbara's body?

CHARLES. Beloved: I am done with all bodies. They are all alike: all cats are grey in the dark. It is the souls and the brains that are different. In the end one learns to leave the body out. And then Barbara is packed off to Paris, and is not asked back by me, though I have no doubt there is some man in the case.

CATHERINE. Why spend you so much time with me here – so much more than you used to?

CHARLES. Beloved: do I plague you? I am off.

He makes for the door: she runs to it and bars his egress.

CATHERINE. No: that is not what I meant. Go back and sit down.

Charles obediently goes back to the couch, where they sit side by side.

CHARLES. And what did you mean, beloved?

CATHERINE. You spend too much time away from court. Your brother is stealing the court away from you. When he is here his rooms are crowded: yours are empty.

CHARLES. I thank heaven for it. The older I grow, the less I can endure that most tiresome of all animals, the courtier. Even a dissolute court, as they say mine is – I suppose they mean a court where bawdy stories are told out loud instead of whispered – is more tedious than a respectable one. They repeat themselves and repeat themselves endlessly. And I am just as bad with my old stories about my flight after the battle of Worcester. I told the same one twice over within an hour last Tuesday. This morning Barbara called me an old wreck.

CATHERINE [*flaming up*] She dared! Send her to the Tower and let her rot there.

CHARLES. She is not so important as that, beloved. Nor am I. And we must forgive our enemies when we can afford to.

CATHERINE. I forgive my enemies, as you well know, Charles. It is my duty as a Catholic and a Christian. But it is not my duty to forgive y o u r enemies. And you never forgive mine.

CHARLES. An excellent family arrangement for a royal pair. We can exchange our revenges and remain good Christians. But Barbara may be right. When a king is shunned, and his heir is courted, his death is not far off.

CATHERINE. You must not say things like that: I not can bear it. You are stronger in your mind than ever; and nobody can keep up with you walking.

CHARLES. Nevertheless, beloved, I shall drop before you do. What will happen to you then? that is what troubles me. When I am dead you must go back to Portugal, where your brother the king will take care of you. You will never be safe here, because you are a Catholic queen.

CATHERINE. I not think I shall care what becomes of me when you are gone. But James is a Catholic. When he is king what have I to fear? Or do you believe your son Monmouth will prevent him from succeeding you and become a Protestant king?

CHARLES. No. He will try, poor boy; but Jamie will kill him. He is his mother's son; and his mother was nothing. Then the Protestants will kill Jamie; and the Dutch lad will see his chance and take it. He will be king: a Protestant king. So you must make for Portugal.

CATHERINE. But such things not could happen. Why are you, who are afraid of nothing else, so afraid of the Protestants?

CHARLES. They killed my great grandmother. They killed my father. They would kill you if I were not a little too clever for them: they are trying hard enough, damn them! They are great killers, these Protestants. Jamie has just one chance. They may call in Orange

Billy before they kill him; and then it will hardly be decent for Billy to kill his wife's father. But they will get rid of Jamie somehow; so you must make for home the moment I have kissed you goodbye for the last time.

CATHERINE [*almost in tears*] You not must talk of it – [*She breaks down*].

CHARLES [*caressing her*] Beloved: you will only lose the worst of husbands.

CATHERINE. That is a lie: if anyone else said it I would kill her. You are the very best husband that ever lived.

CHARLES [*laughing*] Oh! Oh! Oh! The merry monarch! Beloved: can anything I can ever do make up to you for my unfaithfulness?

CATHERINE. People think of nothing but that, as if that were the whole of life. What care I about your women? your concubines? your handmaidens? the servants of your common pleasures? They have set me free to be something more to you than they are or can ever be. You have never been really unfaithful to me.

CHARLES. Yes, once, with the woman whose image as Britannia is on every British penny, and will perhaps stay there to all eternity. And on my honor nothing came of that: I never touched her. But she had some magic that scattered my wits: she made me listen for a moment to those who were always pressing me to divorce my patient wife and take a Protestant queen. But I could never have done it, though I was furious when she ran away from me and married Richmond.

CATHERINE. Oh, I know, I know: it was the only time I ever was jealous. Well, I forgive you: why should a great man like you be satisfied with a little thing like me?

CHARLES. Stop. I cannot bear that. I am not a great man; and neither are you a little woman. You have more brains and character than all the rest of the court put together.

CATHERINE. I am nothing except what you have made me. What did I know when I came here? Only what the nuns teach a Portuguese princess in their convent.

CHARLES. And what more had I to teach you except what I learnt when I was running away from the battle of Worcester? And when I had learnt that much there was an end of me as a king. I knew too much.

CATHERINE. With what you have taught me I shall govern Portugal if I return to it?

CHARLES. I have no doubt of it, beloved; but whether that will make you any happier I have my doubts. I wish you could govern the English for me.

CATHERINE. No one can govern the English: that is why they will never come to any good. In Portugal there is the holy Church: we know what we believe; and we all believe the same things. But here the Church itself is a heresy; and there are a thousand other heresies: almost as many heresies as there are people. And if you ask any of them what his sect believes he does not know: all he can say is that the men of the other sects should be hanged and their women whipped through the town at the cart's tail. But they are all against the true Church. I do not understand the English; and I do not want to govern them.

CHARLES. You are Portuguese. I am Italian, French, Scottish, hardly at all English. When I want to know how the great lump of my subjects will take anything I tell it to Barbara. Then I tell it to Chiffinch. Then I tell it to Jamie. When I have the responses of Barbara, Chiffinch, and Jamie, I know how Tom, Dick and Harry will take it. And it is never as I take it.

CATHERINE. In Portugal we not have this strange notion that Tom, Dick and Harry matter. What do they know about government?

CHARLES. Nothing; but they hate it. And nobody teaches them how necessary it is. Instead, when we teach them anything we teach them grammar and dead languages. What is the result? Protestantism and parliaments instead of citizenship.

CATHERINE. In Portugal, God be praised, there are no Protestants and no parliaments.

CHARLES. Parliaments are the very divvle. Old Noll began by thinking the world of parliaments. Well, he tried every sort of parliament, finishing with a veritable reign of the saints. And in the end he had to turn them all out of doors, neck and crop, and govern through his major-generals. And when Noll died they went back to their parliament and made such a mess of it that they had to send for me.

CATHERINE. Suppose there had been no you?

CHARLES. There is always somebody. In every nation there must be the makings of a capable council and a capable king three or four times over, if only we knew how to pick them. Nobody has found out how to do it: that is why the world is so vilely governed.

CATHERINE. But if the rulers are of noble birth –

CHARLES. You mean if they are the sons of their fathers. What good is that?

CATHERINE. You are a king because you are the son of your father. And you are the best of kings.

CHARLES. Thank you. And your brother Alfonso was king of Portugal because he was the son of his father. Was he also the best of kings?

CATHERINE. Oh, he was dreadful. He was barely fit to be a stable boy; but my brother Pedro took his crown and locked him up; and Pedro also is my father's son.

CHARLES. Just so: six of one and half a dozen of the other. Heredity is no use. Learning Latin is no use: Jack Churchill, who is an ignoramus, is worth fifty scholars. If Orange Billy dies and one of my nieces succeeds him Jack will be King of England.

CATHERINE. Perhaps the Church should select the king – or the queen.

CHARLES. The Church has failed over and over again to select a decent Pope. Alexander Borgia was a jolly fellow; and I am the last man alive to throw stones at him; but he was not a model Pope.

CATHERINE. My father was a great king. He fought the Spaniards and set Portugal free from their yoke. And it was the people who chose him and made him do it. I have sometimes wondered whether the people should not choose their king.

CHARLES. Not the English people. They would choose Titus Oates. No, beloved: the riddle of how to choose a ruler is still unanswered; and it is the riddle of civilization. I tell you again there are in England, or in any other country, the makings of half a dozen decent kings and councils; but they are mostly in prison. If we only knew how to pick them out and label them, then the people could have their choice out of the half dozen. It may end that way, but not until we have learnt how to pick the people who are fit to be chosen before they are chosen. And even then the picked ones will be just those whom the people will not choose. Who is it that said that no nation can bear being well governed for more than three years? Old Noll found that out. Why am I a popular king? Because I am a lazy fellow. I enjoy myself and let the people see me doing it, and leave things as they are, though things as they are will not bear thinking of by those who know what they are. That is what the people like. It is what they would do if they were kings.

CATHERINE. You are not lazy: I wish you were: I should see more of you. You take a great deal too much exercise: you walk and walk and nobody can keep up with you; you are always gardening or sailing or building and talking to gardeners and sailors and shipwrights and bricklayers and masons and people like that, neglecting the court. That is how your brother gathers the court round him and takes it away from you.

CHARLES. Let him. There is nothing to be learnt at court except that a courtier's life is not a happy one. The gardeners and the watermen, the shipwrights and bricklayers and carpenters and masons, are happier and far far more contented. It is the worst of luck to be born a king. Give me a skilled trade and eight or ten shillings a week, and you and I, beloved, would pig along more happily than we have ever been able to do as our majesties.

CATHERINE. I not want to pig along. I was born to rule; and if the worst comes to the worst and I have to go back to my own country I shall shew the world that I can rule, and that I am not the ninny I am made to look like here.

CHARLES. Why dont you do it, beloved? I am not worth staying with.

CATHERINE. I am torn ten different ways. I know that I should make you divorce me and marry a young Protestant wife who would bring you a son to inherit the crown and save all this killing of Monmouth and James and the handing over of your kingdom to the Hollander. I am tempted to do it because then I should return to my own beautiful country and smell the Tagus instead of the dirty Thames, and rule Portugal as my mother used to rule over the head of my worthless brother. I should be somebody then. But I cannot bring myself to leave you: not for all the thrones in the world. And my religion forbids me to put a Protestant on the throne of England when the rightful heir to it is a good Catholic.

CHARLES. You shall not, beloved. I will have no other widow but you.

CATHERINE. Ah! you can coax me so easily.

CHARLES. I treated you very badly when I was a young man because young men have low tastes and think only of themselves. Besides, odsfish! we could not talk to oneanother. The English they taught you in Portugal was a tongue that never was spoke on land or sea; and my Portuguese made you laugh. We must forget our foolish youth: we are grown-up now.

CATHERINE. Happy man! You forget so easily. But think of the difference in our fortunes! All your hopes of being a king were cut off: you were an exile, an outcast, a fugitive. Yet your kingdom dropped into your mouth at last; and you have been a king since you were old enough to use your power. But I! My mother was determined from my birth that I should be a queen: a great queen: Queen of England. Well, she had her way: we were married; and they call me queen. But have I ever reigned? Am I not as much an exile and an outcast as ever you were? I am not Catherine of England: I am Catherine of Bragança: a foreign woman with a funny name that they cannot pronounce. Yet I have the blood of rulers in my veins and the brains of rulers in my head.

CHARLES. They are no use here: the English will not be ruled; and there is nothing they hate like brains. For brains and religion you must go to Scotland; and Scotland is the most damnable country on earth: never shall I forget the life they led me there with their brains and their religion when they made me their boy king to spite Old Noll. I sometimes think religion and brains are the curse of the world. No, beloved, England for me, with all its absurdities!

CATHERINE. There can be only one true religion; and England has fifty.

CHARLES. Well, the more the merrier, if only they could let oneanother live. But they will not do even that.

CATHERINE. Have you no conscience?

CHARLES. I have; and a very troublesome one too. I would give a dukedom to any doctor that would cure me of it. But somehow it is not a conscience of the standard British pattern.

CATHERINE. That is only your witty nonsense. Our consciences, which come from God, must be all the same.

CHARLES. They are not. Do you think God so stupid that he could invent only one sort of conscience?

CATHERINE [shocked] What a dreadful thing to say! I must not listen to you.

CHARLES. No two consciences are the same. No two love affairs are the same. No two marriages are the same. No two illnesses are the same. No two children are the same. No two human beings are the same. What is right for one is wrong for the other. Yet they cannot live together without laws; and a law is something that obliges them all to do the same thing.

CATHERINE. It may be so in England. But in Portugal the Holy Church makes all Catholics the same. My mother ruled them though she was a Spaniard. Why should I not do what my mother did?

CHARLES. Why not, indeed? I daresay you will do it very well, beloved. The Portuguese can believe in a Church and obey a king. The English robbed the Church and destroyed it: if a priest celebrates Mass anywhere in England outside your private chapel he is hanged for it. My great grandmother was a Catholic queen: rather than let her succeed to the throne they chopped her head off. My father was a Protestant king: they chopped his head off for trying to govern them and asking the Midlands to pay for the navy. While the Portuguese were fighting the Spaniards the English were fighting oneanother. You can do nothing with the English. How often have I told you that I am no real king: that the utmost I can do is to keep my crown on my head and my head on my shoulders. How often have you asked me to do some big thing like joining your Church, or some little thing like pardoning a priest or a Quaker condemned to some cruel punishment! And you have found that outside the court, where my smiles and my frowns count for everything, I have no power. The perjured scoundrel, Titus Oates, steeped in unmentionable vices, is lodged in my palace with a pension. If I could have my way he would be lodged on the gallows. There is a preacher named Bunyan who has written a book about the Christian life that is being read, they tell me, all the world over; and I could not release him from Bedford Gaol, where he rotted for years. The world will remember Oates and Bunyan; and I shall be The Merry Monarch. No: give me English birds and English trees, English dogs and Irish horses, English rivers and English ships; but English m e n! No, no, NO.

CATHERINE. And Englishwomen?

CHARLES. Ah! there you have me, beloved. One cannot do without women: at least I cannot. But having to manage rascals like Buckingham and Shaftesbury, and dodgers like Halifax, is far worse than having to manage Barbara and Louise.

CATHERINE. Is there really any difference? Shaftesbury is trying to have me beheaded on Tower Hill on a charge of plotting to poison you sworn to by Titus Oates. Barbara is quite ready to support him in that.

CHARLES. No, beloved. The object of having you beheaded is to enable me to marry a Protestant wife and have a Protestant heir. I have pointed out to Barbara that the Protestant wife would not be so kind to her as you are, and would have her out of the kingdom before she could say Jack Robinson. So now she has thrown over Shaftesbury; and when I have thrown him over, as I shall know how to do presently, there will be an end of him. But he will be succeeded by some stupider rascal, or, worse still, some stupid fellow who is not a rascal. The clever rascals are all for sale; but the honest dunderheads are the very divvle.

CATHERINE. I wish you were not so clever.

CHARLES. Beloved: you could not do without my cleverness. That is why you must go back to Portugal when I am gone.

CATHERINE. But it makes your mind twist about so. You are so clever that you think you can do without religion. If only I could win you to the Church I should die perfectly happy; and so would you.

CHARLES. Well, I promise you I will not die a Protestant. You must see to that when the hour strikes for me: the last hour. So my very belovedest will die happy; and that is all I care about. [*Caressing her*] Does that satisfy you?

CATHERINE. If only I could believe it.

CHARLES. You mean I am the king whose word no man relies on.

CATHERINE. No: you are not that sort of king for me. But will it be a real conversion? I think you would turn Turk to please me.

CHARLES. Faith I believe I would. But there is more in it than that. It is not that I have too little religion in me for the Church: I have too much, like a queer fellow I talked with this morning. [*The clock strikes five*]. Odsfish! I have a Council meeting. I must go. [*He throws off his dressing gown*]. My boots! What has become of my boots?

CATHERINE. There are your boots. And wait until I make you decent.
Whilst he pulls his boots on, she fetches his coat and valets him into it. He snatches up his hat and stick and puts the hat on.

CATHERINE. No no: you have forgotten your wig. [*She takes his hat off and fetches the wig*]. Fancy your going into the Council Chamber like that! Nobody would take you for King Charles the Second without that wig. Now. [*She puts the wig on him; then the hat. A few final pats and pulls complete his toilet*]. Now you look every inch a king. [*Making him a formal curtsey*] Your Majesty's visit has made me very happy. Long live the King!

CHARLES. May the Queen live for ever!
He throws up his arm in a gallant salute and stalks out. She rises and throws herself on her knees at her prie-dieu.

Buoyant Billions:

A Comedy of No Manners

with

Preface

The Author Explains

Preface

I commit this to print within a few weeks of completing my 92nd year. At such an age I should apologize for perpetrating another play or presuming to pontificate in any fashion. I can hardly walk through my garden without a tumble or two; and it seems out of all reason to believe that a man who cannot do a simple thing like that can practise the craft of Shakespear. Is it not a serious sign of dotage to talk about oneself, which is precisely what I am now doing? Should it not warn me that my bolt is shot, and my place silent in the chimney corner?

Well, I grant all this; yet I cannot hold my tongue nor my pen. As long as I live I must write. If I stopped writing I should die for want of something to do.

If I am asked why I have written this play I must reply that I do not know. Among the many sects of Peculiar People which England produces so eccentrically and capriciously are the Spiritualists. They believe in personal immortality as far as any mortal can believe in an unimaginable horror. They have a cohort of Slate Writers and Writing Mediums in whose hands a pencil of any sort will, apparently of its own volition, write communications, undreamt-of by the medium, that must, they claim, be supernatural. It is objected to these that they have neither novelty, profundity, literary value nor artistic charm, being well within the capacity of very ordinary mortals, and are therefore dismissed as fraudulent on the ground that it is much more probable that the mediums are pretending and lying than performing miracles.

As trueblue Britons the mediums do not know how to defend themselves. They only argue-bargue. They should simply point out that the same objection may be raised against any famous scripture. For instance, the Peculiars known as Baconians believe, with all the evidence against them, that the plays attributed to Shakespear must have been written by somebody else, being unaccountably beyond his knowledge and capacity. Who that somebody else was is the mystery; for the plays are equally beyond the capacity of Bacon and all the later rival claimants. Our greatest masterpiece of literature is the Jacobean translation of the Bible; and this the Christian Churches declare to be the word of God, supernaturally dictated through Christian mediums and transcribed by them as literally as any letter dictated by a merchant to his typist.

Take my own case. There is nothing in my circumstances or personality to suggest that I differ from any other son of a downstart gentleman driven by lack of unearned income to become an incompetent merchant and harp on his gentility. When I take my pen or sit down to my typewriter, I am as much a medium as Browning's Mr Sludge or Dunglas Home, or as Job or John of Patmos. When I write a play I do not foresee nor intend a page of it from one end to the other: the play writes itself. I may reason out every sentence until I have made it say exactly what it comes to me to say; but whence and how and why it comes to me, or why I persisted, through nine years of unrelieved market failure, in writing instead of in stockbroking or turf bookmaking or peddling, I do not know. You may say it was because I had a talent that way. So I had; but that fact remains inexplicable. What less could Mr Sludge say? or John Hus, who let himself be burnt rather than recant his 'I dont know. Instruct me'?

When I was a small boy I saw a professional writing medium, pencil in hand, slash down page after page with astonishing speed without lifting his pencil from the blank paper we fed on to his desk. The fact that he was later transported for forgery did not make his performance and his choice of mediumship as his profession less unaccountable. When I was an elderly man, my mother amused herself with a planchette and a ouija, which under her hands produced what are called spirit writings abundantly. It is true that these screeds might have been called wishful writings (like wishful thinkings) so clearly were they as much her own story-telling inventions as the Waverley novels were Scott's. But why did she choose and practise this senseless activity? Why was I doing essentially the same as a playwright? I do not know. We both got some satisfaction from it or we would not have done it.

This satisfaction, this pleasure, this appetite, is as yet far from being as intense as the sexual orgasm or the ecstasy of a saint, though future cortical evolution may leave them far behind. Yet there are the moments of inexplicable happiness of which Mr J. B. Priestley spoke in a recent broadcast as part of his experience. To me they have come only in dreams not oftener than once every fifteen years or so. I do not know how common they are; for I never heard anyone but Mr Priestley mention them. They have an exalted chronic happiness, as of earth become heaven, proving that such states are possible for us even as we now are.

The happiest moment of my life was when as a child I was told by my mother that we were going to move from our Dublin street to Dalkey Hill in sight of the skies and seas of the two great bays between Howth and Bray, with Dalkey Island in the middle. I had already had a glimpse of them, and of Glencree in the mountains, on Sunday excursions; and they had given me the magic delight Mr Ivor Brown has described as the effect on him of natural scenery. Let who can explain it. Poets only can express it. It is a hard fact, waiting for some scientific genius to make psychology of it.

The professional biologists tell us nothing of all this. It would take them out of the realm of logic into that of magic and miracle, in which they would lose their reputation for omniscience and infallibility. But magic and miracle, as far as they are not flat lies, are not divorced from facts and consequently from science: they are facts: as yet unaccounted for, but none the less facts. As such they raise problems; and genuine scientists must face them at the risk of being classed with Cagliostro instead of with Clerk-Maxwell and Einstein, Galileo and Newton, who, by the way, worked hard at interpreting the Bible, and was ashamed of his invention of the Infinitesimal Calculus until Leibniz made it fashionable.

Now Newton was right in rating the Calculus no higher than a school-boy's crib, and the interpretation of the Bible as far more important. In this valuation, which seems so queer to us today, he was not in the least lapsing from science into superstition: he was looking for the foundation of literary art in the facts of history. Nothing could be more important or more scientific; and the fact that the result was the most absurd book in the English language (his Chronology) does not invalidate in the least his integrity as a scientific investigator, nor exemplify his extraordinary mental gifts any less than his hypothesis of gravitation, which might have occurred to anyone who had seen an apple fall when he was wondering why moving bodies did not move in straight lines away into space. Newton was no farther off the scentific target in his attribution of infallibility to Archbishop Ussher than most modern biologists and self-styled scientific socialists in their idolatry of Darwin and Marx. The scientist who solves the problem of the prophet Daniel and John of Patmos, and incidentally of Shakespear and myself, will make a longer stride ahead than any solver of physical problems.

My readers keep complaining in private letters and public criticisms that I have not solved all the problems of the universe for them. As I am obviously neither omnipotent, omniscient, nor infallible, being not only not a god nor even the proprietor of The Times (as they all assume), they infuriate me. Instead of reminding them calmly that, like Newton, all I know is but a grain of sand picked up on the verge of the ocean of undiscovered knowledge, I have some difficulty in refraining from some paraphrase of 'An evil and idolatrous generation clamors for a miracle.' But as Mahomet kept his temper under the same thoughtless pressure, so, I suppose, must I.

This is all I can write by way of preface to a trivial comedy which is the best I can do in my dotage. It is only a prefacette to a comedietta. Forgive it. At least it will not rub into you the miseries and sins of the recent wars, nor even of the next one. History will make little of them; and the sooner we forget them the better. I wonder how many people really prefer bogus war news and police news to smiling comedy with some hope in it! I do not. When they begin I switch off the wireless.

Ayot Saint Lawrence, July 1947

Act I

The World Betterer

A modern interior. A well furnished study. Morning light. A father discussing with his son. Father an elderly gentleman, evidently prosperous, but a man of business, thoroughly middle class. Son in his earliest twenties, smart, but artistically unconventional.

FATHER. Junius, my boy, you must make up your mind. I had a long talk with your mother about it last night. You have been tied to her apron string quite long enough. You have been on my hands much too long. Your six brothers all chose their professions when they were years younger than you. I have always expected more from you than from them. So has your mother.

SON. Why?

FATHER. I suppose because you are our seventh son; and I myself was a seventh son. You are the seventh son of a seventh son. You ought to have second sight.

SON. I have. At first sight there is no hope for our civilization. But one can still make money in it. At second sight the world has a future that will make its people look back on us as a mob of starving savages. But second sight does not yet lead to success in business nor in the professions.

FATHER. That is not so. You have done unusually well at everything you have tried. You were a success at school. I was assured that you had the makings of a born leader of men in you.

SON. Yes. They made me a prefect and gave me a cane to beat the boys they were too lazy to beat themselves. That was what they called teaching me leadership.

FATHER. Well, it gave you some sense of responsibility: what more could they do? At the university you did not do so well; but you could have if you had chosen to work for honors instead of joining rather disreputable clubs and working on your own lines, as you called them. As it was, you did not disgrace yourself. We looked to you to outshine your brothers. But they are all doing well; and you are doing nothing.

SON. I know. But the only profession that appeals to me is one that I cannot afford.

FATHER. How do you know that you cannot afford it? Have I ever stinted you in any way? Do you suppose I expect you to establish yourself in a profession or business in five minutes?

SON. No: you have always been a model father. But the profession I contemplate is not one that a model father could recommend to his son.

FATHER. And what profession is that, pray?

SON. One that is always unsuccessful. Marx's profession. Lenin's profession. Stalin's profession. Ruskin's profession. Plato's profession. Confucius, Gautama, Jesus, Mahomet, Luther, William Morris. The profession of world betterer.

FATHER. My boy, great prophets and poets are all very well; but they are not practical men; and what we need are practical men.

SON. We dont get them. We need men who can harness the tides and the tempests, atom splitting engineers, mathematicians, biologists, psychologists. What do we get? Windbag careerists. Proletarians who can value money in shillings but not in millions, and think their trade unions are the world. As a world betterer I shall spend most of my life hiding from their police. And I may finish on the scaffold.

FATHER. Romantic nonsense, boy. You are in a free country, and can advocate any sort of politics you please as long as you do not break the law.

SON. But I want to break the law.

FATHER. You mean change the law. Well, you can advocate any change you please; and if you can persuade us all to agree with you, you can get elected to Parliament and bring your changes before the House of Commons.

SON. Too slow. Class war is rushing on us with tiger springs. The tiger has sprung in Russia, in Persia, in Mexico, in Turkey, in Italy, Spain, Germany, Austria, everywhere if you count national strikes as acts of civil war. We are trying to charm the tiger away by mumbling old spells about liberty, peace, democracy, sanctions, open doors, and closed minds, when it is scientific political reconstruction that is called for. So I propose to become a political reconstructionist. Are you in favor of reconstruction?

FATHER. I do not see any need for it. All the people who are discontented are so because they are poor. I am not poor; and I do not see why I should be discontented.

SON. Well, I am discontented because other people are poor. To me living in a world of poor and unhappy people is like living in hell.

FATHER. You need not speak to them. You need not know them. You do not mix with them. And they are not unhappy.

SON. How am I to get away from them? The streets are full of them. And how do I know that we shall not lose all our money and fall into poverty ourselves? Fancy you and mother ending your days in a work-house, or trying to live on an old age pension! That happens, you know.

FATHER. In our case it happens the other way. There is no need to mention it outside; but one of my grandfathers, the founder of our present fortune, began as a porter in a hotel. Thanks to his ability and the social system that gave it scope, we are now safely fixed in a social circle where rich men become richer instead of poorer if they are sensible and well conducted. Our system works very satisfactorily. Why reconstruct it?

SON. Many people feel like that. Others feel as I do. If neither of us will budge, and no compromise is possible, what are we to do? Kill one-another?

FATHER. Nonsense! There are constitutional ways of making all possible political changes.

SON. Voting instead of fighting. No use. The defeated party always fights if it has a dog's chance when the point is worth fighting for and it can find a leader. The defeated dictator always fights unless his successor takes the precaution of murdering him.

FATHER. Not in England. Such things happen only on the Continent. We dont do them here.

SON. We do. We did it in Ireland. We did it in India. It has always been so. We resist changes until the changes break us.

FATHER. Well, what does all this come to? If people wont change what good is there in your being a world betterer, as you call it?

SON. What good is there in going on as we are? Besides, things will not stay as they are. However hard we try to stick in our old grooves, evolution goes on in spite of us. The more we strive to stay as we are, the more we find that we are no longer where we were.

FATHER. Yet we are not always having revolutions.

SON. They occur, though nobody understands them. When the feudal aristocracy collapsed before the plutocratic middle class Henry the Seventh had to fight the battle of Bosworth Field. When the plutocrats got the upper hand of the monarchy Cromwell had to cut off the king's head. The French Revolution tried hard to be Liberal and Parliamentary. No use: the guillotine was overworked until the executioners struck; and Napoleon had to fight all Europe. When the Russians did away with the Tzardom they had to fight not only all the rest of the world but a civil war as well. They first killed all the

83

counter-revolutionists; and then had to kill most of the revolutionists. Revolution is dirty work always. Why should it be?

FATHER. Because it is unconstitutional. Why not do things constitutionally?

SON. Because the object of a revolution is to change the constitution; and to change the constitution is unconstitutional.

FATHER. That is a quibble. It is always possible to vote instead of fighting. All the blood shed in revolutions has been quite unnecessary. All the changes could have been effected without killing anybody. You must listen to reason?

SON. Yes; but reason leads just as clearly to a catholic monarchy as to an American republic, to a Communist Soviet as to Capitalism. What is the use of arguing when the Pope's arguments are as logical as Martin Luther's, and Hilaire Belloc's as H. G. Wells's? Why appeal to the mob when ninetyfive per cent of them do not understand politics, and can do nothing but mischief without leaders? And what sort of leaders do they vote for? For Titus Oates and Lord George Gordon with their Polish plots, for Hitlers who call on them to exterminate Jews, for Mussolinis who rally them to nationalist dreams of glory and empire in which all foreigners are enemies to be subjugated.

FATHER. The people run after wicked leaders only when they cannot find righteous ones. They can always find them in England.

SON. Yes; and when they find them why do they run after them? Only to crucify them. The righteous man takes his life in his hand whenever he utters the truth. Charlemagne, Mahomet, St Dominic: these were righteous men according to their lights; but with Charlemagne it was embrace Christianity instantly or die; with Mahomet the slaying of the infidel was a passport to Heaven; with Dominic and his Dogs of God it was Recant or burn.

FATHER. But these things happened long ago, when people were cruel and uncivilized.

SON. My dear father: within the last thirty years we have had more horrible persecutions and massacres, more diabolical tortures and crucifixions, more slaughter and destruction than Attila and Genghis Khan and all the other scourges of God ever ventured on. I tell you, if people only knew the history of their own times they would die of horror at their own wickedness. Karl Marx changed the mind of the world by simply telling the purseproud nineteenth century its own villainous history. He ruined himself; his infant son died of poverty; and two of his children committed suicide. But he did the trick.

FATHER. The Russian madness will not last. Indeed it has collapsed already. I now invest all my savings in Russian Government Stock. My stockbroker refuses to buy it for me; but my banker assures me that it is the only perfectly safe foreign investment. The Russians pay in their own gold.

SON. And the gold goes to rot in American banks, though whole nations are barely keeping half alive for lack of it.

FATHER. Well, my boy, you are keeping alive pretty comfortably. Why should you saw through the branch you are sitting on?

SON. Because it is cracking; and it seems to me prudent to arrange a soft place to drop to when it snaps.

FATHER. The softest place now is where you are. Listen to me, my boy. You are cleverer than I am. You know more. You know too much. You talk too well. I have thought a good deal over this. I have tried to imagine what old John Shakespear of Stratford-upon-Avon, mayor and alderman and leading citizen of his town, must have felt when he declined into bankruptcy and realized that his good-for-nothing son, who had run away to London after his conviction as a poacher, and being forced to marry a girl he had compromised, was a much greater man than his father had ever been or could hope to be. That is what may happen to me. But there is a difference. Shakespear had a lucrative talent by which he prospered and returned to his native town as a rich man, and bought a property there. You have no such talent. I cannot start you in life with a gift of capital as I started your brothers, because the war taxation has left me barely enough to pay my own way. I can do nothing for you: if you want to better the world you must begin by bettering yourself.

SON. And until I better the world I cannot better myself; for nobody will employ a world betterer as long as there are enough selfseekers for all the paying jobs. Still, some of the world betterers manage to survive. Why not I?

FATHER. They survive because they fit themselves into the world of today. They marry rich women. They take commercial jobs. They spunge on disciples from whom they beg or borrow. What else can they do except starve or commit suicide? A hundred years ago there were kings to spunge on. Nowadays there are republics everywhere; and their governments are irresistible, because they alone can afford to make atomic bombs, and wipe out a city and all its inhabitants in a thousandth of a second.

SON. What does that matter if they can build it again in ten minutes? All the scientists in the world are at work finding out how to dilute and

85

control and cheapen atomic power until it can be used to boil an egg or sharpen a lead pencil as easily as to destroy a city. Already they tell us that the bomb stuff will make itself for nothing.

FATHER. I hope not. For if every man Jack of us can blow the world to pieces there will be an end of everything. Shakespear's angry ape will see to that.

SON. Will he? He hasnt done so yet. I can go into the nearest oil shop and for less than a shilling buy enough chemical salts to blow this house and all its inhabitants to smithereens. A glass retort, a pestle and mortar, and a wash bottle are all I need to do the trick. But I dont do it.

FATHER. The trade unions did it in Manchester and Sheffield.

SON. They soon dropped it. They did not even destroy the slums they lived in: they only blew up a few of their own people for not joining the unions. No: mankind has not the nerve to go through to the end with murder and suicide. Hiroshima and Nagasaki are already rebuilt; and Japan is all the better for the change. When atom splitting makes it easy for us to support ourselves as well by two hours work as now by two years, we shall move mountains and straighten rivers in a hand's turn. Then the problem of what to do in our spare time will make life enormously more interesting. No more doubt as to whether life is worth living. Then the world betterers will come to their own.

FATHER. The sportsmen will, anyhow. War is a sport. It used to be the sport of kings. Now it is the sport of Labor Parties.

SON. What could kings and parties do without armies of proletarians? War is a sport too ruinous and vicious for men ennobled by immense power and its splendid possibilities.

FATHER. Power corrupts: it does not ennoble.

SON. It does if it is big enough. It is petty power that corrupts petty men. Almighty power will change the world. If the old civilizations, the Sumerians, the Egyptians, the Greeks, the Romans, had discovered it, their civilizations would not have collapsed as they did. There would have been no Dark Ages. The world betterers will get the upper hand.

FATHER. Well, it may be so. But does not that point to your settling down respectably as an atom splitting engineer with the government and the police on your side?

SON. Yes, if only I had any talent for it. But I seem to have no talent for anything but preaching and propaganda. I am a missionary without an endowed established Church.

FATHER. Then how are you to live? You must do something to support yourself when I am gone.

SON. I have thought of insuring your life.

FATHER. How are you to pay the premium?

SON. Borrow it from mother, I suppose.

FATHER. Well, there is some sense in that. But it would not last your lifetime: it would only give you a start. At what?

SON. I could speak in the parks until I attracted a congregation of my own. Then I could start a proprietary chapel and live on the collections.

FATHER. And this is what I am to tell your mother!

SON. If I were you I wouldnt.

FATHER. Oh, you are incorrigible. I tell you again you are too clever: you know too much: I can do nothing with you. I wonder how many fathers are saying the same to their sons today.

SON. Lots of them. In your time the young were post-Marxists and their fathers pre-Marxists. Today we are all post-Atomists.

FATHER. Damn the atomic bomb!

SON. Bless it say I. It will make world bettering possible. It will begin by ridding the world of the anopheles mosquito, the tsetse fly, the white ant, and the locust. I want to go round the world to investigate that, especially through the Panama Canal. Will you pay my fare?

FATHER. Yes, anything to keep you from tomfooling in the parks. And it will keep your mother quiet for a while.

SON. Better say nothing until I am gone. She would never let me go: her seventh son is her pet. It is a tyranny from which I must escape.

FATHER. And leave me to weather the storm! Well, goodbye.

SON. Goodbye. You are a damned good father; and I shall not forget it.

They kiss; and the son goes.

Act II

The Adventure

The shore of a broad water studded with half-submerged trees in a tropical landscape, covered with bush except for a clearance by the waterside, where there is a wooden house on posts, with a ladder from the stoep or verandah to the ground. The roof is of corrugated iron, painted green. The Son, dressed in flannel slacks, a tennis shirt, and a panama hat, is looking about him like a stranger. A young woman, dressed for work in pyjama slacks and a pullover, comes out of the house and, from the top of the steps, proceeds to make the stranger unwelcome.

SHE. Now then. This clearance is private property. Whats your business?

HE. No business, dear lady. Treat me as a passing tramp.

SHE. Well, pass double quick. This isnt a doss house.

HE. No; but in this lonely place the arrival of any stranger must be a godsend. Besides, I am hungry and thirsty.

SHE. Most tramps are. Get out.

HE. No: positively no, until I have had refreshments.

SHE. I have a dog here.

HE. You have not. It would have barked. And dogs love me.

SHE. I have a gun here.

HE. So have I. Both useless, except to commit suicide. Have you a husband?

SHE. What is that to you?

HE. If you have, he is only a man, lady. I also am a man. But you do not look married. Have you any milk in the house? Or a hunk of bread and an onion?

SHE. Not for you.

HE. Why not? Have you any religion?

SHE. No. Get out.

HE. Ah, that complicates matters. I thought you were a hospitable friendly savage. I see you are a commercial minded British snob. Must I insult you by offering to pay for my entertainment? Or impress you by introducing myself as a graduate of Oxford University?

SHE. I know that stunt, my lad. The wandering scholar turns up here about twice a week.

HE. 'My lad' eh? That is an endearment. We are getting on. What about the milk?

SHE. You can get a meal where the lake steamers stop, two miles farther on.

HE. Two miles! In this heat! I should die.

SHE [*patiently*] Will you pass on and not come troubling where you are not wanted. [*She goes into the house and slams the door*].

An elderly native arrives with a jar of milk and a basket of bread and fruit. He deposits them on the stoep.

THE NATIVE [*calling to the lady inside*] Ahaiya! Missy's rations. Pink person loafing round.

She opens the door and hands a coin to the native; then slams the door before, after an angry glance at the intruder, leaving the meal on the stoep.

HE [*to the native*] You bring me samee. Half dollar. [*He exhibits the coin*].

THE NATIVE. Too much. Twentyfive cent enough.

HE [*producing a 25c. piece and giving it to him*] The honest man gets paid in advance and has his part in the glory of God.

THE NATIVE. You wait here. No walk about.

HE. Why not?

THE NATIVE. Not good walk about. Gater and snake.

HE. What is gater?

THE NATIVE. Alligator, sir. Much gater, much rattler.

HE. All right. I wait here.

THE NATIVE. Yes, sir. And you no speak holy woman. Speak to her forbidden. She speak with great spirits only. Very strong magics. Put spell on you. Fetch gaters and rattlers with magic tunes on her pipe. Very unlucky speak to her. Very lucky bring her gifts.

HE. Has she husband?

THE NATIVE. No no no no. She holy woman. Live alone. You no speak to her, sir. You wait here. Back quick with chop chop. [*He goes*].

SHE [*opening the door again*] Not gone yet?

HE. The native says you are a holy woman. You are treating me in a very unholy manner. May I suggest that you allow me to consume your meal? You can consume mine yourself after he brings it? I am hungrier than you.

SHE. You are not starving. A fast will do you no harm. You can wait ten minutes more at all events. If you persist in bothering me I will call the gaters and the rattlers.

HE. You have been listening. That is another advance.

SHE. Take care. I can call them.

HE. How?

SHE. In the days of my vanity, when I tried to be happy with men like you, I learnt how to play the soprano saxophone. I have the instrument here. Twenty notes from it will surround you with hissing rattling things, with gaping jaws and slashing tails. I am far better protected against idle gentlemen here than I should be in Piccadilly.

HE. Yes, holy lady; but what about your conscience? A hungry man asks you for food. Dare you throw him to the gaters and rattlers? How will that appear in the great day of reckoning?

SHE. Neither you nor I will matter much when that day comes, if it ever does. But you can eat my lunch to shut your mouth.

HE. Oh, thanks!

SHE. You need not look round for a tumbler and a knife and fork. Drink from the calabash: eat from your fingers.

HE. The simple life, eh? [He attacks the meal].

SHE. No. In the simple life you ring for the servants. Everything is done for you; and you learn nothing.

HE. And here you wait until that kindly native comes and feeds you, like Elijah's ravens. What do you learn from that?

SHE. You learn what nice people natives are. But you begin by trying to feed yourself and build your own shack. I have been through all that, and learnt what a helpless creature a civilized woman is.

HE. Quite. That is the advantage of being civilized: everything is done for you by somebody else; and you havnt a notion of how or why, unless you read Karl Marx.

SHE. I read Karl Marx when I was fifteen. That is why I am here instead of in London looking for a rich husband.

HE. We are getting on like old friends. Evidently I please you.

SHE. Why do you want to please me now that you have your meal?

HE. I dont know. Why do we go on talking to oneanother?

SHE. I dont know. We are dangerous to oneanother. Finish your food; and pass on.

HE. But you have chosen to live dangerously. So have I. It may break our hearts if I pass on.

SHE. Young man: I spent years waiting for somebody to break my heart before I discovered that I havnt got one. I broke several men's hearts in the process. I came here to get rid of that sort of thing. I can stand almost anything human except an English gentleman.

HE. And I can stand anything except an English lady. That game is up. Dancing and gambling, drinking cocktails, tempting women and running away when they meet you half-way and say 'Thats quite all right, sonny: dont apologize.' Hunting and shooting is all right; but you need to be a genuine countrified savage for it; and I am a town bird. My father is a chain shopkeeper, not a country squire.

SHE. Same here: my father is a famous lucky financier. Born a proletarian. Neither of us the real thing.

HE. Plenty of money and no roots. No traditions.

SHE. Nonsense. We are rooted in the slums and suburbs, and full of their snobbery. But failures as ladies and gentlemen.

HE. Nothing left but to live on father's money, eh?

SHE. Yes: parasites: that is not living. Yet we have our living selves for all that. And in this wild life you can taste yourself.

HE. Not always a pleasant taste, is it?

SHE. Every animal can bear its own odor.

HE. That remark has completely destroyed my appetite. The coarse realism with which women face physical facts shocks the delicacy of my sex.

SHE. Yes: men are dreamers and drones. So if you can eat no more, get out.

HE. I should much prefer to lie down and sleep in the friendly shadow of your house until the heat of the day has done its worst.

SHE. If you want a house to shade you, build one for yourself. Leave mine in peace.

HE. That is not natural. In native life the woman keeps the house and works there: the man keeps the woman and rests there.

SHE. You do not keep the woman in this case. She has had enough of you. Get out.

HE. As I see things the woman does not say get out.

SHE. Do you expect her to say come in? As you see things, the man works out of doors. What does he work at, pray?

HE. He hunts, fishes, and fights.

SHE. Have you hunted or fished for me?

HE. No. I hate killing.

SHE. Have you fought for me?

HE. No. I am a timid creature.

SHE. Cowards are no use to women. They need killers. Where are your scalps?

HE. My what?

SHE. Your trophies that you dare kill. The scalps of our enemies.

HE. I have never killed anybody. I dont want to. I want a decent life for everybody because poor people are as tiresome as rich people.

SHE. What is the woman to eat if you do not kill animals for her?

HE. She can be a vegetarian. I am.

SHE. So am I. But I have learnt here that if we vegetarians do not kill animals the animals will kill us. It is the flesh eaters who let the animals live, and feed and nurse them. We vegetarians will make an end of them. No matter what we eat, man is still the killer and woman the life giver. Can you kill or not?

HE. I can shoot a little, though few experienced country gentlemen would care to be next to me at a shoot. But I do not know how to load the gun: I must have a loader. I cannot find the birds: they have to be driven to me by an army of beaters. And I expect a good lunch afterwards. I can also hunt if somebody will fetch me a saddled horse, and stable it for me and take it off my hands again when the hunt is over. I should be afraid not to fight if you put me into an army and convinced me that if I ran away I should be shot at dawn. But of what use are these heroic accomplishments here? No loaders, no beaters, no grooms, no stables, no soldiers, no King and country. I should have to learn to make bows and arrows and assegais; to track game; to catch and break-in wild horses; and to tackle natives armed with poisoned arrows. I should not have a dog's chance. There are only two things I can do as well as any native: eat and sleep. You have enabled me to eat. Why will you not let me sleep?

SHE. Because I want to practise on the saxophone. The rattlers will come and you will never awake.

HE. Then hadnt you better let me sleep indoors?

SHE. The saxophone would keep you awake.

HE. On the contrary, music always sends me fast asleep.

SHE. The only sleep that is possible here when I am playing the saxophone is the sleep of death.

HE [*rising wearily*] You have the last word. You are an inhospitable wretch.

SHE. And you are an infernal nuisance [*she goes into the house and slams the door*].

   The native returns with another meal. He puts it down near the door, at which he raps.

THE NATIVE [*cries*] Ahaiya! Missy's meal.

HE. Say, John: can you direct me to the nearest witch doctor? Spell maker. One who can put terrible strong magics on this house.

THE NATIVE. Sir: magics are superstitions. Pink trash believe such things: colored man, no.

HE. But havnt you gods and priests who can bring down the anger of the gods on unkind people?

THE NATIVE. Sir: there is but one god, the source of all creation. His dwelling is in the sun: therefore though you can look upon all other things you cannot look at the sun.

HE. What do you call him?

THE NATIVE. Sir: his name is not to be pronounced without great reverence. I have been taught that he has other names in other lands; but here his holy name [*he bends his neck*] is Hoochlipoochli. He has a hundred earthly brides; and she who dwells within is one of them.

HE. Listen to me, John. We white men have a god much much greater than Hoochlipoochli.

THE NATIVE. Sir: that may be so. But you pink men do not believe in your god. We believe in ours. Better have no god at all than a god in whom you do not believe.

HE. What do you mean by our not believing? How do you know we do not believe?

THE NATIVE. He who believes in his god, obeys his commands. You expect your god to obey yours. But pardon me, sir: I am forbidden to converse on such high matters with the unlearned. I perceive by your assurance that you are a highly honorable person among your own people; but here you are a heathen, a barbarian, an infidel. Mentally we are not on the same plane. Conversation between us, except on such simple matters as milk and vegetables, could lead only to bewilderment and strife. I wish you good morning, sir.

HE. Stay, presumptuous one. I would have you to know that I am a Master of Arts of the University of Oxford, the centre of all the learning in the universe. The possession of such a degree places the graduate on the highest mental plane attainable by humanity.

THE NATIVE. How did you obtain that degree, sir, may I respectfully ask?

HE. By paying a solid twenty pounds for it.

THE NATIVE. It is impossible. Knowledge and wisdom cannot be purchased like fashionable garments.

HE. In England they can. A sage teaches us all the questions our examiners are likely to ask us, and the answers they expect from us.

THE NATIVE. One answers questions truthfully only out of one's own wisdom and knowledge.

HE. Not at Oxford. Unless you are a hundred years behind hand in science and seven hundred in history you cannot hope for a degree there.

THE NATIVE. Can it be true that the doctrines of your teachers are less than a thousand years old?

HE. The most advanced of them would have felt quite at home with Richard the Third. I should like to have heard them discussing Columbus with him.

THE NATIVE. Then, sir, you must indeed venerate me; for the doctrines of my teachers have lasted many thousands of centuries. Only the truth could survive so long.

HE. I venerate nobody. Veneration is dead. Oxford doctrine has made a gentleman of me. You, it seems, have been made a sage by a similar process. Are we any the better or wiser?

THE NATIVE. Sir: you have lost your faith; but do not throw the hatchet after the handle. Pink men, when they find that their beliefs are only half true, reject both halves. We colored men are more considerate. My grandfather saw the great evils of this world, and thought they shewed the terrible greatness of Hoochlipoochli. My father saw them also, but could not reconcile the existence of evil with divine justice and benevolence. He therefore believed not only in Hoochlipoochli but in Poochlihoochli, the god of hell, whom you pink men call The Devil. As for me, I cannot believe everything my ancestors believed. I believe as they did that justice and benevolence are mighty powers in the world, but that they have no effective existence save in ourselves, and that except to the extent to which you and I and our like are just and benevolent there is no justice and no benevolence.

HE. And consequently no Hoochlipoochli.

THE NATIVE. Not at all. You are throwing the hatchet after the handle. His kingdom is within us; but it is for us to administer it. Something within me makes me hunger and thirst for righteousness. That something must be Hoochlipoochli.

HE. Was it Hoochlipoochli who set you talking pidgin English to me though you can talk philosopher's English better than most Englishmen?

THE NATIVE. Sir: you began by speaking pidgin to me. You addressed me as John, which is not my name. In courtesy I spoke as you spoke.

HE. Still, when you told me that the woman here is one of Hoochlipoochli's many hundred earthly wives, you were humbugging me.

THE NATIVE. Sir: Hoochlipoochli possesses all of us more or less; and so every woman is his bride. I desired only your good when I bade you beware of her; for it is true that when she plays on her strange instrument the serpents of the bush and the monsters of the lake are charmed, and assemble here to listen.

SHE [*throwing open her door and appearing on the threshold with the saxophone in her hand*] And if you do not stop talking and maddening me with the sound of your cackle I shall strike up.

HE. Strike up by all means. I shall enjoy a little music.

SHE. We shall see. I have had enough of you.

She preludes on the saxophone.

Hissing and rattlings in the bush. An alligator crawls in. The two men fly for their lives.

Act III

The Discussion

A drawingroom in Belgrave Square, London, converted into a Chinese temple on a domestic scale, with white walls just enough rose tinted to take the glare off, and a tabernacle in vermilion and gold, on a dais of two broad shallow steps. Divan seats, softly upholstered against the walls, and very comfortable easy chairs of wickerwork, luxuriously cushioned, are also available. There is a sort of bishop's chair at one corner of the tabernacle. The effect is lovely and soothing, as only Chinese art could make it.

A most incongruous figure enters: a middle-aged twentieth century London solicitor, carrying a case of papers. He is accompanied and ushered by a robed Chinese priest, who fits perfectly into the surroundings.

THE SOLICITOR [*looking round him*] Whats all this? I should have been shewn into the library. Do you understand who I am? Sir Ferdinand Flopper, Mr Buoyant's solicitor?

THE PRIEST. It is Mr Buoyant's wish that you should meet his children in this holy place. Did he not mention it in your instructions?

SIR FERDINAND. No. This place is not holy. We are in Belgrave Square, not in Hong Kong.

THE PRIEST. Sir: in many old English houses there is a room set apart as a meditation parlor.

SIR FERDINAND. Pooh! They have been abolished.

THE PRIEST. Yes. The English people no longer meditate.

SIR FERDINAND. Does Mr Buoyant?

THE PRIEST. His soul needs refreshment. He is a mighty man of business. in his hands all things turn into money. Souls perish under such burdens. He comes here and sits for half an hour while I go through my act of worship, of which he does not understand a single word. But he goes out a new man, soothed and serene. You may call this his oratory.

SIR FERDINAND. I shall certainly not call it anything of the sort. His oratory would be a Church of England oratory.

THE PRIEST. He has not found peace in the Church of England.

SIR FERDINAND. And you tell me that he has found it here, in this

96

outlandish apartment where he does not understand a word of the service!

THE PRIEST. In the Church of England he understood too much. He could not believe. And the people in their Sunday clothes were so forbidding!

SIR FERDINAND. Forbidding!!

THE PRIEST. Sunday clothes and poker faces. No peace, no joy. But for the music they would all go mad. That is, perhaps, why you do not go to church.

SIR FERDINAND. Who told you I do not go to church?

THE PRIEST. Nobody told me. But do you?

SIR FERDINAND. I am here on business, and cannot waste my morning on religious discussions. Will you be good enough to direct me to the library?

THE PRIEST. You would find it a rather dismal apartment after this one. And its atmosphere is mentally paralyzing. Mr Buoyant's instructions are that your advice to his family must be given here. But no religious service is to be imposed on you.

SIR FERDINAND. Nothing can be imposed on me. The atmosphere here is most unsuitable. Does the family know I have arrived?

THE PRIEST. Here they are.

The family, consisting of a middle-aged widower, a young man, two married ladies, an unmarried girl of 20, and an irreverent youth of 17, enters. The widower introduces them.

THE WIDOWER. Good morning, Sir Ferdinand. We are the family of your client Mr Bastable Buoyant, better known as Old Bill Buoyant the Billionaire. I am a widower. The ladies are my brothers' wives. One brother is absent: he leaves everything to his wife. The two children are our sister Darkie and our brother Fiffy, registered as Eudoxia Emily and Frederick.

They bow to Sir Ferdinand as they are introduced, and seat themselves on the divan, the husbands on opposite sides from their wives.

The two juniors also plant themselves on opposite sides well to the fore. Sir Ferdinand, returning their bows rather stiffly, seats himself in the bishop's chair.

THE PRIEST. I leave you to your deliberations. Peace be with you!

He goes, the family waving him a salute.

SIR FERDINAND. As I have only just been called in, and am a stranger to you all, I am naturally somewhat at a loss. How much do you know already of the business I am to put before you?

DARKIE [*taking the lead at once decisively*] Nothing whatever. Business means money; and none of us knows anything about money because our father knows everything about it. But I know all about housekeeping because our mother knew nothing about it and cared less. She preferred painting. We had extraordinarily clever parents; and the result is that we are a family of helpless duffers.

SECONDBORN. That is true. So much has been done for us we have learnt to do hardly anything for ourselves. I am a bit of a mathematician, but earn nothing by it.

MRS SECONDBORN [*an aggressive woman*] Mathematics; that is his fad. Start a Buoyant on a fad; and he is happy and busy with it for the rest of the year.

THE YOUTH. We are too damnably rich, you see. The boss making billions all the time.

DARKIE. We have bits and scraps of taste and talents for scholarship, painting, playing musical instruments, writing, and talking. One brother is a champion amateur boxer. Another is a historian and knows eleven languages. He is also a pedestrian and walks 3000 miles every year on principle. We are all more or less like that, because daddy began with eight shillings a week and taught himself to read and write when he was seventeen and wanted to write to his mother. She could read handwriting.

THE WIDOWER. Darkie is explaining to you that as we are entirely dependent on our father for our incomes we can defend ourselves against his tyranny only by acquiring the culture of which an uneducated man stands in awe.

MRS THIRDBORN [*gentle, beautiful, and saintly*] Oh, he is not a tyrant.

THE WIDOWER. He might be, if we were not obviously his social superiors.

MRS SECONDBORN. In justice to the old devil I must say that, as far as I can make out, he has never spoken a cross word to any of you.

DARKIE. I never said he did. I was going on to explain my own exceptional position in the family. Am I boring you, Sir Ferdinand?

SIR FERDINAND. Not at all. We have plenty of time before lunch. So if your position is exceptional, I had better know what it is.

DARKIE. Well, as I am the only female, I am the spoilt darling and pampered pet of the lot. I have no talents, no accomplishments, except what I picked up doing just what I liked and was given everything I asked for. That has been harder than any schooling; and I sometimes blame my parents for not having thrashed the life out of me instead of leaving me to learn life's lessons by breaking my shins against them and falling into every booby trap. I was so

overpetted that I had to learn or die. So if there is anything real to be
done I have to see to it.

MRS THIRDBORN [*very kindly*] Dont mind her, Sir Ferdinand. She always
talks the greatest nonsense about herself.

DARKIE. I daresay I do. Anyhow I have finished now. Go ahead, Sir
Ferdinand.

SIR FERDINAND. One question first please. Mr Buoyant must have had
legal advice during all these years. Is there not a family solicitor?

THE WIDOWER. No. He does not believe in having the same solicitor
every time.

DARKIE. He thinks it is throwing away experience. He always calls in a
different doctor when he is ill.

THE YOUTH. He picks up his solicitor for the job, like picking up a taxi.

THE WIDOWER. There is something to be said for his plan. He has learnt
much about doctors and solicitors by it.

SECONDBORN. He now advises his doctors and instructs his solicitors.

SIR F. If so, why does he call them in at all?

MRS SECONDBORN. If he didnt, and any of us died, or any money he is
trustee for went wrong, he might be prosecuted for negligence or
conversion or something.

SIR F. True. But this raises questions of professional etiquet. I have some
misgivings as to whether I can act in the case.

THE YOUTH. If the boss says you can, you may bet your bottom dollar
it will be all right.

DARKIE. He makes so much money that whatever he says, goes.

SIR F. Not legally.

THE WIDOWER. No doubt. But it works pragmatically.

SIR F. I hardly know what to say. You are such an unusually outspoken
family, and your father such an extraordinary man, that I should like
to know more of you. You belong to a new generation, quite unlike
mine. I am at sea here. May I continue provisionally as a friendly
acquaintance rather than as a solicitor?

DARKIE. The very thing!

THE YOUTH. Silence all.

DARKIE. Go ahead, Sir Ferdinand. Whats the latest?

SIR F. You know, I presume, that your father's money, now practically
unlimited, has been made, and is still being made, on the money
market, by buying stocks and shares and selling them again at a profit.
Such profits are not taxed, as they are classed as capital, not as income.
Consequently it has been possible for your father to remain enormously
rich, although the war taxation has abolished rich men as a class.

THE YOUTH. So much the better for us.

SIR F. Not altogether. The Chancellor of the Exchequer may tax money market incomes, either as such or as gambling. In that case The Buoyant Billions will dry up abruptly. In any case they will stop with his death, which cannot now be far off. Your incomes will be taxed like everyone elses, if you have any incomes. Have you?

THE WIDOWER. All I know is that what money I need appears to my credit in my bank passbook as cash or dividends on the few investments my stockbroker has advised.

SIR F. Does that apply all round?

SECONDBORN. To me, yes.

DARKIE. I told you so, Sir Ferdinand. None of us knows anything about making money because our father knows all about it.

SIR F. Has he never taught you anything about it?

THE WIDOWER. He couldnt. He does not understand it himself. He makes money by instinct, as beavers build dams.

SECONDBORN. Whenever I have taken his financial advice I have lost by it. I now leave it to my banker.

SIR F. Then I am afraid I must warn you all that you will presently become very poor. You will have to let your country houses and live in gate lodges and gardeners' cottages. Your ladies will have to do the housework. Your clothes will have to last you for years. I am here to impress these hard facts on you.

THE WIDOWER. But surely this shortage will not last for ever. The Labor Government, which is responsible for these robberies of the rich, will be defeated at the next election.

SIR F. Do not depend on that. All the king's horses and all the king's men cannot bring back the unearned incomes of the nineteenth century. The Socialists and Trade Unionists will see to that.

DARKIE. None of us women knows how to do housework.

SIR F. I am afraid you will have to learn.

MRS SECONDBORN. The whole thing is utterly ridiculous. The war is over; and there will always be rich and poor. The Chancellor is a beggar on horseback. He will be sent back to the gutter at the next election.

SIR F. Nobody can object to these revolutionary changes more than I do; but they are occurring among my clients every day.

MRS SECONDBORN. Nonsense! We must live. What are we to do?

SIR F. Reduce your expenditure. Live as poorer people than yourselves now live.

MRS SECONDBORN. Oh yes, poor people. But we are not poor people. We cannot live that way.

MRS THIRDBORN. Why not? Our riches have not made us happy. Our
Lord's mother was the wife of a carpenter. I have always thought of
her as a woman who did her own housework. I am sure I could learn.
Is it not easier for a camel to pass through the eye of a needle than for
a rich woman to enter the kingdom of heaven?

MRS SECONDBORN. Oh, you are religious. Much good your religion
will do us!

THE WIDOWER. Dont let us quarrel about religion.

THE YOUTH. The old man isnt dead yet. He will make billions, taxes or
no taxes. Lets make the most of him while he lasts.

SECONDBORN. I find it hard to believe that he will ever die. He is a
human calculating machine. Calculating machines dont die.

SIR F. They wear out. He cannot live for ever.

THE WIDOWER. I used to play the cornet fairly well. If only my wife
were alive to play my accompaniments on a street piano I should
not starve.

SIR F. None of you need starve. On your father's reputation you will
live on company directorships. You need not know anything about
the business; your name on the prospectus will be sufficient. I must
now pass on to another matter. Mr Buoyant has added to his in-
struction this sentence. 'My elder daughter is provided for and need
not be present. She can take care of herself.' Have you a sister, Miss
Buoyant?

DARKIE. I have a stepsister.

SIR F. [surprised] Was your father twice married?

THE WIDOWER. He was; but we try to forget it. We are ashamed of it.

MRS THIRDBORN. I am not ashamed of it.

MRS SECONDBORN. Thats only your religion; you have no natural
feelings. Of course we are ashamed of it.

SIR F. May I ask what was wrong about it?

THE WIDOWER. Nothing wrong. But when our father married he was a
very poor man; and he married a very common woman. She had
never in her life had a satisfying dinner; and she died of overeating
when they could afford it. They had one daughter.

MRS SECONDBORN. A quite impossible person.

SIR F. In what way?

DARKIE. She can do everything we cant do. She can cook. She can make
beds. She can make her own clothes. She can sweep and scrub. She
can nurse. She learnt it all before she was ten, and was sent to a ladies'
school.

MRS SECONDBORN. Nothing could make a real lady of her. She dresses like a lady, and can talk like a lady, and can behave like a lady when she likes; but she does not belong to us. Her ten years of poverty and commonness makes a difference we cannot get over. She knows things a lady ought not to know.

MRS THIRDBORN. Including some things nobody ought to know. But it is not her fault.

MRS SECONDBORN. She has no manners at home, and no education. She keeps them for visitors. No class.

SIR F. My dear good people, you are behind the times. It is now a disgrace to have been born rich. Fashion is led by the wives of Cabinet Ministers whose fathers and husbands began on five shillings a week: they boast of it. Your stepsister is probably ashamed of you. May I ask where she is at present?

THE WIDOWER. In Panama, we believe.

SIR F. Panama!

THE YOUTH. On the banks of the canal all alone in a shack put up by herself and a few natives.

SECONDBORN. An interesting experience. When I feel that I can no longer bear civilized society I retreat into pure mathematics. But I need not go to Panama for that, thank Heaven.

MRS SECONDBORN. No: because I provide a comfortable home for you, where you see whom you like when you like. This woman lives like a savage in a swamp full of snakes and alligators and natives.

SECONDBORN. My dear: the world is so wicked and ignorant and unreasonable that I must get away from it occasionally.

MRS SECONDBORN. You do it to get away from me. You think I dont know; but I do. Am I wicked and ignorant and unreasonable?

SECONDBORN. Occasionally, my dear. Only occasionally. Not always.

MRS SECONDBORN. Well, of all the monstrous accusations –

SIR F. Need we go into your domestic affairs? We really must not be personal.

MRS SECONDBORN. Whatever is not personal is not human.

The woman from Panama dashes into the temple, in travelling dress, and in a blazing rage.

SHE. What is all this? Why was I not told? [*To Sir F.*] Who are you?

SIR F. I am Mr Buoyant's solicitor, in consultation with his family. May I ask whom I am addressing?

SHE. You are addressing old Bill Buoyant's firstborn, next to himself the head of the family.

SIR F. Then you are expressly excluded from this family council on the ground that you are already provided for. The rest may have to face ruin when your father dies.

SHE. Well, here I am and here I stay. When they are all ruined they will expect me to keep them on my annuity. I cant and wont. So now give me a chair.

THE YOUTH [*giving her his chair*] Here you are, Clemmy. [*He plants it in front of the altar at the side opposite to Sir Ferdinand; fetches another for himself; and resumes his place*].

SIR F. Did you say Clemmy? The name in my instructions is Babzy.

SHE. Babzy is my vulgar father's vulgar pet name for his vulgar first baby. I was christened Clementina Alexandra; but Babzy is shorter: my father would not change it. Clemmy to the others.

MRS SECONDBORN. Have you come home for good?

SHE. That wont matter to you, Julia. For my home is here, in Daddy's house, not in yours. Daddy is growing old; and old men sometimes do foolish things with their money. None of you knows anything about money; so I had better keep an eye on you and him. Where is Daddy?

SIR F. Mr Buoyant is staying away purposely. He has no gift of expression; and his children, he tells me, are too much for him as talkers, and generally arrive at wrong conclusions by talking their feet off the ground. I am quoting his own words. Having done my best to act for him without making the least impression on your very interesting relatives, I really do not know why I am staying, especially as you appear to be taking my place. I had better go.

SHE. No. Stay for the fun of it. Whats your name, by the way?

SIR F. Envelopes should be addressed to Sir Ferdinand Flopper, Bart.

SHE. What! The great Sir Ferdinand?

SIR F. You are good enough to put it that way. Now may I ask you a question?

SHE. Ask a dozen if you like.

SIR F. You did not come back from Panama to attend this meeting. You must have left before it was decided on.

SHE. How clever of you to think of that! I came because I was attacked by the symptoms of a very dangerous disease.

They all shew great concern, exclaiming Oh *in their various ways.*

SIR F. Oh! You came for medical advice. I beg your pardon.

SHE. No. It is not a doctor's job. I found myself what is called falling in love. I had illusions, infatuations, impulses that were utterly unreasonable and irresistible. Desires in which my body was taking command of my soul. And all for a man of whom I knew nothing: a passing vagabond who had begged a meal from me. He came to me next day and said he had fallen in love with me at first sight, and that he was going quite mad about me. He warned me to run away and leave no address, as he would follow me to the ends of the earth if he knew where I was; and we should both make fools of ourselves by getting married. So I fled; and here I am. He does not know my name, nor I his. But when I think of him everything is transfigured and I am magically happy. Unreadable poems like the Song of Solomon delight me: bagatelles by Beethoven deepen into great sonatas: every walk through the country is an exploration of the plains of heaven. My reason tells me that this cannot possibly be real; that the day will come when it will vanish and leave me face to face with reality; perhaps tied to a husband who may be anything from a criminal to an intolerable bore. So I have run away and put the seas between me and this figure that looks like a beautiful and wonderful celestial messenger – a Lohengrin – but really does not exist at all except in my imagination. So now you know, all of you. Let us change the subject.

SIR F. Not, if you please, until I have reminded you that very few men are criminals, and that most married couples spend the whole day apart, the woman in the house, the man in the office or study or workshop. And there is such a possibility as divorce.

THE WIDOWER. Besides, take my case. My late wife and I were so indispensable to oneanother that a separation would have been for us a desolating calamity. Yet I repeatedly found myself irresistibly attracted biologically by females with whom I could not converse seriously for five minutes. My wife needed some romance in her life when I ceased to be romantic to her and became only her matter-of-fact husband. To keep her in good humor and health I had to invite and entertain a succession of interesting young men to keep her supplied with what I call Sunday husbands.

MRS SECONDBORN. That is a perfectly different thing. You have low tastes, which you occasionally gratify. I take an interest in young men; but I do not misconduct myself with them.

SECONDBORN. That, my love, is because your sense of property is stronger than your biological instinct. I am your property. Therefore you are damnably jealous.

MRS SECONDBORN. I deny it. I am not jealous.

THE WIDOWER. I think Sir Ferdinand's mind would be clearer on the subject if, like me, he had been married twice. My first marriage, which was quite biological, was a failure. What people called our love turned into something very like hatred. But biological tastes are not low tastes. Our two children were great successes: beautiful children with good characters. But nobody could live in the same house with their mother.

SIR F. [*very gravely*] Excuse me. I do not think you should speak of your dead wife in such terms.

THE WIDOWER. Oh, she is not dead: I let her divorce me. We are now quite good friends again. But to understand this question it is not enough to have been married once. Henry the Eighth would be the leading authority if he were alive. The prophet Mahomet was married more than fourteen times. And what about Solomon?

SIR F. Do pray let us keep religion out of this discussion. Surely religion is one thing, and the British marriage law another.

All the rest laugh, except Mrs Secondborn, who snorts.

SIR F. What is there to laugh at? Can we not be sensible and practical? We are dealing with the hard cash of your incomes, not with Solomon and Mahomet. We are not Mormons. Their wives in British law were only concubines.

THE WIDOWER. I hold that concubines are a necessary institution. In a nation wellbred biologically there should be concubines as well as wives and husbands. Some marriages are between couples who have no children because they have hereditary ailments which they fear to transmit to their offspring. Others are of shrews and bullies who produce excellent bastards, though domestic life with them is impossible. They should be concubines, not husbands and wives. All concubinages are exactly alike. No two marriages are alike.

SIR F. Nonsense! All marriages are exactly alike in law.

THE WIDOWER. So much the worse for law, I am afraid.

MRS THIRDBORN. No two love affairs are alike. I was in love three times before I married a friend who was not in love with me nor I with him. We were both sane. Yet we can say honestly 'Whom God hath joined' –

SIR F. Oh, do please leave God out of the question. Marriage is a legal institution; and God has nothing to do with legal institutions.

MRS THIRDBORN. God keeps butting in somehow.

SIR F. Surely that is not the way to speak of the Almighty. If you must drag in religion, at least do so in becoming language.

MRS THIRDBORN. When you really believe in God you can make fun of Him. When you are only pretending you pull long faces and call Him Gawd.

MRS SECONDBORN. Dont forget that when you wake up from your dreams and delusions about your husband you have your children to love. You may be only too glad to be rid of your crazy notions about your husband. The kids fill his place.

MRS THIRDBORN. Not after they are six, when they go to school and begin to be independent of you and form a new relation with their teachers. Only husband and wife come to feel that they belong to oneanother and are really parts of oneanother. That is one of the mysteries of marriage.

MRS SECONDBORN. Besides, the illusions dont affect people who have common sense. I never read the Song of Solomon, nor bothered about Beethoven; but I always knew whether it was a fine day or a wet one without any nonsense about the plains of heaven. Dick's weaknesses were as obvious to me then as they are now. But I could put up with them. I liked him because he was so unlike me. [*To her husband*] And it was the same with you, wasnt it, Dick?

SECONDBORN. Not quite. I had my share of the illusions. But when they vanished they did not matter much. I had got used to you. Let us look at this mathematically. The sex illusion is not a fixed quantity: not what mathematicians call a constant. It varies from zero in my wife's case to madness in that of our stepsister. Reason and experience, which hold it in check, are also variable. Our stepsister is highly observant and reasonable. My wife is totally unreasonable.

MRS SECONDBORN. Which of us two is the reasonable one? Who keeps the house for you? Who looks after your clothes? Who sees that you get your meals regularly and do not eat and drink more than is good for you? Reason! I have to reason with you every day, and can get nothing out of you but incomprehensible ravings about variables and functions. Your mind never stays put for ten minutes at a time.

SECONDBORN. My dearest: nothing in the world ever stays put for ten seconds. We can know it only relatively at any moment. Yet most people can think only absolutely. Relatively, variably, mathematically, they cannot think at all. Everything for them is either soot or white-wash. They undertake to make a new world after every war without brains enough to add *a* to *b*.

MRS SECONDBORN. Are you happy with me or are you not?

SECONDBORN. I am never happy. I dont want to be happy. I want to be alive and active. Bothering about happiness is the worst unhappiness.

DARKIE. Oh, let us talk sense. [*To her stepsister*] Clemmy: your room is not ready for you: to clear it will take weeks. And there are no maids to be got now.

SHE. English maids are no use to me. I have brought a Panama native: he will clear my room for me in twenty minutes.

THE WIDOWER. Then our business is finished. Sir Ferdinand has told us that our incomes will stop when our father dies. He has advised us that we can live on directorships on the strength of our famous name and its associations with billions. I hope so. What more is there to be said?

THE YOUTH. What about me? Nobody will make me a director. I am a world betterer.

SIR F. World betterer! What new hare are you starting now?

THE YOUTH. All intelligent men of my age are world betterers today.

SIR F. Pooh! You will drop all that nonsense when you take your university degree.

THE WIDOWER. Impossible. Our father gave us all the money we needed on condition that we would never engage in money making, nor take a university degree.

SIR F. Not go to a university!

SECONDBORN. You misunderstand. We have all spent three years at college. Our father sent us there to acquire the social training the communal life of a university gives. But he insisted on our leaving without a degree.

SIR F. In Heaven's name, why?

SECONDBORN. One of his notions. He holds that dictated mental work on uncongenial subjects is overwork which injures the brain permanently. So we are not university graduates; but we are university men none the less. If a man is known to have been at Oxford or Cambridge nobody ever asks whether he had taken a degree or not.

SIR F. But that does not justify false pretences.

THE YOUTH. University degrees are the falsest of pretences. Graduates as a class are politically and scientifically obsolete and ignorant. Even in the elementary schools children spend nine years without learning how to speak their native language decently or write it easily.

THE WIDOWER. We are not impostors, Sir Ferdinand, because we ran away from our examinations. What culture a university can give, we possess. However, if you have any scruples –

SIR F. I have scruples. I have principles. I have common sense. I have sanity. They seem to have no place in the affairs of this family.

MRS THIRDBORN. Listen to me, Sir Ferdinand. You must understand that my father-in-law's dearest wish was to be a teacher and a preacher. But as he had original ideas no one would employ him as a preacher nor listen to him as a teacher. He could do nothing but make money: though he regarded it as the curse of his life. He made it in the city all day and returned to his home every evening to forget it, and teach his children to speak their minds always and never to mistake saying the proper thing for the truth.

SIR F. But surely the truth is always the proper thing.

MRS THIRDBORN. Yes; but the proper thing is not always God's truth.

SIR F. [*bothered*] You give things such a twist! We really shall get nowhere unless you will speak in an expected manner.

The Panama native, attired as a British valet, enters hastily and comes straight to Her.

NATIVE. Pink lady: the man has come.

SHE. Here!!!

NATIVE. In this house. He will not be denied. He has divine guidance. He has seen you again at the singing theatre here in London. God led him to Panama.

SHE. Shew him up.

The Native bows his assent and goes out.

SIR F. May I ask who is this man?

SHE. He is the man I am in love with: the object of my illusions, my madness. If he followed me across the Atlantic, and tracked me back again, he must be as mad as I am.

NATIVE [*at the door, announcing*] The man of destiny. [*He withdraws*].

The Son, elegantly dressed, enters.

HE [*to Her, standing in the middle of the temple after looking at the company in dismay*] Am I intruding? I had hoped to find you alone.

SHE. The Buoyants are never alone. Let me introduce you. My stepbrothers, Tom and Dick. Mrs Dick and Mrs Harry: a grass widow. Tom is a widower. Darkie: my unmarried stepsister. Fiffy: the youngest. Sir Ferdinand Whopper, our father's latest and most eminent solicitor.

SIR F. My name is not Whopper: it is Flopper.

SHE. My mistake. They rhyme.

HE. Bon soir la compagnie. This room is like a temple. Are you engaged in an act of worship?

MRS THIRDBORN. All the world is a temple of the Holy Ghost. You may be quite at your ease here, resting your soul.

SIR F. In what capacity do you claim to join us, may I ask?

HE. Only in pursuit of old Bill Buoyant's billions. I am by profession a world betterer. I need money for investigation and experiment. I saw Miss Buoyant one night at the opera. She attracted me so strongly that I did not hear a note of the music. I found out who she was but not what she is. I know nothing of her tastes, her intelligence, her manners, her temper: in short, of anything that would make it possible for me to live with her; yet I feel that I must possess her. For this I have no excuse. Nature has struck this blow at me: I can neither explain it nor resist it: I am mad about her. All I can do is to marry her for her money if I can persuade her to marry me.

SIR F. Do I understand that you propose to marry this lady for her money, and are apologizing for wanting to marry her for love as well?

HE. I said nothing about love. Love means many different things: love of parents and children, love of pet animals, love of whisky or strawberry ices, love of cricket or lawn tennis, also love of money. My case is a specific one of animal magnetism, as inexplicable as the terrestrial magnetism that drags a steel ship to a north or south pole that is not the astronomical pole. The ship can be demagnetized: who can demagnetize me? No one. We have not even a name for this mystery.

SIR F. I should call it the voice of nature.

HE. How much farther does that get you? Calling things names does not explain them: it is the trade of sham scientists who do not know what science means.

SECONDBORN. That is true. Are you a mathematician?

HE. I know the multiplication table, and can do very simple sums: that is all; but though I cannot do equations, I am mathematician enough to know that nothing is stationary: everything is moving and changing.

SHE. What complicates the affair is that I am in love with this man. And I dare not marry a man I love. I should be his slave.

SIR F. Really you are all quite mad. Is not your being in love with him a reason for marrying him if he is in love with you, as he appears to be in spite of his outrageous boast of being a fortune hunter?

SHE. You may leave money out of the question. Though I was brought up never to think of money, I have never spent all my annuity; and with what I could spare I have doubled my income on the money market. I have inherited my father's flair for finance. Money makes itself in my hands in spite of his preaching. When I want a husband I can afford to pay for him.

HE. That is very satisfactory. Why not marry me?

SHE. We might regret it. Love marriages are the most unreasonable, and probably the most often regretted.

HE. Everything we do can be regretted. There is only one thing that a woman is certain to regret.

SHE. What is that, pray?

HE. Being unmarried.

SHE. I deny it. The day of ridiculous old maids is over. Great men have been bachelors and great women virgins.

HE. They may have regretted it all the same.

SIR F. I must remind you, Miss Buoyant, that though many women have regretted their marriages there is one experience that no woman has ever regretted, and that experience is motherhood. Celibacy for a woman is *il gran rifiuto*, the great refusal of her destiny, of the purpose in life which comes before all personal considerations: the replacing of the dead by the living.

MRS THIRDBORN. For once, dear Sir Ferdinand, you are not talking nonsense. Child bearing is an experience which it is impossible to regret. It is definitely ordained.

SECONDBORN. Regret is essentially mathematical. What are the mathematical probabilities? How many marriages are regretted? How much are they regretted? How long are they regretted? What is the proportion of divorces? The registrar of marriages should have a totalizator balancing these quantities. There should be one in every church. People would then know what chances they are taking. Should first cousins marry? Should Catholics and Protestants marry? Should lepers marry? At what ages should they marry? Without these statistics you cannot give scientific answers to these questions: you have only notions and guesswork to go on.

HE. Our fancies come first: they are irresistible. They must have a meaning and a purpose. Well, I have a strong fancy for your stepsister; and she confesses to a strong fancy for me. Let us chance it.

DARKIE. What about your own experience, Sir Ferdinand?

SHE. Yes. How did your own marriage turn out? Did you marry for love?

SIR F. I am not married. I am a bachelor.

They laugh at him.

SIR F. What are you all laughing at? Am I expected to substitute personal experiences for legal advice? May I not advise women though I am not a woman? I am here to advise a family which I can only describe charitably as a family of lunatics. Does not the value of my advice lie in the fact that I am not myself a lunatic?

THE YOUTH. But you are a lunatic. And you havnt given us any advice.

SECONDBORN. What have you given us? Instead of facts, escapist romance from the cinemas. Instead of mathematical and relative measurements, a three dimensional timeless universe. Instead of logic, association of ideas, mostly nonsensical ideas. Instead of analysis, everything in totalitarian lumps. Nothing scientific.

SIR F. I am a lawyer, not a scientist.

SECONDBORN. Until law and science, politics and religion, are all one, the scientists, the lawyers, the clergymen, the politicians will be foolish tinkers who think they can mend the world because they can mend holes in a saucepan.

DARKIE. Do let us get back to tin tacks. Is Clemmy going to marry him or is she not? If she says yes I bet she will have her own way whatever he does.

THE WIDOWER. The woman always does. I have gone twice to my weddings like a lamb to the slaughter house. My two wives were triumphant. I bought new clothes, oiled and brushed my hair, and was afraid to run away. My second marriage was a success: I knew what to expect. Second marriages are the quietest and happiest. The twice married, if one of them dies, marry a third time even at the most advanced age.

SIR F. Then marriage is not a failure as an institution. With reasonable divorce laws, not at all.

HE [to Her] You hear?

SHE. Sit down, will you. Dont stand over me, pontificating.

HE. I beg your pardon. [He sits down on the altar step in the middle].

SHE. You make everything beautiful to me. You give me a happiness I have never experienced before. But if I marry you all this will cease. If I dont marry you – if you die – if we never meet again, it may last all my life. And there are rights I will give to no man over me.

SIR F. Conjugal rights. They cannot now be enforced. Not effectively. Do not let them hinder you. What are the gentleman's means? that is the question.

SHE. What am I to do with my means? that also is the question.

HE. What all independent women do with their means. Keep a husband on them.

MRS THIRDBORN. Is a husband a dog or a cat to be kept as a pet? I never heard such nonsense.

HE. Dogs are sometimes better bargains. I am not so sure about cats.

MRS SECONDBORN [rising] Come home, Dick. I have had enough of this. It will just end in their getting married like other people. Come home. [She storms out].

MRS THIRDBORN [rising] Sir Ferdinand's law has failed us. Dick's science has failed us. Fiff's boyish dreams have failed us: he has not yet bettered the world. We must leave it in God's hands [She goes out].

SECONDBORN [rising] It always comes to that: leave it to God, though we do not know what God is, and are still seeking a general mathematical theory expressing Him. All we know is that He leaves much of it to us; and we make a shocking mess of it. We must be goodnatured and make the best of it. Goodbye, Mr Golddigger. [He follows his wife out].

THE WIDOWER [rising] As I have no wife to decide for me, I must go of my own accord.

SIR F. [*rising*] As nobody pays the slightest attention to my advice, I will accompany you. [*The three go out*].

DARKIE [*rising*] Come on, Fiff. Lets leave them alone together.

HE. Thank you.

Darkie and Fiff go out.

HE. Well?

SHE. I will think about it.

The Chinese Priest returns, followed by the Native swinging a censer.

THE PRIEST. Will you have the kindness to follow your friends and leave me to purify this temple of peace. It has been terribly profaned for the last hour. Father Buoyant will be here presently for his rest, his meditation, his soothing, his divine recreation. You have poisoned its atmosphere with your wranglings. I must change its air and restore its peace lest it kill Father Buoyant instead of giving him a foretaste of heaven. Go now: you must not breathe here any longer.

SHE [*rising*] Daddy made me sit still and be silent here when I was in my restless teens. I detested it. The scent of incense sickens me. [*To Him*] Come, you. We must think it over.

She goes out. He waves his hand to the Priest and follows.

THE PRIEST. What freaks these pinks are! Belonging neither to the west, like you, nor to the east, like me.

THE NATIVE [*swinging the censer*] Neither to north nor south; but in that they resemble us. They have much to teach us.

THE PRIEST. Yes; but they are themselves unteachable, not understanding what they teach.

THE NATIVE. True: they can teach; but they cannot learn.

THE PRIEST. Freaks. Dangerous freaks. The future is with the learners.

The temple vanishes, blacked out.

Act IV

The End

When the temple reappears the censer is on the altar. The Priest and the Native are rearranging the chairs.

Old Bill Buoyant comes in. A greybeard, like any other greybeard; but a gorgeous golden dressing gown and yellow slippers give him a hieratic air.

OLD BILL. Have they all cleared out?

PRIEST. All. The temple is cleansed.

OLD BILL. Good. Who is your friend?

NATIVE. I am the servant of your daughter.

OLD BILL. Which daughter?

NATIVE. From Panama.

OLD BILL. Good. Has she left the house yet?

NATIVE. Not without me. I drive her car.

OLD BILL. Good. Tell her to come and see me here.

NATIVE. At your service, O sage. [*He salaams and goes out*].

OLD BILL. Shall I profane the temple if I kiss my daughter here? I am fond of her.

PRIEST. Truly no. The temple will sanctify your kiss.

OLD BILL. Good. It is curious how happy I always feel here. I am not a religious man. I do not go to church.

PRIEST. You meditate.

OLD BILL. No. Meditation is not in my line: I speculate. And my speculations turn out well when I spend an hour here and just empty my mind.

PRIEST. When the mind is empty the gods take possession. And the gods know.

OLD BILL. Yes: I suppose thats it. But it's a queer business: I thought I was the very last man in the world to put my nose into a temple. However, you know all this. I am repeating myself, and boring you. Leave me to myself. [*He seats himself in the bishop's chair*].

PRIEST. I repeat the service every day; yet it does not bore me: there is always something new in it. They tell me it is the same with your orchestral symphonies: the great ones cannot be heard too often. But as you desire, I leave you to your aftercalm.

OLD BILL. So long, Mahatma.

The Priest nods gravely, and is going when She and He come in.

THE PRIEST. Peace be with you three. [*He goes*].

SHE [*rushing to Old Bill and kissing him*] Daddyest!

OLD BILL [*returning her embrace*] My Babzy! Who is the man?

SHE. I dont know. He wants to marry me.

OLD BILL. Does he indeed? Do you want to marry him?

SHE. I am considering it. I am not dead set against it.

OLD BILL. Whats his name?

SHE. I dont know.

OLD BILL. The devil you dont!

SHE [*to Him*] Whats your name?

HE. Smith. Only Smith. Christened Junius.

OLD BILL. Have you nothing else to say for yourself?

JUNIUS. Nothing whatever.

OLD BILL. Any profession?

HE. World betterer. Nothing paying.

SHE. If I marry him I shall have to keep him and manage for him. But that is not altogether a drawback. I do not mean to be any man's kept slave.

OLD BILL [*to Junius*] What about you? Do you want to be any woman's kept man?

JUNIUS. I dont want anything but your daughter. I dont know why. I know nothing about her; and she knows nothing about me. I am simply mad on the subject.

OLD BILL [*to Her*] Are you mad on the subject?

SHE. Not so mad as he is. I can do without him. If not, I should be his slave.

OLD BILL. Do you hear that, young man? You will be the slave.

JUNIUS. I suppose so. But I must risk it. So must she. You can understand this. You have made your billions by taking risks.

OLD BILL. I have seen men ruined by taking risks. I have a sort of instinct about them which brings me out all right. For old Bill Buoyant there are no risks. But for you, perhaps ? ? ?

JUNIUS. Well, there may be none for your daughter. She may inherit your genius.

OLD BILL. She does. But my genius tells me not to throw away my daughter on a young lunatic.

JUNIUS. You are jealous, eh? Let me remind you that all parents must see their children walk out sooner or later. Mothers-in-law are stock jokes. Nobody jokes about fathers-in-law; but they are troublesome enough when they hold on too long.

SHE. Parents cannot be turned out into the woods to die. We are not savages. Daddy will always be a part of my life.

JUNIUS. Not always. How long do you intend to live, old man?

OLD BILL. Not for ever: God forbid! [*To Her*] The fellow is right, darling. Leave me out of the question.

SHE. I cant leave you out, Daddy. But you will know your natural place in my house: you have always known it in your own. I can trust you.

JUNIUS. I have no objection to your father as long as he lasts. He has the billions.

OLD BILL. The billions will stop when I die. Would you be as keen if there were no billions?

JUNIUS. Just as keen. How often must I tell you that I am mad about her? But we shall want the money. I have earned nothing so far.

OLD BILL [*to Her*] He has an eye for facts, this chap. I rather like him.

SHE. Yes: so do I. He has no illusions about himself nor about me. After all, if he turns out badly I can divorce him.

OLD BILL. Well, our parting must come someday; and if you and I were the wisest father and daughter on earth the upshot would be just as much a toss-up as if we were the two damndest fools. Still, there are certain precautions one can take.

JUNIUS. A joint annuity, for instance.

OLD BILL. Your sense of money is very clear, young man. But I have already bought her an annuity for her life. Not for yours. Any further precautions you must take yourself.

JUNIUS. I must agree. The Life Force has got me. I can make no conditions.

OLD BILL [*to Her*] Well, will you marry him?

SHE. I will consider it.

JUNIUS. If you consider it you will refuse. There would be no marriages if the two started considering.

OLD BILL. That is the first stupid thing you have said, young man. All marriages are very anxiously considered; but considering has never yet prevented a marriage. If you are her man she will have you, consideration or no consideration.

SHE. What do you advise, Daddy?

OLD BILL. Oh, take him, take him. I like him; and he will do as well as another. You may regret it; but you will regret it worse if you are afraid to try your luck.

JUNIUS. I am surprised and deeply obliged to you, Mr Buoyant. I expected you to use all your influence against me. You are a model father-in-law.

SHE. I feel as if I were going to commit suicide.

JUNIUS. In a sense, you are. So am I. The chrysalis dies when the dragonfly is born.

SHE. I am no chrysalis. I am a working bee: you are a drone.

JUNIUS. That is nature's arrangement. We cannot change it.

OLD BILL. A working husband is no husband at all. When I had to work, my wife was only my housekeeper: she saw next to nothing of me except when I came home at night hungry and tired and dirty. When I did nothing but send telegrams to my stockbroker – I dont call that work – and buy fancy waistcoats and diamond cravat pins, she began to enjoy her marriage and love me. And long as she has been dead now, I have never been unfaithful to her, nor ever shall be.

JUNIUS. But you married again.

OLD BILL. It was not the same thing. I wanted more children because I was so fond of the one I had. But it was not the same.

JUNIUS. Did you never think of bettering the world with your money?

OLD BILL. What the devil do I care about the world? What did it care about me when I was poor? Dont talk your world bettering cant to me if we are to get on together. I am not going to buy any of your shares.

JUNIUS. I apologize. My shares pay no dividends. I will not pursue the subject. When are we to get married? Name the day.

OLD BILL. Dont frighten her. When she names it, you will be frightened.

JUNIUS. I am frightened already. But we must dare. By the way, where shall we live? Not in Panama, I hope.

SHE. No. In Panama I should be nervous about you when you were out of my sight. You cannot charm the rattlers and gaters as I can.

JUNIUS. Why not? I can learn the saxophone.

SHE. True; but we should be out of reach of Daddy. We shall live in Park Lane.

JUNIUS. You know, of course, that there are plenty of rattlers and gaters of the human variety in Park Lane?

SHE. Yes; and you may be one of them.

JUNIUS. You have an answer for everything. What a prospect for me!

SHE. We are both taking chances. We shall live where I like.

JUNIUS. Or where I like. I can assert myself.

SHE. So can I. We shall see which of us wins. Stop chattering; and go out and buy a marriage licence.

JUNIUS [*taken aback*] Oh, I say! This is very sudden.

OLD BILL. Frightened, eh? Go. Get it over. You will have to arrange for two witnesses.

JUNIUS. I wish I could arrange for an anesthetist. The operation is terrifying.

SHE. Dont forget to buy a wedding ring. Have you money enough?

JUNIUS. I have what is left of the thousand pounds my father started me with. Panama made a big hole in it.

OLD BILL. Off with you, damn you. You are stealing my daughter from me. I hope she will soon tire of you and come back to me. [*To Her*] Give him one of your rings to get the fit right. Never mind the witnesses: Tom and Dick will do.

JUNIUS [*to Her*] Wouldnt you like to be married in church and have the banns called? That would give us three weeks to think it over.

SHE. No. Now or never.

JUNIUS. I am being rushed.

OLD BILL. You will spend your life being rushed if you live with Babz. Better get used to it at once.

SHE. A ring that will fit your middle finger will be big enough for my third. I have bigger hands. I was brought up to use them. You werent.

JUNIUS. You must put up with that. My hands are those of a philosopher: yours of a charwoman. Oh, why, WHY am I infatuated with you? I know so many apparently superior women.

SHE. Same here. Daddy is worth ten of you.

JUNIUS. You think so. But if you only knew how quickly I can lose money. He can only make it.

OLD BILL. Leave me out of it: I shall not last much longer: you have a lifetime to give her. Away with you to the registry office and stop talking.

JUNIUS. I go. But I'm not sure I shall ever come back, [*He goes out*].

SHE. I half hope he wont.

JUNIUS [*coming back*] By the way, whats your Christian name?

SHE. Clementina Alexandra.

JUNIUS. Righto! [*Making a note of it*] Cle-Men-Tina Alexandra. [*He goes*].

SHE. [*throwing her arms round Old Bill's neck and kissing him*] Daddy! Daddy! Daddy!

 The Native comes in and closes the door carefully. Babz quickly releases her father.

THE NATIVE [*to Her*] Sir Flopper, the illustrious law servant of God, has waited until your venerable father is disengaged. May he enter?

OLD BILL. Yes. Shew him in.

THE NATIVE [*looks to Her for confirmation*]??

SHE. Yes. Shew him in.

THE NATIVE [*throwing the door open*] Enter, Excellency.

Sir Ferdinand comes in. The Native withdraws.

SIR FERDINAND [*to Old Bill*] Pardon. I thought you were alone.

OLD BILL. Get out, Babzy.

SHE. Au revoir, Sir Ferdinand.

He opens the door for her and bows gravely as she passes out, then closes the door, and, after an inviting gesture from Old Bill, sits down in the chair vacated by her.

SIR FERDINAND. First let me say that I am not here professionally.

OLD BILL. Why not? You must live.

SIR FERDINAND. My reason is that I am totally incapable of advising you on the subject of your extraordinary family. They are outside my experience. If I were a medical adviser I should certify them as insane.

OLD BILL. And me?

SIR FERDINAND. Well, hardly yet. Your instructions were rational enough. I put your financial case before your sons as you desired. I was interrupted by the arrival from America of the lady who has just left us. I was interrupted again by the arrival of a young man who proposed to marry her for her money. Your daughter made no objection: she seemed to prefer it to a disinterested proposal. Your family did not demur. I am prepared to learn that you do not demur. In any other family he would have been kicked out of the house.

OLD BILL. I like the fellow.

SIR FERDINAND. Like the fellow! Like an impudent fortune hunter! In Heaven's name, why?

OLD BILL. He asks straight questions and gives straight answers. So does my daughter. I taught her to do it. It was all I could teach her. Didnt you notice it?

SIR FERDINAND. I did indeed. And I have come to tell you I can no longer act as your solicitor. My brother Cyril is a doctor, head of a mental hospital for incurables. He is the man you should consult. Lawyers are useless here.

OLD BILL. Come, come, Flopper! You know as well as I do that people who marry for money are happy together as often as other people. It is the love matches that break down because Providence wants sound children and does not care a snap of its fingers whether the parents are happy or not. It makes them mad about one another until the children are born, and then drops them like hot potatoes. Money guarantees comfort and what you call culture. Love guarantees nothing. I know this. You know it. My daughter knows it. The young man knows it.

Are we mad because we act and speak accordingly? Are you sane because you pretend to be shocked by it? It is you who should go to the mental hospital.

SIR FERDINAND. That also is a matter for medical, not legal opinion. I will not discuss it. I have only to tell you that I explained to your second family as you instructed me, that the source of their incomes would dry up at your death, and they must then fend for themselves.

OLD BILL. Good. What did they say to that?

SIR FERDINAND. Nothing. I had to suggest that they should live by directorships founded on your reputation.

OLD BILL. Guinea pigs. No use: that game is up. The new Labor Government gives such jobs to superannuated Trade Union secretaries.

SIR FERDINAND. Then why have you not provided for your second family as you did for your first daughter?

OLD BILL. It is not the same. They dont belong to me as she does.

SIR FERDINAND. They will starve.

OLD BILL. No they wont. They can live on their wives' incomes. I took care of that.

SIR FERDINAND. Well, that is all I have to say. I shall accept no fees for it; but I shall be glad to keep up our acquaintance, if that will be agreeable to you.

OLD BILL. Why?

SIR FERDINAND. Pure curiosity.

OLD BILL. I dont believe you.

SIR FERDINAND [*rising, offended*] Do you accuse me of lying?

OLD BILL. Yes. There must be some attraction. Which woman is it? One of my sons' wives, eh?

SIR FERDINAND [*sitting down again, deflated*] Well, really! No: they are married women. You have two unmarried daughters.

OLD BILL. Darkie? I actually forgot Darkie. Think of that!

SIR FERDINAND. Do not misunderstand me. I am a bachelor, not a libertine. I want a daughter.

OLD BILL. Good. Ive always had an uneasy conscience about Darkie. Ive never been able to give her the affection Ive heaped on Babzy. She has never had a father. Take her; and be a father to her. Come as often as you please: you are one of the family now.

SIR FERDINAND. You take my breath away. This is too sudden. A minute ago I did not know why I wanted to keep on terms with you all. You have shoved it down my throat.

OLD BILL. That is the Buoyant way: it saves a lot of time. Now that you know, you had better stay to lunch.

SIR FERDINAND. No. I must go home and think it over. Never fear: I shall not back out.

Darkie comes in.

OLD BILL. Here she is. Telepathy. It runs in the family.

DARKIE. Oh! I beg your pardon. I did not know you were engaged. It is only to ask whether you will have asparagus or broad beans for lunch.

OLD BILL. Sparrowgrass? Yes: plenty of it. [*She turns to go*]. Wait a bit. Sir Ferdinand Flopper here has fallen for you. He wants to be your father.

DARKIE. I dont want a father. Ive never had a real father: I'm not accustomed to it. I'm only a housekeeper.

OLD BILL. Well, my child, you can have a real father now, a baronet. Try him. You can drop him if he doesnt suit. Somebody to spoil you as Ive spoilt Babzy.

DARKIE. I dont want to be spoilt. I like housekeeping; and Im not sentimental. If I ever want to be spoilt I shall get married. I am sorry to disappoint you, Sir Ferdinand; but daughtering is a game I have no turn for.

DARKIE. I see. But at least youll not mind my keeping up my acquaintance with the family.

DARKIE. Not a bit. Let me know what you like to eat and drink: that is all. I must go now to see about father's lunch. Tata.

She goes out.

OLD BILL. Dumbfounded, eh?

SIR FERDINAND. Completely. What a house this is! She was not a bit surprised, though she was quite unprepared.

OLD BILL. We Buoyants are always prepared for the worst.

SIR FERDINAND. Or the best, I hope. My offer is hardly a misfortune, as I see it.

OLD BILL. It isnt. Dont fancy you have escaped her. She asked about your grub. She is glad to have one more to housekeep for. You may consider yourself adopted.

SIR FERDINAND. I am past considering anything.

OLD BILL. Youll get used to it.

SIR FERDINAND. Yes: I suppose I shall. The curious thing is, I am beginning to like it.

OLD BILL. Good. [*Looking at his watch*] I wonder whether that chap is coming back. He ought to be here by now.

The Widower enters.

THE WIDOWER. Look here, Ee Pee: the young man from Panama says he is going to be married to Clemmy. He wants me and Dick to be witnesses. Is that all right?

OLD BILL. Yes. Quite all right. Has he got the licence?

THE WIDOWER. Yes. And he has borrowed my wife's wedding ring for the ceremony. He was short of pocket money for a new one. The money for the licence cleaned him out.

OLD BILL. Then he has come back?

THE WIDOWER. Yes. A bit upset, naturally; but he means business.

OLD BILL. Good.

SIR FERDINAND. Excuse me: but what does Ee Pee mean? Esteemed Parent?

OLD BILL. No. Earthly Providence. Darkie's invention.

SIR FERDINAND. Ah! Precisely.

The youth Fiffy comes in.

FIFFY. Look here, Ee Pee. Clemmy and the man from Panama are going to marry. He has got the licence.

OLD BILL. Well, what is that to you, you young rip?

FIFFY. Only that the chap is a World Betterer. I thought you had enough of that from me.

OLD BILL. So I have. The pair of you want to better the world when you dont know enough of it to manage a fish and chips business.

FIFFY. True, O king. But we are needed in the world bettering business, not in fish and chips. Still, one World Betterer is enough in one family.

OLD BILL. Keep out of it then, you. You were born to talk and say nothing, to write and do nothing. That pays.

FIFFY. To make sure, I shall marry for money, as the Panama chap is doing. Dont you agree, Sir Ferdinand?

SIR FERDINAND. Yes, if you can find the lady. Dress better; and oil your hair.

Babzy comes back with her two stepsisters-in-law.

SHE. Dick, dear: shall I marry the man from Panama?

SECONDBORN. My dearest Clemmy: I cannot advise you. You must take chances; but they are not calculable mathematically. We have no figures to go on: the proportion of happy love marriages to happy marriages of convenience has never been counted.

MRS SECONDBORN. Do stop talking heartless nonsense, Dick. Has the man any means or expectations? Is he a gentleman? He speaks like a gentleman. He dresses like a gentleman. But he has not the feelings of a gentleman. He says things that no gentleman would dream of saying. That is all we know about him. Dont marry him, Clemmy.

SECONDBORN. My dear: she must take chances or not marry at all.

MRS SECONDBORN. Oh, bother your chances! Chances! Chances! Chances! You are always talking about chances. Talk sense.

SECONDBORN. You tell me so almost every day, dear. I took my chance when I married you. But I do not regret it. You are the stupidest woman on earth; but you are a part of my life.

MRS SECONDBORN. Well, ask Sir Ferdinand which of us is right. Clemmy has low tastes; but that is no reason why she should throw herself away on a nobody.

SIR FERDINAND. I do not think, Mr Buoyant, that you can treat this question altogether as a mathematical one. You must take account of feelings, passions, emotions, intuitions, instincts, as well as cold quantities and figures and logic.

SECONDBORN [*rising to the occasion eloquently*] And who dares say that mathematics and reasoning are not passions? Mathematic perception is the noblest of all the faculties! This cant about their being soulless, dead, inhuman mechanisms is contrary to the plainest facts of life and history. What has carried our minds farther than mathematical foresight? Who has done more for enlightenment and civilization than Giordano Bruno, Copernicus, Galileo, Newton, Descartes, Rutherford, Einstein, all of them far seeing guessers carried away by the passion for measuring truth and knowledge that possessed and drove them? Will you set above this great passion the vulgar concupiscences of Don Juan and Casanova, and the romance of Beatrice and Francesca, of Irish Deirdre, the greatest bores in literature, mere names incidentally immortalized by a few lines in a great poem?

MRS THIRDBORN. They had hearts, Dick.

SECONDBORN. Hearts! What are hearts without brains? You mean that they had glands: pituitary glands, adrenal glands, thyroid glands, pouring hormones into their blood. Do you suppose that there is no mathematical hormone? Our anatomists have not yet discovered it; but it is there, undiscovered and invisible, pouring into our brains, controlled by our enzymes and catalysts as surely as our appetites for beef and brandy. La Rochefoucauld told you two centuries ago that though the appetite we call love is in everybody's mouth very few have ever experienced it. God is not Love: Love is not Enough: the appetite for more truth, more knowledge, for measurement and precision, is far more universal: even the dullest fools have some glimmer of it. My wife here never tires of playing bridge and solving crossword puzzles as she tires of housekeeping. Her love for me is very variable: it turns to hate in its terrible reactions. Mathematical passion alone has no reaction: our pleasure in it promises a development in which life will be an intellectual ecstasy surpassing the ecstasies of saints. Think of that, Clara. Take your chance, Clemmy. Forgive my prolixity. Ive done.

He flings himself back into his chair.

MRS SECONDBORN [*humbled*] Well, Dick, I will say that you are wonderful when you speak your piece, though I never understand a word. You must be the greatest man in the family: you always make me feel like a fool. I am proud of you. I may lose my temper sometimes; but I never hate you.

Darkie comes in.

OLD BILL. Ah! there you are. Youve missed something.

DARKIE. No: Ive been listening at the door.

FIFFY. By George, Dick, you were splendid. World bettering be damned! I shall qualify as a doctor and look for that hormone.

Junius comes in with the licence in his hand.

JUNIUS. Well, Ive come back after all. Here is the licence. Ive got the witnesses. Is it yes or no?

SHE. I suppose I must take my chance. Yes.

DARKIE. What I want to know is how many of you are staying for lunch.

The curtain falls and ends the play.

The Author Explains

(Replies to a questionnaire by Stephen Winsten and Esmé Percy, in holograph facsimile. *World Review*, London, September 1949)

(*1*) *Why did you call your new play a 'Comedy of No Manners' when this is the best-mannered play you have written? In Act I, father and son are exceptionally courteous.*
They are not courteous. They are simply frank, which is the extremity of no manners. This takes the play out of the well category [*sic*] called Comedy of Manners.

(*2*) *If, as the result of taxation, there will be no more wealthy folk, what will Worldbetterers do if they cannot marry 'for money'?*
Just what they do at present when they cannot attract wealthy wives.

(*3*) *All the wisdom seems to have been put into the mouths of Native and Eastern. Have you given up hope on the Pinks?*
Read the play again. The pink women are as wise as the yellow men; and none of the white men are nitwits. But east is east and west is west throughout.

(*4*) *In* Good King Charles *Kneller seems to have the better of Newton in argument. Here, in* Buoyant Billions, *you go all out for the mathematician. Does it mean you have changed your mind?*
I do not go all out for anybody or anything. I am a playwright, not a Soot or Whitewash doctrinaire. I give Newton his own point of view and Kneller his own also. There is neither change nor contradiction on my part.

(*5*) *In* Buoyant Billions *it is the male who is the pursuing animal: a change from* Man and Superman?
There is no pursuing animal in the play. There are two people who fall in love at first sight and are both terrified at finding themselves mad on the subject, and caught in a trap laid by the Life Force. Do you expect me to keep writing Man & Superman over and over again?

(*6*) *Do you suggest that Buoyant's training of his children made it difficult for them to cope with changed circumstances?*
No. It is difficult for everybody to cope with changed circumstances.

Farfetched Fables

with
Preface

Preface

As I have now entered my 93rd year, my fans must not expect from me more than a few crumbs dropped from the literary loaves I distributed in my prime, plus a few speculations as to what may happen in the next million light years that are troubling me in the queer second wind that follows second childhood.

Being unable to put everything in the heavens above and on the earth beneath into every page I write, as some of my correspondents seem to expect, I have had to leave some scraps and shavings out; and now I gather up a few of them and present them in the childish form of Far-fetched Fables. Philosophic treatises, however precise and lucid, are thrown away on readers who can enjoy and sometimes even understand parables, fairy tales, novels, poems, and prophecies. Proverbs are more memorable than catechisms and creeds. Fictions like The Prodigal Son, The Good Samaritan, The Pilgrim's Progress, and Gulliver's Travels, stick in minds impervious to the Epistles of Paul, the sermons of Bunyan, and the wisecracks of Koheleth and Ecclesiasticus. Hard workers who devour my plays cannot all tackle my prefaces without falling asleep almost at once.

The Panjandrums of literature will no doubt continue to assume that whoever can read anything can read everything, and that whoever can add two and two, bet on a horse, or play whist or bridge, can take in the tensor calculus. I know better, and can only hope that a batch of childish fables may stick in some heads that my graver performances overshoot.

The New Psychobiology

Nowadays biology is taking a new turn in my direction. What I called metabiology when I wrote The Doctor's Dilemma has made a step towards reality as psychobiology. The medical profession has split violently into psychotherapists and old-fashioned pill and bottle prescribers backed by surgeons practising on our living bodies as flesh plumbers and carpenters. When these surgeons find a tumor or a cancer they just cut it out. When your digestion or excretion goes wrong the bottlemen dose you with hydrochloric acid or chalk-and-opium ('the old mixture') as the case may be. When these treatments fail, or when they are impracticable, they tell you sympathetically that you must die; and die you do, unless you cure yourself or are cured by a disciple of Mrs Eddy practising Christian Science.

The more intelligent, observant, and open-minded apothecaries and Sawbonesses, wakened up by an extraordinarily indelicate adventurer named Sigmund Freud, and by the able Scotch doctor Scot Haldane (J. B. S. Haldane's father), become more and more sceptical of the dogma that a healthy body insures a healthy mind (*mens sana in corpore sano*) and more and more inclined to believe that an unhealthy body is the result of a diseased mind. As I write, a treatise on Mental Abnormality by Dr Millais Culpin has just been published. It would have been impossible when I wrote The Doctor's Dilemma. In spite of its author's efforts to be impartial, it is convincing and converting as to his evident belief that the old mechanistic surgery and *materia medica* cost many lives.

Am I a Pathological Case?

This leads my restlessly speculative mind further than Dr Culpin has ventured. Is literary genius a disease? Shakespear, Walter Scott, Alexandre Dumas, myself: are we all mental cases? Are we simply incorrigible liars? Are players impostors and hypocrites? Were the Bible Christians right when they disowned Bunyan because the incidents he described had never occurred nor had the characters of whom he told such circumstantial tales ever existed? He pleaded that Jesus had taught by parables; but this made matters worse; for the Bibliolators never doubted that the Prodigal Son and the Good Samaritan were historical personages whose adventures had actually occurred. To them Bunyan's plea, classing the parables with Esop's Fables and the stories of Reynard the Fox, was a blasphemy. The first Freudians used to recite a string of words to their patients, asking what they suggested, and studying the reaction, until they wormed their way into the sufferer's sub-conscious mind, and unveiled some forgotten trouble that had been worrying him and upsetting his health. By bringing it to light they cured the patient.

When this Freudian technique was tried on me it failed because the words suggested always something fictitious. On the salt marshes of Norfolk I had been struck by the fact that when the horses stood round timidly at a distance, a handsome and intelligent donkey came and conversed with me after its fashion. I still have the photograph I took of this interesting acquaintance. The word Ass would have recalled this experience to any normal person. But when it was put to me, I immediately said Dogberry. I was once shewn the dagger with which Major

Sirr killed Lord Edward Fitzgerald; but the word dagger got nothing from me but Macbeth. Highway or stile produced Autolycus, Interpreter the Pilgrim's Progress, blacksmith Joe Gargery. I was living in an imaginary world. Deeply as I was interested in politics, Hamlet and Falstaff were more alive to me than any living politician or even any relative. Can I then be given credit for common sanity? Can I make any effective excuse except Bunyan's excuse, which is no excuse at all? If I plead that I am only doing what More and Bunyan, Dickens and Wells did I do not exonerate myself: I convict them.

All I can plead is that as events as they actually occur mean no more than a passing crowd to a policeman on point duty, they must be arranged in some comprehensible order as stories. Without this there can be no history, no morality, no social conscience. Thus the historian, the story teller, the playwright and his actors, the poet, the mathematician, and the philosopher, are functionaries without whom civilization would not be possible. I conclude that I was born a story teller because one was needed. I am therefore not a disease but a social necessity.

Divine Providence

Providence, which I call The Life Force, when not defeated by the imperfection of its mortal instruments, always takes care that the necessary functionaries are born specialized for their job. When no specialization beyond that of common mental ability is needed, millions of 'hands' (correctly so called industrially) are born. But as they are helpless without skilled craftsmen and mechanics, without directors and deciders, without legislators and thinkers, these also are provided in the required numbers. Chaucer and Shakespear, Dante and Michael Angelo, Goethe and Ibsen, Newton and Einstein, Adam Smith and Karl Marx arrive only once at intervals of hundreds of years, whilst carpenters and tailors, stockbrokers and parsons, industrialists and traders are all forthcoming in thousands as fast as they are needed.

I present myself therefore as an instrument of the Life Force, writing by what is called inspiration; but as the Life Force proceeds experimentally by Trial-and-Error, and never achieves a 100 per cent success, I may be one of its complete failures, and certainly fall very short not only of perfection but of the Force's former highest achievements. For instance I am much less mentally gifted than, say, Leibniz, and can only have been needed because, as he was so gifted as to be unintelligible to the mob, it remained for some simpler soul like myself to translate his monads and his universal substance, as he called the Life Force, into fables which, however farfetched, can at least interest, amuse, and perhaps enlighten those capable of such entertainment, but baffled by Leibniz's algebraic symbols and his philosophic jargon.

Here I must warn you that you can make no greater mistakes in your social thinking than to assume, as too many do, that persons with the rarest mental gifts or specific talents are in any other respect superior beings. The Life Force, when it gives some needed extraordinary quality to some individual, does not bother about his or her morals. It may even, when some feat is required which a human being can perform only after drinking a pint of brandy, make him a dipsomaniac, like Edmund Kean, Robson, and Dickens on his last American tour. Or, needing a woman capable of bearing first rate children, it may endow her with enchanting sexual attraction yet leave her destitute of the qualities that make married life with her bearable. Apparently its aim is always the attainment of power over circumstances and matter through science, and is to this extent benevolent; but outside this bias it is quite unscrupulous, and lets its agents be equally so. Geniuses are often spendthrifts, drunkards, libertines, liars, dishonest in money matters, backsliders of all sorts, whilst many simple credulous souls are models of integrity and piety, high in the calendar of saints.

Mental Capacity Differs and Divides

When reading what follows it must not be forgotten that though we differ widely in practical ability and mental scope, the same basic income, or ration, or minimum wage, or national dividend, or whatever the newspapers call it for the moment, will suffice for mayor and scavenger, for admiral and cabin boy, for judge and executioner, for field marshal and drummer boy, for sexton and archbishop, bank manager and bank porter, sister of charity and prison wardress, and who not. What is more, they are all equally indispensable. An industrial magnate once wrote asking me did I realize that his army of laborers would be destitute and helpless without him. I replied that if he did not realize that without them he would be a nobody he was no gentleman. This closed the correspondence.

Equality of income is an obvious corollary. Yes; but how much income? A national dividend of, say, thirteen shillings a week per family, which was the share agricultural laborers got in the nineteenth century, kept them alive for thirty years or so, but left no surplus for education and culture: in short, for civilization. Now without cultured homes civilization is impossible. Without culture possible in every home democratic civilization is impossible, because equality of opportunity is impossible. The present combination of class culture and general savagery produces civil war, called class war, until strikes, lock-outs, and police batons are succeeded by shot and shell. Then the final destruction of civilization is threatened.

Consequently the basic income to be aimed at must be sufficient to establish culture in every home, and wages must be levelled up, not down, to this quota by increased production. When the quota is achieved, arithmetical inequality will no longer matter; for the eugenic test is general intermarriageability; and though the difference between £5 a week and £50 makes the recipients practically exogamous, millionaires could not marry at all if they scorned brides from homes with £5000 a year. There is no harm in a few people having some spare money, called capital, to experiment with; for the basic income will keep them in the normal grooves.

So much for the economics of the situation produced by differences in mental capacity! Having dealt with it in former writings, I mention it here only for new readers saturated with the common notion that income ought to vary with mental capacity, personal talent, and business ability. Such equations are wildly impossible, and have nothing to do with the insane misdistribution of national income produced by nineteenth century plutocracy. And so I pass on to political ethics.

Most of us so far are ungovernable by abstract thought. Our inborn sense of right and wrong, of grace and sin, must be embodied for us in a supernatural ruler of the universe: omnipotent, omniscient, all wise, all benevolent. In ancient Greece this was called making the word flesh, because the Greeks did not then discriminate between thought and the words that expressed it. The Bible translators have Englished it too literally as the word made flesh.

But as the minds of the masses could not get beyond their trades and their localities, their God could not be omnipresent; and a host of minor gods sprang up. The Greeks added to Zeus and Chronos vocational deities: Vulcan the blacksmith, Athene (Minerva) the thinker, Diana the huntress, Aphrodite (Venus) the sexmistress. They reappear in Christianity as Peter the fisherman, Luke the painter, Joseph the carpenter, Saint Cecilia the musician, and the rest.

But this also was too wide a classification for the very simple souls, who carried the localization of their gods to the extent of claiming exclusive property for their own city in each saint, and waging civil war in the name of the black image of the Blessed Virgin in their parish church against the worshippers of her white image in the next village.

Satanic Solution of the Problem of Evil

A difficulty was raised by the fact that evil was in the world as well as good, and often triumphed over the good. Consequently there must be a devil as well as a divinity: Poochlihoochli as well as Hoochlipoochli, Ahriman as well as Ormudz, Lucifer, Beelzebub and Apollyon as well as the Holy Trinity, the Scarlet Woman as well as Our Lady: in short as many demons as saints.

At first, however, this setting up against God of a rival deity with a contrary ideology was resented as a Manichean heresy, because plague, pestilence and famine, battle, murder and sudden death, were not regarded with horror as the work of Shelley's Almighty Fiend, but with awe as evidence of the terrible greatness of God, the fear of him being placed to his credit as the beginning of wisdom. The invention of Satan is a heroic advance on Jahvism. It is an attempt to solve the Problem of Evil, and at least faces the fact that evil *is* evil.

Thus the world, as we imagine it, is crowded with anthropomorphic supernatural beings of whose existence there is no scientific proof. None the less, without such belief the human race cannot be civilized and governed, though the ten per cent or so of persons mentally capable of civilizing and governing are mostly too clever to be imposed on by fairy tales, and in any case have to deal with hard facts as well as fancies and fictions.

Mendacity Compulsory in Kingcraft and Priestcraft

This lands them in the quaintest moral dilemmas. It drives them to falsehoods, hypocrisies, and forgeries most distressing to their intellectual consciences. When the people demand miracles, worship relics, and will not obey any authority that does not supply them, the priest must create and nourish their faith by liquefying the blood of Saint Januarius, and saying Mass over a jawbone labelled as that of Saint Anthony of Padua. When the people believe that the earth is flat, immovable, and the centre of the universe, and Copernicus and Leonardo convince both Galileo the scientist and the Vatican that the earth is a planet of the sun, the Pope and the cardinals have to make Galileo recant and pretend that he believes what the people believe, because, if the Church admits that it has ever been mistaken, its whole authority will collapse, and civilization perish in anarchy. If Joshua could not make the sun stand still, there is a blunder in the Bible. When the Protestants blew the gaff to discredit the Vatican, and the secret could no longer be kept by forbidding Catholics to read the Bible, the people were not logical enough to draw subversive inferences. They swallowed the contradiction cheerfully.

Meanwhile the people had to be threatened with a posthumous eternity in a brimstone hell if they behaved in an uncivilized way. As burning brimstone could not hurt a spirit, they had to be assured that their bodies would be resurrected on a great Day of Judgment. But the official translators of the Bible in England were presently staggered by a passage in the Book of Job, in which that prophet declared that as worms would destroy his body, in the flesh he should not see God. Such a heresy, if published, would knock the keystone out of the arch of British civilization. There was nothing for it but to alter the word of God, making Job say that though worms would destroy his body yet in his flesh he should see God. The facts made this forgery necessary; but it was a forgery all the same.

A later difficulty was more easily got over. The apostles were Communists so Red that St Peter actually struck a man and his wife dead for keeping back money from the common stock. The translators could not pretend that St Peter was a disciple of the unborn Adam Smith rather than of Jesus; so they let the narrative stand, but taught that Ananias and Sapphira were executed for telling a lie and not for any economic misdemeanor. This view was impressed on me in my childhood. I now regard it as a much graver lie than that of Ananias.

'The lie' said Ferdinand Lassalle 'is a European Power.' He might, however, have added that it is none the worse when it does a necessary job; for I myself have been a faker of miracles. Let me tell one of my old stories over again.

G. B. S. Miracle Faker

When I was a vestryman I had to check the accounts of the Public Health Committee. It was a simple process: I examined one in every ten or so of the receipted accounts and passed it whilst my fellow members did the same; and so enough of the accounts got checked to make their falsification too risky.

As it happened, one which I examined was for sulphur candles to disinfect houses in which cases of fever had occurred. I knew that experiments had proved that the fumes of burning sulphur had no such effect. Pathogenic bacilli like them and multiply on them.

I put the case to the Medical Officer of Health, and asked why the money of the ratepayers should be spent on a useless fumigant. He replied that the sulphur was not useless: it was necessary. But, I urged, the houses are not being disinfected at all. 'Oh yes they are' he said. 'How?' I persisted. 'Soap and water and sunshine' he explained. 'Then why sulphur?' 'Because the strippers and cleaners will not venture into an infected house unless we make a horrible stink in it with burning sulphur.'

I passed the account. It was precisely equivalent to liquefying the blood of Saint Januarius.

Some twenty years later I wrote a play called Saint Joan in which I made an archbishop explain that a miracle is an event that creates faith, even if it is faked for that end. Had I not been a vulgar vestryman as well as a famous playwright I should not have thought of that. All playwrights should know that had I not suspended my artistic activity to write political treatises and work on political committees long enough to have written twenty plays, the Shavian idiosyncrasy which fascinates some of them (or used to) and disgusts the Art For Art's Sake faction, would have missed half its value, such as it is.

Parental Dilemmas

The first and most intimate of the moral dilemmas that arise from differences in mental ability are not between classes and Churches, but in the daily work of bringing up children. The difference between Einstein and an average ploughman is less troublesome than the difference between children at five, at ten, and at fifteen. At five the Church catechism is only a paradigm: I learnt it at that age and still remember its phrases; but it had no effect on my conduct. I got no farther with it critically than to wonder why it obliged me, when asked what my name was, to reply that it was N or M, which was not true.

What did affect my conduct was my nurse's threat that if I was naughty or dirty the cock would come down the chimney. I confidently recommend this formula to all parents, nurses, and kindergarten teachers, as it effects its purpose and then dies a natural death, fading from the mind as the child grows out of it without leaving any psychic complexes.

But the same cannot be said for more complicated schemes of infant civilization. If they begin with Law's Serious Call, as many pious parents think they should, they may be worse than no scheme at all. I knew a man whose youth was made miserable by a dread of hell sedulously inculcated from his infancy. His reaction against it carried him into Socialism, whereupon he founded a Labor Church in which all the meetings began by calling on the speakers to pray: a demand which so took aback my Fabian colleagues that one of them began with 'Heavenly Father: unaccustomed as I have been many years to address you, I *etc. etc.*' The Labor Church did not last; but the reaction did; and the last I heard of its founder was that he was helping the movement against Victorian prudery in a very practical way as a Nudist photographer, the basis of that prudery being the fact that the clothing, or rather upholstering, of Victorian women was much more aphrodisiac than their unadorned bodies.

As to the Socialist orator who parodied 'Unaccustomed as I am to public speaking,' he died in the bosom of the Roman Catholic Church.

I tell these anecdotes because they give an impression, better than any abstract argument could, of the way in which highly intelligent children of pious families, or of irreligious ones capable of nothing more intellectual than sport and sex, reacted against their bringing-up. One day, at a rehearsal of one of my plays, an actress who was a Roman Catholic consulted me in some distress because her adolescent son had become an atheist. I advised her not to worry; for as family religions have to be cast off as thoughtless habits before they can be replaced by genuine religious convictions, she might safely leave her son's case to God.

Edmund Gosse was the son of a Plymouth Brother, and was baptized by total immersion, of which he wrote a highly entertaining description in his book called Father and Son. The immersion had washed all the father's pious credulity out of the son. George Eliot, also piously brought up, began her reaction by translating Emil Strauss's Life of Jesus, which divested the worshipped Redeemer of supernatural attributes, and even questioned the sanity of his pretension to them.

The All or Nothing Complex

In those days we were all what I called Soot or Whitewash merchants, pilloried as All or Nothings in Ibsen's Brand. When one link in our mental chain snapped we did not pick up the sound links and join them, we threw the chain away as if all its links had snapped. If the story of Noah's Ark was a fable, if Joshua could not have delayed the sunset in the Valley of Ajalon, if the big fish could not have swallowed Jonah nor he survive in its belly, then nothing in the Bible was true. If Jehovah was a barbarous tribal idol, irreconcilable with the God of Micah, then there was no God at all, and the heavens were empty. On the other hand if Galileo, the man of science, knew better than Joshua, and Linneus and Darwin better than Moses, then everything that scientists said was true. Thus the credulity that believed in the Garden of Eden with its talking serpent, and in the speeches of Balaam's ass, was not cured. It was simply transferred to Herbert Spencer and John Stuart Mill. The transfer was often for the worse, as when baptism by water and the spirit, consecrating the baptized as a soldier and a servant of the Highest, was replaced by the poisonous rite of vaccination on evidence that could not have imposed on any competent statistician, and was picked up by Jenner from a dairy farmer and his milkmaids.

Catholicism Impracticable

The lesson of this is that a totally Catholic Church or Communist State is an impossible simplification of social organization. It is contrary to natural history. No Church can reconcile and associate in common worship a Jehovah's Witness with William Blake, who called Jehovah Old Nobodaddy. Napoleon, who pointed to the starry sky and asked 'Who made all that?' did not kneel beside those who replied that it made itself, or retorted 'We dont know: and neither do you.' I, as a Creative Evolutionist, postulate a creative Life Force or Evolutionary Appetite seeking power over circumstances and mental development by the method of Trial and Error, making mistake after mistake, but still winning its finally irresistible way. Where in the world is there a Church that will receive me on such terms, or into which I could honestly consent to be received? There are Shaw Societies; but they are not Catholic Churches in pretence, much less in reality. And this is exactly as it should be, because, as human mental capacity varies from grade to grade, those who cannot find a creed which fits their grade have no established creed at all, and are ungovernable unless they are naturally amiable Vicars of Bray supporting any government that is for the moment established. There are hosts of such creedless voters, acting strongly as a conservative force, and usefully stabilizing government as such. But they make reforms very difficult sometimes.

The Tares and the Wheat

I therefore appreciate the wisdom of Jesus's warning to his missionaries that if they tore up the weeds they would tear up the wheat as well, meaning that if they tried to substitute his gospel for that of Moses instead of pouring the new wine into the old bottles (forgive the Biblical change of metaphor) nothing would be left of either Jesus or Moses. As I put it, the conversion of savagery to Christianity is the conversion of Christianity to savagery.

This is as true as ever. Not only are the immediate black converts of our missionaries inferior in character both to the unconverted and the born converted, but all the established religions in the world are deeply corrupted by the necessity for adapting their original inspired philosophic creeds to the narrow intelligences of illiterate peasants and of children. Eight thousand years ago religion was carried to the utmost reach of the human mind by the Indian Jainists, who renounced idolatry and blood sacrifice long before Micah, and repudiated every pretence to know the will of God, forbidding even the mention of his name in the magnificent temples they built for their faith.

But go into a Jainist temple today: what do you find? Idols everywhere. Not even anthropomorphic idols but horse idols, cat idols, elephant idols and what not? The statues of the Jainist sages and saints, far from being contemplated as great seers, are worshipped as gods.

The Thirtynine Articles

For such examples it is not necessary to travel to Bombay. The articles of the Church of England begin with the fundamental truth that God has neither body, parts, nor passions, yet presently enjoin the acceptance as divine revelation of a document alleging that God exhibited his hind quarters to one of the prophets, and when he had resolved to destroy the human race as one of his mistakes, was induced to make an exception in the case of Noah and his family by a bribe of roast meat. Later articles instruct us to love our fellow-creatures, yet to obey an injunction to hold accursed all who do good works otherwise than in the name of Christ, such works being sinful. In one article it is at first assumed that the swallowing of a consecrated wafer is only the heathen rite of eating the god (transubstantiation) and as such abominable, and then that it is holy as a memorial of the last recorded supper of Jesus. No man can be ordained a minister of the Church of England unless he swears without any mental reservation that he believes these contradictions. I once held lightly that candidates of irresistible vocation might swear this blamelessly because they were under duress. But one day I was present at the induction of a rector. When the bishop asked the postulant to tell a flat lie which both of them knew to be a lie, and he told it without a blush, the impression made on me was so shocking that I have felt ever since that the Church of England must revise its articles at all hazards if it is to be credited with the intellectual honesty necessary to its influence and authority. Shake that authority, and churchgoing will be nothing more than parading in our best clothes every Sunday.

A Hundred Religions and Only One Sauce

As it is, Christianity has split into sects, persuasions, and Nonconformities in all directions. The Statesman's Year-Book has given up trying to list them. They range from Pillars of Fire, Jehovah's Witnesses, Plymouth Brothers, and Glasites, to Presbyterians, Methodists, Congregationalists, Baptists, Friends (Quakers), and Unitarians. Within the Established Church itself there are Ritualists, Anglo-Catholics who call their services Masses and never mention the Reformation, Laodicean Broad Churchmen, and Low Church Protestants. The Friends abhor ritual and dictated prayers, and repudiate cathedral services and Masses as playacting, whilst the Anglo-Catholics cannot think religiously without them. Presbyterians and Congregationalists differ from the clergy of the Established Church on the political issue of episcopal or lay Church government. The Unitarians reject the Trinity and deny deity to Jesus. Calvinists deny universal atonement, preached by our missionaries, who are practically all Independents.

Common to these irreconcilable faiths is the pretension that each is the true Catholic Church, and should hand over all whom it cannot convert to the State (the Secular Arm) to be exterminated for the crime of heresy by the cruellest possible methods, even to burning alive. This does not mean that all rulers who order such extermination are horribly cruel. 'Bloody Mary' believed that heretics must be liquidated; but she was not responsible for the political circumstance that the secular criminal law was atrociously cruel, and that no other agency could effect the liquidation. Calvin agreed that Servetus must be killed; but he objected humanely to his being burned. Charles II, humane (indeed, as some think, too humane in his kindness to his dozen dogs and half dozen mistresses), could not question the necessity for punishing the Regicides with death; but he loathed the butchering of them in the hideous manner ordained centuries earlier for the punishment of William Wallace, and stopped it as soon as he dared. It was still unrepealed during my own lifetime; and has only just (1948) been repealed in Scotland.

So far I have not been imprisoned, as poorer men have been in my time, for blasphemy or apostasy. I am not technically an apostate, as I have never been confirmed; and my godparents are dead. But having torn some of the Thirtynine Articles to rags, I should have been pilloried and had my ears cropped had I lived in the days of the British Inquisition called the Star Chamber. Nowadays Nonconformity and Agnosticism are far too powerful electorally for such persecution. But the Blasphemy Laws are still available and in use against obscure sceptics, whilst I suffer nothing worse than incessant attempts to convert me. All the religions and their sects, Christian or Moslem, Buddhist or Shinto, Jain or Jew, call me to repentance, and ask me for subscriptions. I am not so bigoted as to dismiss their experiences as the inventions of liars and the fancies of noodles. They are evidence like any other human evidence; and they force me to the conclusion that every grade of human intelligence can be civilized by providing it with a frame of reference peculiar to its mental capacity, and called a religion.

The Marxist Church

The Marxist Church, called Cominform, is like all the other Churches. Having ceased to believe in the beneficently interfering and overruling God of Adam Smith and Voltaire, no less than in the vicarage of the Pope and his infallibility in council with the College of Cardinals, Cominform makes Karl Marx its Deity and the Kremlin his Vatican. It worships his apostles at its conventicles and in its chapels, with Das Kapital as its Bible and gospel, just as Cobdenist Plutocracy used to make a Bible of Adam Smith's Wealth of Nations with its gospel of The Economic Harmonies and its policy of Free Trade.

I am myself much idolized. I receive almost daily letters from devout Shavians who believe that my income is unlimited, my knowledge and wisdom infinite, my name a guarantee of success for any enterprise, my age that of Jesus at his death, and the entire Press at my command, especially The Times, of which I am assumed to be the proprietor.

If this is not idolatry the word has no meaning. The fact that I am ascertainably, and indeed conspicuously, only a superannuated (not supernatural) journalist and playwright does not shake the faith of my idolaters in the least. Facts count for nothing. I am told that I should be shot in Russia if I dared to pontificate against the Government there as I often do here, and that Freedom of the Press, the glory of England, does not and cannot exist under Communist tyranny.

Should I be Shot in Russia?

As a matter of fact the Russian newspapers are full of complaints and grievances. There is a Government Department whose function it is to receive and deal with such complaints. Here in England I, an old journalist and agitator, know only too well that both platform and press are gagged by such an irresponsible tyranny of partisan newspaper proprietors and shamelessly mendacious advertizers, and by the law against seditious and blasphemous libel, that my speeches were never reported, and my letters and articles inserted only when I could combine what I believed and wanted to say with something that the paper wanted to have said, or when I could disguise it as an attractively readable art criticism, the queer result being that my reputation was made in Conservative papers whilst the Liberal, Radical, and Socialist editors dared not mention my name except in disparagement and repudiation. I owe more of my publicity to The Times than to any other daily newspaper. The same is true of my Fabian colleagues. The Webbs, now in Westminster Abbey, never could get into the British daily newspapers. In Russia, when Fabians were despised there as bourgeois Deviators, the Webbs were translated by Lenin.

As a playwright I was held up as an irreligious pornographer, and as such a public enemy, not to say a thoroughpaced cad, for many years by an irresponsible censorship which could not be challenged in parliament or elsewhere. No such misfortune has happened to me in Russia.

What damns our foreign policy here is our ignorance of history of home affairs. In the imagination of our amateur politicians England is a Utopia in which everything and everybody is 'free,' and all other countries 'police States.' I, being Irish, know better.

To return to the inveteracy of idolatry. Ten years ago disciples of a rival celebrity were sending me portraits of an Austrian Messiah named Hitler, described by Mr Winston Churchill as a bloodthirsty guttersnipe, yet more fanatically deified in Germany than Horatio Bottomley in England.

One of the puzzles of history is whether Jesus, denounced by the ladies and gentlemen of his time as a Sabbath breaker, a gluttonous man, and a winebibber, and finally executed for rioting in the temple, really believed in his claim to be Messiah, or was forced to assume that character because he could not make converts on any other terms, just as Mahomet found that he could not govern the Arabs without inventing a very sensual paradise and a very disgusting hell to keep them in order. Whether he invented his conversations with the Archangel Gabriel, or, like Joan of Arc, really heard voices when he listened for the voice of God, we shall never know. I have just had a letter from a man who, having made repeated attempts to give up smoking, had failed, until one day, walking through Hyde Park, he heard a Gospel preacher cry 'Listen for the voice of God and it will come to you.' This stuck in his mind. He listened, not piously but experimentally; and sure enough a voice said to him 'Quit smoking: quit smoking.' This time he quitted without the smallest difficulty.

Compatibilities

Differences of creed must be tolerated, analyzed, discussed, and as far as possible reconciled. My postulate of a provident and purposeful Life Force that proceeds by trial-and-error, and makes mistakes with the best intentions, is not in effect irreconcilable with belief in a supernatural benignant Providence at war with a malignant Satan. We cannot 'make our souls' in the same assembly; but in the same building we can. Therefore if our cathedrals and churches are to be open to all faiths, as they in fact are, for contemplation and soul making, their different rituals must be performed at different hours, as they are at the Albert Hall in London, the Usher Hall in Edinburgh, the Free Trade hall in Manchester, the Montford Hall in Leicester, and wherever two or three gathered together may hear Messiah or the great Masses of Bach and Beethoven on Sunday or Monday, and watch a boxing show on Tuesday or Wednesday. The rituals differ, but not enough to provoke their votaries to burn one another at the stake or refuse to dine together on occasion. The sporting peer who becomes famous as the owner of a Derby winner meets the winner of a Nobel Prize without the least embarrassment; and I have never suffered the smallest discourtesy except one in a Manchester club, and then only because my criticisms of Shakespear stopped this side of idolatry.

It may seem that between a Roman Catholic who believes devoutly in Confession and a modern free-thinking scientist there can be neither sympathy nor co-operation. Yet there is no essential difference between Confession and modern Psychotherapy. The post-Freudian psychoanalyst relieves his patient of the torments of guilt and shame by extracting a confession of their hidden cause. What else does the priest do in the confessional, though the result is called cure by one and absolution by the other? What I, a Freethinker, call the Life Force, my pious neighbors call Divine Providence: in some respects a better name for it. Bread and wine are changed into living tissue by swallowing and digestion. If this is not transubstantiation what *is* transubstantiation? I have described the surprise of a Fabian lecturer on being asked to open a political meeting with prayer. When I was invited to address the most important Secular Society in England I found that I had to supply the sermon in a ritual of hymns and lessons in all respects like a religious Sunday service except that the lessons were from Browning and the hymns were aspirations to 'join the choir invisible.' Later on, when I attended a church service in memory of my wife's sister, and was disposed to be moved by it, the lesson was the chapter from the Bible which describes how the Israelites in captivity were instructed by a deified Jonathan Wild to steal the jewelry of the Egyptians before their flight into the desert. The Leicester Atheists were in fact more pious than the Shropshire Anglicans.

Bohemian Anarchism

The anarchy which the priests feared when they gagged Galileo actually came to pass much more widely than the epidemics which the Medical Officer of Health dreaded when he gagged me about the sulphur candles. In my early days as a Socialist lecturer I was once opposed by a speaker who had been an apostle of Robert Owen's New Moral World, the first version of British Socialism. His ground was that too many of his fellow apostles took the new moral world as an emancipation from all the obligations of the old moral world, and were dishonest and licentious. Prominent in my own generation of Marxists was one who, I believe, would have gone as a martyr to the scaffold or the stake rather than admit that God existed, or that Marx and Darwin were fallible. But when money or women were concerned, he was such a conscienceless rascal that he was finally blackballed by all the Socialist societies.

Do not misunderstand me. I am not stigmatizing all Owenites, Marxists, and Darwinists as immoral; but it must be borne in mind that all revolutionary and reform movements are recruited from those who are not good enough for the existing system as well as those who are too good for it. All such movements attract sinners as well as saints by giving them a prominence as platform orators and pamphleteers out of all proportion to their numbers and deserts. They justify their delinquencies as assertions of principle, and thus give Socialism a reputation for anarchism, irreligion, and sexual promiscuity which is association of ideas, not logic. No eminence in a specific department implies even ordinary ability in any other, nor does any specific personal depravity imply general depravity. I may fairly claim to be an adept in literature; but in dozens of other departments I am a duffer. I have often quoted a certain ex-Colonel who said to me 'I know for certain that the Rector is the father of his housemaid's illegitimate child; and after that you may tell me that the Bible is true: I shall not believe you.' It does not follow that the Colonel was not a military genius, nor the Rector an eloquent preacher and efficient clergyman.

Nevertheless we cannot legislate for every individual separately, nor provide a special policeman to keep him (or her) in order. All civilized persons except certified lunatics and incorrigible criminals must for elementary purposes be held equally capable and responsible. Those who cannot read any book more abstruse than Esop's Fables, nor get beyond the multiplication table (if so far) in mathematics, can understand the Ten Commandments well enough to be legislated for in the mass.

Sham Democracy

In the face of these hard facts most of the current interpretations of the word Democracy are dangerous nonsense. The fundamental notion that the voice of the people is the voice of God is a sample. What people? Were Solon and Sully, Voltaire and Adam Smith, Plato and Aristotle, Hobbes and Tom Paine and Marx, the people? Were Lord George Gordon, Titus Oates, and Horatio Bottomley the people? Were General Roberts and Henry Irving, nominated by Gallup poll as ideal rulers, the people? Am I the people? Was Ruskin? Were Moses, Jesus, Peter and Paul, Mahomet, Brigham Young? If their voices were all voices of God, God must be a very accomplished ventriloquist.

Democracy means government in the interest of everybody. It most emphatically does not mean government BY everybody. All recorded attempts at that have not only failed but rapidly developed into despotisms and tyrannies. The trade union secretary elected by everybody in his Union, the pirate captain whose crew can make him walk the plank at any moment, are the most absolute despots on earth. Cromwell tried government by a parliament of elected saints and had to turn it into the street as Bismarck turned the Frankfort Parliament in 1862. He tried an oligarchy of majors general, but finally had to make himself Lord Protector and govern despotically as much as it was possible to govern Englishmen at all, which, as he bitterly complained, was not very much. Much or little, votes for everybody, politically called Adult Suffrage, always produces anarchy, which, being unbearable, produces by reaction overwhelming majorities in favour of Regressions called Restorations, or Napoleonic Emperors and South American dictator-presidents. Democratic government of the people by the people, professed ideologically nowadays by all Governments and Oppositions, has never for a moment existed.

Real democracy leaves wide open the question as to which method best secures it: monarchies, oligarchies, parliaments nominated or elected with or without proportional representation, restricted franchise, intervals between general elections, or other 'checks and balances' devised to prevent glaring abuses of virtually irresponsible power. None of them has ever made Voltaire's *Monsieur Tout le Monde* master of the situation. Adult suffrage did not prevent two so-called world wars and a royal abdication on which the people were no more consulted than I was. Political adventurers and 'tin Jesuses' rose like rockets to dictatorships and fell to earth like sticks, or were succeeded, as Napoleon was, by Bourbonic bosses. The Russian Bolsheviks, having invented the Soviet System, and brought their country to the verge of ruin and a little over by All or Nothing Catastrophism, were forced by the facts to make room in Bolshevism for more private enterprise than there is in England. The moment it did so, the basic difference between British and Russian economic policy vanished or criss-crossed. Lenin and Stalin had to cry *Laisser-faire* to all the enterprises not yet ripe for nationalization. The Labor Party in England nationalized as many industries as it could manage, and regulated private employers, controlled prices, rationed food and clothing, imposed purchase taxes on luxuries, and increased the bureaucracy both in numbers and power whilst jealously restricting official salaries more grudgingly with a view to equality of income than the Kremlin. Stalin's Russo-Fabian slogan, Socialism in a Single Country, is countered by Churchill's manifestos of Plutocratic Capitalism Everywhere and Down with Communism, which is more than Trotsky claimed for international Marxism.

With all this staring them in the face, and no intention whatever of going back to turnpike roads, toll bridges, private detectives and prizefighters for police, sixpenny linkmen for municipal electric lighting, cadis under palm trees for judges, condottieri and privateers for national defence, profiteers for Exchequer Chancellors: in short, the substitution of private enterprise for the omnipresent Communism without which our civilization could not endure for a week, our politicians and partisans keep shouting their abhorrence of Communism as if their Parties were cannibal tribes fighting and eating one another instead of civilized men driven by sheer pressure of facts into sane co-operation.

The Political Time Lag

The worst features of our sham-democratic misgovernment are caused, not by incurable mental incapacity, but by an ignorance that is essentially mathematical. None of our politicians seems to know that political action, like all earthly action, must take place in a world of four dimensions, not three. The fourth dimension is that of Time. To ignore it is to be pre-Einstein, which is as out-of-date as to be pre-Marx. Fortunately it can be taught, just as the theories of rent and value can be taught; and those who learn it see that our British parliamentary system is far too slow for twentieth century social organization. The Soviet system in Russia outstrips it because, being faster, it is more immediately responsive to the continual need for reforms and adaptations to changing circumstances. It includes all the conventional democractic checks and safeguards against despotism now so illusory, and gives them as much effectiveness as their airy nature is capable of. Incidentally it gives Stalin the best right of any living statesman to the vacant Nobel peace prize, and our diplomatists the worst. This will shock our ignoramuses as a stupendous heresy and a mad paradox. Let us see.

When the horrors of unregulated selfish private enterprise forced both Conservatives and Cobdenists to devise and pass the Factory Acts, it took the British Parliament a time lag of 50 years to make them effective. Home Rule for Ireland took thirty years to get through Parliament, and was decided after all by a sanguinary civil war.

In the simplest home affairs the time lag extends to centuries. For instance, the practice of earth burial, with its cemeteries crowding the living out by the dead, its poisonous slow putrefactions, its risk of burial alive, and its cost, should be forbidden and replaced by cremation. It was discussed 80 years ago when I was a boy. Yet not even the cremation of an Archbishop (Temple: one of our best) has overcome our dread of doing anything that everyone else is not yet doing, nor the bigoted opposition of the Churches which preach the Resurrection of The Body without considering that a body can be resurrected from dust and ashes as feasibly as from a heap of maggots. Our crematory gardens of rest are still countable only in dozens, and cremations only in thousands, even in big cities. In lesser towns the figure is zero.

Adult Suffrage is Mobocracy

Adult Suffrage is supposed to be a substitute for civil war. The idea is that if two bodies of citizens differ on any public point they should not fight it out, but count heads and leave the decision to the majority. The snag in this is that as the majority is always against any change, and it takes at least thirty years to convert it, whilst only ten per cent or thereabouts of the population has sufficient mental capacity to foresee its necessity or desirability, a time lag is created during which the majority is always out-of-date. It would be more sensible to leave the decision to the minority if a qualified one could be selected and empanelled. Democratic government needs a Cabinet of Thinkers (Politbureau) as well as a Cabinet of

Administrators (Commissars). Adult Suffrage can never supply this, especially in England, where intellect is hated and dreaded, not wholly without reason, as it is dangerous unless disciplined and politically educated; whilst acting and oratory, professional and amateur, are popular, and are the keys to success in elections.

The Marxist Class War

The conflict of economic interest between proprietors and proletarians was described by H. G. Wells as past and obsolete when it had in fact just flamed up in Spain from a bandying of strikes and lock-outs into raging sanguinary civil war, as it had already done in Russia, with the difference that in Russia the proletarians won, whereas in Spain they were utterly defeated through lack of competent ministers and commanders.

The struggle is confused by a cross conflict between feudal and plutocratic ideologies. The feudal proprietariat is all for well policed private property and *Laisser-faire*, the proletariat all for State industry with abolition of feudal privilege and replacement of private or 'real' property by property on social conditions; so that a proprietor shall hold his land, his shares, his spare money (called capital) on the same terms as his umbrella: namely that he shall not use it to break his neighbor's head nor evict him from his country and homestead to make room for sheep or deer.

Both parties insist on the supreme necessity for increased production; but as the Plutocrats do all they can to sabotage State industry, and the Proletarians to sabotage private enterprise, the effect is to hinder production to the utmost and demonstrate the vanity of two-party government.

What is to be Done?

I am asked every week what is my immediate practical remedy for all this. Also what is my solution of the riddle of the universe? When I reply that I dont know, and have no panacea, I am told that I am not constructive, implying that practical people are constructive and do know. If they are and do, why are we in our present perilous muddle?

I can only suggest certain definite and practicable experiments in social organization, on a provisional hypothesis or frame of reference (a necessary tool of thought) that will serve also as a credible religion. For nomenclatory purpose I may be called a Fabian Communist and Creative Evolutionist if I must have a label of some sort. At present I am stuck all over with labels like a tourist's trunk. I cannot call myself the Way and the Life, having only a questionable hypothesis or two to offer; but that is the heroic label that all Worldbetterers aspire to, and some have even dared to claim.

Some 30 years or so ago I wrote a play called As Far As Thought Can Reach. Perhaps I should have called it as far as my thought could reach; but I left this to be taken for granted.

Political Mathematics

What we need desperately is an anthropometric slide-rule by which we can classify and select our rulers, most of whom are at present either rich nonentities, venal careerists, or round pegs in square holes. Now it is no use my singing at the top of my voice that democracy is impossible without scientific anthropometry. I might as well be the Town Crier offering a reward for an imaginary lost dog. How are we to begin?

Sixty years ago Sidney Webb created a Progressive Party on the new County Councils by sending to all the candidates at the first election a catechism setting forth a program of Socialist reforms, and demanding whether they were in favor of them or not. As Nature abhors a vacuum the program flew into empty heads and won the election for them. This, as far as I know, was the first non-party test ever applied to membership of a public authority in England since benefit of clergy was legal and the professions were closed to all but members of the Church of England. This at least provided some evidence as to whether the candidate could read, write, and even translate a little dog Latin. It was better than no test at all.

But it is now quite insufficient in view of the enormous increase of public functions involved by modern Socialism. We already have in our professional and university examinations virtual panels of persons tested and registered as qualified to exercise ruling functions as Astronomers Royal, Archbishops, Lord Chief Justices, and public schoolmasters. Even police constables are instructed. Yet for the ministers who are supported to direct and control them we have no guarantee that they can read or write, or could manage a baked potato stall successfully.

Now people who cannot manage baked potato stalls nor peddle bootlaces successfully cannot manage public departments manned with school-tested permanent executives. Consequently these executives constitute a bureaucracy, not a democracy. Elections do not touch them: the people have no choice. When they have passed the competitive examinations by which they are tested, they are there for life, practically irremovable. And so government goes on.

Unfortunately the tests tend to exclude born rulers. Knowledge of languages, dead and foreign, puts a Mezzofanti, useless as a legislator or administrator, above a Solon who knows no language but his own. It puts facility in doing set sums in algebra by rule of thumb above inborn mathematical comprehension by statesmen who cannot add up their washing bills accurately. Examinations by elderly men of youths are at least thirty years out of date: in economics, for instance, the candidate who has been taught that the latest views are those of Bastiat and Cobden, ignoring those of Cairnes and Mill, is successful, especially if he ranks those of Karl Marx as blasphemous, and history as ending with Macaulay. The questions that will be asked and the problems set at the examinations, with the answers and solutions that will be accepted by the elderly examiners, soon become known, enabling professional crammers to coach any sixth form schoolboy to pass in them to the exclusion of up-to-date candidates who are ploughed because they know better than their examiners, yet are as unconscious of their mental superiority as a baby is of the chemistry by which it performs the complicated chemical operation of digesting its food.

Evidently the present curriculum and method should be radically changed. When I say this, the reply is 'Granted; but how?' Unfortunately I dont know; and neither does anyone else; but as somebody must make a beginning here are a few of the best suggestions I can think of.

Rent and Value the Ass's Bridges

First, there is the economic Ass's Bridge: the theory of rent, and with it inextricably the theory of exchange value. Unless a postulant for first class honors in politics can write an essay shewing that he (or she) has completely mastered these impartial physical and mathematical theories, the top panel must be closed against him. This would plough Adam Smith, Ricardo, Ruskin, and Marx; but they could read up the subject and return to the charge. Stanley Jevons would pass it, though after he had knocked out Ricardo and the rest with his correct mathematical theory he taught that a State parcel post is an impossibility. For when he returned to England after serving in the Gold Escort in Australia, and became a university professor, he taught anything and everything the old examiners expected him to teach, and so might have failed in a character test.

Statistics Vital

The panel for health authorities should require a stringent test in statistics. At present the most unbearable tyranny is that of the State doctor who has been taught to prescribe digitalis and immobilization, plus a diet of alcoholic stimulants, for heart disease, and to amputate limbs and extirpate tonsils as carpenters and plumbers deal with faulty chair legs and leaking pipes. He may, like Jenner, be so ignorant of the rudiments of statistics as to believe that the coincidence of a decrease in the number of deaths from a specific disease following the introduction of an alleged prophylactic proves that the prophylactic is infallible and that compulsion to use it will abolish the disease. Statisticians, checking the figures by the comparisons they call controls, may prove up to the hilt that the prophylactic not only fails to cure but kills. When vaccination was made compulsory as a preventive of smallpox the controls were cholera, typhus, and endemic fever: all three rampant when I was born. They were wiped out by sanitation; whilst under compulsory vaccination, enforced by ruthless persecution, smallpox persisted and culminated in two appalling epidemics (1871 and 1881) which gave vaccination its deathblow, though its ghost still walks because doctors are ignorant of statistics, and, I must add, because it is lucrative, as it calls in the doctor when the patient is not ill. In the army some thirty inoculations are practically compulsory; and vaccination is made a condition of admission to the United States and other similarly deluded countries. The personal outrage involved is so intolerable that it will not be in the least surprising if vaccination officers are resisted, not with facts and figures but with fists, if not pistols.

The remedy, however, is not to compel medical students to qualify as statisticians, but to establish a Ministry of Statistics with formidable powers of dealing with lying advertisements of panaceas, prophylactics, elixirs, immunizers, vaccines, antitoxins, vitamins, and professedly hygienic foods and drugs and drinks of all sorts. Such a public department should be manned not by chemists analyzing the advertized wares and determining their therapeutical value, but by mathematicians criticizing their statistical pretensions. As there is an enormous trade in such wares at present the opposition to such a Ministry will be lavishly financed; but the need for it is too urgent to allow any consideration to stand in its way; for the popular demand for miracles and deities has been transferred to 'marvels of science' and doctors, by dupes who think they are emancipating themselves from what in their abysmal ignorance they call medieval barbarism when they are in fact exalting every laboratory vivisector and quack immunizer above Jesus and St James. Mrs Eddy, a much sounder hygienist than Jenner, Pasteur, Lister, and their disciples, had to call her doctrine Christian Science instead of calling the popular faith in pseudo-scientific quackery Anti-Christian Nonsense.

The Esthetic Test

The next test I propose may prove more surprising. For the top panel I would have postulants taken into a gallery of unlabelled reproductions of the famous pictures of the world, and asked how many of the painters they can name at sight, and whether they have anything to say about them, or are in any way interested in them. They should then be taken into a music room furnished with a piano, and asked to sing or whistle or hum or play as many of the leading themes of the symphonies, concertos, string quartets, and opera tunes of Mozart and Beethoven, and the Leit-motifs of Wagner, as they can remember. Their performances may be execrable; but that will not matter: the object is not to test their executive skill but to ascertain their knowledge of the best music and their interest in and enjoyment of it, if any.

I would have them taken then into a library stocked with the master-pieces of literature. They should be asked which of them they had ever read, and whether they read anything but newspapers and detective stories. If the answer be Yes, they can be invited to indicate the books they know.

I am quite aware of the possibility of misleading results. Dr Inge, an unquestionably top notcher, when he was Dean of St Paul's and had to deal with the music there, expressed a doubt whether the Almighty really enjoys 'this perpetual serenading.' William Morris, equally *honoris causa*, could not tolerate a piano in his house. When one was played in his hearing by his neighbors, he would throw up his window and roar curses at them.

But if Dr Inge had been brought up on Beethoven instead of on Jackson's Te Deum, he might have preferred Wagner to Plotinus; and Morris was deeply affected by medieval music, and quite right in loathing the modern steel grand piano of his day as a noisy nuisance. Still, some of the postulants will be tone deaf or color blind. Their comments may be none the less valuable as evidence of their mental capacity.

Subconscious Capacities

More baffling at present are the cases in which the judges will be faced with apparently vacant minds, and met, not with an epigram of which no mediocrity would be capable, but with a blank 'I dont know what you are talking about.' This will not prove that the postulant is a nitwit: it will raise the question whether the question is beyond his mental powers or so far within them that he is unconscious of them. Ask anyone how water tastes, and you will get the reply of Pinero's Baron Croodle 'Water is a doglike and revolting beverage' or simply 'Water has no taste,' or, intelligently, 'Water has no taste for me, because it is always in my mouth.' Ask an idle child what it is doing, and it will not claim that it is breathing and circulating its blood: it will say it is doing nothing. When we co-ordinate our two eyes to look at anything, we do not notice that the images of everything else within our range of vision are doubled. When we listen to an orchestra or an organ we are deaf to the accompanying thunder of beats, partials, and harmonics. Attention is a condition of consciousness. Without it we may miss many 'self-evident truths.' How then are we to distinguish between the unconscious genius and the idiot?

Again, I do not know; but we can at least call in the professional psychotherapists whose business it is to dig up the buried factors of the mind and bring them to light and consciousness. The technique of this therapy has developed since the days when, being asked what the word Ass suggested to me, I replied Dogberry and Balaam. It suggested, not facts and experiences, but fictions. Put the word Calculus to a surgeon and he will name the disease called stone, from which Newton suffered. Put it to a mathematician and he will cite the method of measurement Newton and Leibniz elaborated.

Examinations and Schoolmasters

I avoid calling the tests examinations because the word suggests the schoolmaster, the enemy of mankind at present, though when by the rarest chance he happens to be born a teacher, he is a priceless social treasure. I have met only one who accepted my challenge to say to his pupils 'If I bore you you may go out and play.' Set an average schoolmaster or schoolmarm to test for the panels, and the result will be a set of examination papers with such questions and problems as 'Define the square root of minus one in Peano terms; and if an empty aeroplane travelling at supersonic speed takes a thousand light years to reach the nearest star, how long will it take a London motor bus keeping schedule time to travel from Millbank to Westminster Bridge with a full complement of passengers? Give the name, date, and locality of the birth of Beethoven's great grandmother's cousin's stepsister; and write a tonal fugue on the following theme. Give the family names of Domenichino and Titian; and write an essay not exceeding 32 words on their respective styles and influence on Renaissance art. Give the dates of six of Shakespear's plays, with the acreage occupied by (a) the Globe Theatre, (b) the

Shoreditch Curtain theatre, and (c) the Blackfriars theatre. Estimate the age of Ann Hathaway at her marriage with Shakespear. Enumerate the discrepancies between the narratives of Homer, Plutarch, Holinshed, and Shakespear. Was Bacon the author of Shakespear's plays (5000 words)?'

The Wrong Sort of Memory

And so on. The schoolmaster does not teach. He canes or impositions or 'keeps in' the pupils who cannot answer pointless questions devised to catch them out. Such questions test memory, but secure victory in examinations for the indiscriminate encyclopedic memory, which is the most disabling of all memories. Universities are infested with pedants who have all recorded history at their tongues' ends, but can make no use of it except to disqualify examinees with the priceless gift of forgetting all events that do not matter. Were I to keep always in mind every experience of my 93 years living and reading I should go mad. I am often amazed when, having to refer to old papers filed away and forgotten, I am reminded of transactions which I could have sworn had never occurred, and meetings with notable persons I have no recollection of having ever seen. But this does not disconcert me. Kipling's 'Lest we forget' is often less urgent than 'Lest we remember.'

Certainly, those who forget everything are impossible politically; and I have often wished I had the memory of Macaulay or Sidney Webb, or the patience of my player collaborators who have to memorize speeches I have myself written but of which at rehearsal I cannot quote two words correctly; but on the whole the people who remember everything they ought to forget are, if given any anthority, more dangerous than those who forget some things they had better remember. Dr Inge, commenting on the Irish question, pointed out how difficult is the common government of a nation which never remembers and one which never forgets.

Anyhow, we must keep schoolmasters away from the panel tests. My own school experience has biased me on this point. When the time came to teach me mathematics I was taught simply nothing: I was set to explain Euclid's diagrams and theorems without a word as to their use or history or nature. I found it so easy to pick this up in class that at the end of the half year I was expected to come out well in the examinations. I entirely disgraced myself because the questions did not pose the propositions but gave only their numbers, of which I could recollect only the first five and the one about the square of the hypothenuse.

The next step was algebra, again without a word of definition or explanation. I was simply expected to do the sums in Colenso's schoolbook.

Now an uninstructed child does not dissociate numbers or their symbols from the material objects it knows quite well how to count. To me *a* and *b*, when they meant numbers, were senseless unless they mean butter and eggs and a pound of cheese. I had enough mathematical faculty to infer that if $a = b$ and $b = c$, *a* must equal *c*. But I had wit enough to infer that if a quart of brandy equals three Bibles, and three Bibles the Apostles' Creed, the Creed is worth a quart of brandy, manifestly a *reductio ad absurdum*.

My schoolmaster was only the common enemy of me and my schoolfellows. In his presence I was forbidden to move, or to speak except in answer to his questions. Only by stealth could I relieve the torture of immobility by stealthily exchanging punches (called 'the coward's blow') with the boy next me. Had my so-called teacher been my father, and I a child under six, I could have asked him questions, and had the matter explained to me. As it was, I did exactly what the Vatican felt everybody would do if Galileo picked a hole in the Bible. I concluded that mathematics are blazing nonsense, and thereafter made a fool of myself even in my twenties when I made the acquaintance of the editor of Biometrika, Karl Pearson, who maintained that no theory could be valid until it was proved mathematically. I threw in his teeth my conviction that his specialty was an absurdity. Instead of enlightening me he laughed (he had an engaging smile and was a most attractive man) and left me encouraged in my ignorance by my observation that though he was scrupulous and sceptical when counting and correlating, he was as credulous and careless as any ordinary mortal in selecting the facts to be counted. Not until Graham Wallas, a born teacher, enlightened me, did I understand mathematics and realize their enormous importance.

Some Results

Is it to be wondered at that with such school methods masquerading as education, millions of scholars pass to their graves unhonored and unsung whilst men and women totally illiterate, or at most selftaught to read and write in their late teens, rise to eminence whilst 'university engineers' are drugs in the labor market compared to those who go straight from their elementary schools to the factory, speaking slum English and signing with a mark. Experienced employers tell us they prefer uneducated workmen. Senior Wranglers and Double-Firsts and Ireland Scholars see no more than costermongers in the fact that a saving of 1 per cent per minute of time in writing English means 525,000 per cent per year, and that ten times that much could be saved by adding 15 letters to the alphabet. It took a world war to establish summer time after it had been contemptuously rejected by our pundits as a negligible fad. The fact that by adding two digits to our arithmetic tables we could make 16 figures do the work of twenty (a colossal saving of time for the world's bookkeeping) appeals no more to winners of the mathematical tripos than the infinitesimal calculus to a newly born infant. Political controversy is now (1949) raging on the nationalization of our industries; yet not one word is said nor a figure given as to its basic advantage in the fact that coal can be had in Sunderland for the trouble of picking it up from the sands at low tide, whilst in Whitehaven it has to be hewn out under the sea, miles from the pit head, or that land in the City of London fetches fabulous prices per square foot and twenty miles off will hardly support a goose on the common, thus making it impossible without nationalization to substitute cost-of-production prices, averaged over the whole country, for prices loaded with enormous rents for the proprietors of London land and Seaham mines, not equivalently surtaxed. Doctors and dental surgeons who excuse their high fees on the ground that they are working until half past four in the afternoon earning rent for their landlords, and only the rest of the day for themselves and their families, are so incapable of putting two and two together politically that they vote like sheep for the landlords, and denounce land municipalization as robbery. Had the late famous President Franklin Roosevelt, a thoroughly schooled gentleman-amateur Socialist, been taught the law of rent, his first attempts at The New Deal would not have failed so often. I could cite dozens of examples of how what our Cabinet ministers call Democracy, and what I call Mobocracy, places in authority would-be rulers who assure us that they can govern England, plus the Commonwealth, plus Western Europe, and finally the world, when as a matter of fact they could not manage a village shop successfully.

Capital Accumulation

Capital is spare money saved by postponement of consumption. To effect this in a private property system some people must be made so rich that when they are satiated with every purchasable luxury they have still a surplus which they can invest without privation. In the nineteenth century this arrangement was accepted as final and inevitable by able and benevolent public men like Thomas de Quincey, Macaulay, Austin, Cobden, and Bright, until Karl Marx dealt it a mortal blow by shewing from official records that its delusive prosperity masked an abyss of plague, pestilence and famine, battle, murder, compulsory prostitution, and premature death. Ferdinand Lassalle in Germany had already demonstrated the injustice of its 'iron law of wages.'

England's Shamefaced Leadership

England was by no means silent on the subject. Marx's invective, though it rivalled Jeremiah's, was pale beside the fierce diatribes of Ruskin, who puzzled his readers by describing himself as an old Tory and the Reddest of Red Communists. Carlyle called our boasted commercial prosperity shooting Niagara, and dismissed Cobdenist Free Trade as Godforsaken nonsense. The pious Conservative Lord Shaftesbury and the Radical atheist demagogue Bradlaugh were at one in their agitation for Acts in restraint of the prevalent ruthless exploitation of labor. Robert Owen had called for a New Moral world as loudly as any of our present post war Chadbands. It was he who made current the word Socialism as the alternative to Capitalist plutocracy. When the Russian Bolsheviks went ruinously wrong by ignoring 'the inevitability of gradualness' and attempting a catastrophic transfer of industry and agriculture from private to public ownership, it was the Englishman Sidney Webb and his Fabians who corrected them and devised the new economic policy Lenin had to announce, and Stalin to put in practice. Thus Englishmen can claim to have been pioneers in the revolutionary development of political organization since Cobdenism conquered us.

Unfortunately, whenever English parties effect an advance, they are so ashamed of it that they immediately throw away all credit for it by protesting that they are respectable citizens who would never dream of changing anything, and shouting their abhorrence of all the wicked foreigners who are in effect taking their advice. And then they are surprised when their disciples, especially in Russia, regard them as enemies, and the Marxist Left wins more and more votes from them.

The Threatening Future: Homilies No Use

While the time lag lasts the future remains threatening. The problem of optimum wealth distribution, which Plutocracy, with its inherent class warfare, has hopelessly failed to solve, will not yield to the well-intentioned Utopian amateurs who infest our parliaments and parties, imagining that it can be solved by giving to all of us according to our needs and balancing the account by taking from each of us according to our productive capacity. They might as well decree that we shall do unto others as we would have them do to us, or achieve the greatest good for the greatest number, or soothe our souls with exhortations to love one-another. Homilies cut no ice in administrative councils: the literary talent and pulpit eloquence that has always been calling for a better world has never succeeded, though it has stolen credit for many changes forced on it by circumstances and natural selection. The satirical humor of Aristophanes, the wisecracks of Confucius, the precepts of the Buddha, the parables of Jesus, the theses of Luther, the *jeux d'esprit* of Erasmus and Montaigne, the Utopias of More and Fourier and Wells, the allegories of Voltaire, Rousseau, and Bunyan, the polemics of Leibniz and Spinoza, the poems of Goethe, Shelley, and Byron, the manifesto of Marx and Engels, Mozart's Magic Flute and Beethoven's Ode to Joy, with the music dramas of Wagner, to say nothing of living seers of visions and dreamers of dreams: none of these esthetic feats have made Reformations or Revolutions; and most of them, as far as they have been thrown into the hands of the common people as the Protestant Reformation threw the Bible, have been followed by massacres, witch hunts, civil and international wars of religion, and all forms of persecution, from petty boycotts to legalized burnings at the stake and breakings on the wheel, highly popular as public entertainments. The nineteenth century, which believed itself to be the climax of civilization, of Liberty, Equality, and Fraternity, was convicted by Karl Marx of being the worst and wickedest on record; and the twentieth, not yet half through, has been ravaged by two so-called world wars culminating in the atrocity of the atomic bomb.

As long as atomic bomb manufacture remains a trade secret known to only one State, it will be the mainstay of Peace because all the States (including the one) will be afraid of it. When the secret is out atomic warfare will be barred as poison gas was in 1938–45; and war will be possible as before. How that may happen is the subject of the first two far-fetched fables that follow.

Ayot Saint Lawrence, 1948–9

First Fable

A public park on a fine summer afternoon. Chairs for hire scattered about the sward.

A young woman of respectable appearance arrives and seats herself. A park attendant approaches her; takes two-pence from her; says 'Kew,' short for 'Thank-you'; and gives her a ticket.

A well-dressed young man enters and takes the nearest chair. The attendant takes two-pence as before, and passes on.

YOUNG MAN. Excuse me. Would you rather I sat farther away?

YOUNG WOMAN. As you please. I dont care where you sit.

YOUNG MAN. I hope you dont think me intrusive?

YOUNG WOMAN. I am not thinking about you at all. But you may talk to me if you want to. I dont mind.

YOUNG MAN. Well, I certainly do want to talk to you. In fact that is why I took this chair.

YOUNG WOMAN. I thought so. Well, talk away. What have you to say to me?

YOUNG MAN. Ive never seen you before. But at first sight I find you irresistibly attractive.

YOUNG WOMAN. Lots of men do. What of it?

YOUNG MAN. Some women find me attractive. Are you married?

YOUNG WOMAN. No. Are you?

YOUNG MAN. No. Are you engaged?

YOUNG WOMAN. No. What is it to you whether I am engaged or not?

YOUNG MAN. Need you ask? Ive got into this conversation with a view to our possible marriage.

YOUNG WOMAN. Nothing doing. I'll not marry.

YOUNG MAN. It is odd that so many attractive women are unmarried. Dull ugly frumps never seem to have any difficulty in finding mates. Why wont you marry? I am available.

YOUNG WOMAN. My father was shot in the Great War that now seems such a little one. My eldest brother was killed in Normandy when we were liberating France there. His wife and children were blown to bits by a bomb that wrecked the whole street they lived in. Do you think I'll bear children for that?

YOUNG MAN. They died for England. They made war to end war. Dont you admire bravery? Dont you love your country?

YOUNG WOMAN. What use is bravery now when any coward can launch an atomic bomb? Until men are wise and women civilized they had better not be born. At all events I shall not bring them into this wicked world to kill and be killed.

An excited middle-aged man comes along waving a newspaper and cheering.

M. A. M. Hurrah! Have you heard the news?

YOUNG MAN. No. Whats happened?

M. A. M. No more war. The United Nations have abolished it.

YOUNG MAN [*disparagingly*] Hmm! May I have a look at your paper?

M. A. M. Here it is in black and white. You may keep it. I'll buy another. Hurrah! hurrah!! hurrah!!!

He hands over the paper and rushes away, cheering.

YOUNG WOMAN. What does it say?

YOUNG MAN [*reading the headlines*] 'THE WORLD AT PEACE AT LAST. WASHINGTON AGREES. MOSCOW AGREES. CHINA AGREES. THE WESTERN UNION AGREES. THE FEDERALISTS AGREE. THE COMMUNISTS AGREE. THE FASCISTS AGREE. ATOMIC BOMB MANUFACTURE MADE A CAPITAL CRIME. UNIVERSAL SECURITY GUARANTEED.'

YOUNG WOMAN. Have the armies been disbanded? Have the military academies been closed? Has conscription been abolished?

YOUNG MAN. It doesnt say. Oh yes: here is a stop press paragraph. 'ARMIES WILL IN FUTURE BE CALLED WORLD POLICE. NO MORE CONSCRIPTION.' Hm!

YOUNG WOMAN. You dont seem pleased.

YOUNG MAN. I dont swallow all that rot about no more war. Men will always fight even if they have nothing to fight with but their fists. And the women will egg them on.

YOUNG WOMAN. What does the leading article say?

YOUNG MAN [*turning to the leader page and quoting*] 'Truce of God begins a new chapter in the history of the globe. The atomic bomb has reduced war to absurdity; for it threatens not only both victors and vanquished but the whole neutral world. We do not as yet know for certain that the bomb that disintegrated Hiroshima is not still at work disintegrating. The weather has been curiously unusual ever since. But no nation will ever venture on atomic warfare again.'

YOUNG WOMAN. Do you believe that?

YOUNG MAN. Yes; but it wont stop war. In 1914 the Germans tried poison gas; and so did we. But the airmen who dropped it on the cities could not stay in the air for long; and when they had to come down they found the streets full of the gas, because poison gas is heavier than air and takes many days to disperse. So in the last war gas was not used; and atomic bombs wont be used in the next one.

YOUNG WOMAN. Oh! So you think there will be a next one.

YOUNG MAN. Of course there will, but not with atomic bombs. There is no satisfaction in seeing the world lit up by a blinding flash, and being burnt to dust before you have time to think about it, with every stick and stone for miles around falling and crumbling, all the drains and telephones and electrics torn up and flung into the air, and people who are too far off to be burnt die of radiation. Besides, bombs kill women. Killing men does not matter: the women can replace them; but kill the women and you kill the human race.

YOUNG WOMAN. That wont stop war. Somebody will discover a poison gas lighter than air! It may kill the inhabitants of a city; but it will leave the city standing and in working order.

YOUNG MAN [*thoughtfully, letting the newspaper drop on his knees*] That is an idea.

YOUNG WOMAN. What idea?

YOUNG MAN. Yours. There is a lot of money in it. The Government gave £100,000 to the man who found out how to land our army in Normandy in 1945.

YOUNG WOMAN. Governments will pay millions for any new devilment, though they wont pay twopence for a washing machine. When a Jewish chemist found out how to make high explosive cheaply we made him a present of Jerusalem, which didnt belong to us.

YOUNG MAN [*hopefully*] Yes, by George! So we did.

YOUNG WOMAN. Well, what of it?

YOUNG MAN. I'm a chemist.

YOUNG WOMAN. Does that mean that you are in the atomic bomb business?

YOUNG MAN. No; but I'm on the staff in a chlorine gas factory. The atomic bomb people may be barking up the wrong tree.

YOUNG WOMAN [*rising wrathfully*] So that is what you are! One of these scientific devils who are destroying us! Well, you shall not sit next me again. Go where you belong: to hell. Good day to you.

She goes away.

YOUNG MAN [*still thoughtful*] Lighter than air, eh? [*Slower*] Ligh – ter – than – air?

The scene fades out.

Second Fable

A room in the War Office in London. The Commander-in-Chief at work reading letters. A secretary opening them. The telephone rings. The secretary answers it.

SEC. Yes? . . . [*To the C.-in-C.*] Lord Oldhand from the Foreign Office.

C.-IN-C. Shew him up; and get out.

SEC. He is shewing himself up. He must have heard –
  Lord O. bursts in. The secretary hurries out.

OLDHAND. Ulsterbridge: have you heard the news?

C.-IN-C. Of course Ive heard the news. Here in the War Office we have to get the news in six minutes. At the Foreign Office six years is soon enough for you. Sit down.

OLDHAND [*seating himself*] Is this a time for your Irish jokes? What the devil are we to do? How much do you know?

C.-IN-C. Only that there is not one of God's creatures left alive in the Isle of Wight. I shall have to send every soldier in England to cremate the dead or throw them into the sea. The Home Office will have to find 88,454 civilians to dust the houses with vacuum cleaners and keep the banks and the telephone services and the wireless and water supplies and the lighting and the markets and all the rest of it going.

OLDHAND. Precisely. And all this is your fault.

C.-IN-C. Oldhand: you lie, categorically. How my fault?

OLDHAND. Do you forget that when that fellow who found out how to make volatile poison gas offered us his discovery it was you who turned him down?

C.-IN-C. That cockney blighter? He wanted a hundred thousand pounds for it. And the scientific authorities assured me that every penny spent on anything but atomic research would be wasted.

OLDHAND. Well, he sold it to the South African negro Hitler, Ketchewayo the Second, for a hundred and fifty thousand. Ketch could afford it: his backyard is chock full of diamonds. The fellow made a Declaration of Independence for Zululand with himself as emperor. Capetown, Natal, and Rhodesia went to war with him and involved us in it. That made it your job, didnt it?

C.-IN-C. Not a bit of it. Ketch is far too cunning to go to war with us. He did not go to war with anybody. He dropped his bombs on the Isle of

Wight just to shew Capetown and the rest that the world was at his mercy. He selected the Isle of Wight because it's a safe distance from his own people, just as we selected Hiroshima in 1945. He thinks islands are out-of-the way little places that dont matter to us. But he maintains that his relations with the Commonwealth are friendly; and as you have not declared war on him we are still technically at peace. That makes it your job, not mine, though as usual when there is anything to be done except what was done last time, I shall have to do it.

OLDHAND. You have a very important diplomatic point there, I admit; but it must stand over. Meanwhile let us put our heads together and get to work. The first practical step is to hang this traitor who has sold his accursed invention to the enemy.

C.-IN-C. What! Dont you know that he went to live in the Isle of Wight as the safest civilized place in the world, and is now lying dead there, killed by his own poison gas?

OLDHAND. Serve the scoundrel right! there is the hand of God in this. But your mistake in turning the fellow down was none the less a mistake because he is dead and you are alive – so far. You may be dead tomorrow.

C.-IN-C. So may you.

OLDHAND. Yes; and it will be your doing.

C.-IN-C. How was I to know that the gas was any good? I get dozens of such inventions every week, all guaranteed to make an end of war and establish heaven on earth. I'm a soldier, not a chemist. I have to go by what the scientific authorities tell me. Youre a diplomatist, not a laboratory bloke. Do you know what an isotype is? Do you know what a meson is? I dont: neither do you. What would you have done except what I did? kick the fellow out.

OLDHAND. Listen to me. I am, as you say, a diplomatist; and I think youll admit that I know my job after my fifteen years in the Foreign Office. You know your job too as a soldier: I dont question it. That gives us one great principle in common.

C.-IN-C. And what is that, may I ask?

OLDHAND. It is to regard all our allies as Powers that may at any moment become our enemies. The public thinks it is the other way about; but we know better. We must be prepared for war before everything.

C.-IN-C. We never are, thanks to the damned taxpayers who wont vote us the money. But of course I agree in principle. What then?

OLDHAND. I'll tell you what then. What sort of fellow was this volatile gas man? You interviewed him. What did you make of him?

C.-IN-C. Oh, a middleclass cad through and through. Out for money and nothing else. Big money.

OLDHAND. Just so. Well, what security have we that after selling his invention to Ketchewayo in Africa he did not sell it over again in Europe? All he had to do was to hand over half a sheet of notepaper with a prescription on it and pocket another hundred and fifty thousand. Every State in Europe and America except ourselves may have it up its sleeve for all we know. The gas may come in at that window while we are talking.

C.-IN-C. That is true: it may. Let us hope it wont.

OLDHAND. Hope wont help us if it does. Our first duty is at all cost to get hold of that receipt, and make the gas ourselves. When the other States know that we have plenty of it none of them will dare to start using it. Meanwhile –

C.-IN-C. Meanwhile I have to provide gas masks for everybody in the country, and make wearing of them compulsory. I have to bury the dead; and I cant spare enough soldiers to do it. Youll have to buy a million vultures from Bombay to pick the bones of the dead before they stink us out. We must make every house in the country gas-proof, and rigidly enforce the closing of all windows. We must – [he is interrupted by a siren alarm, followed by an artillery salvo]. What the devil is that?

OLDHAND. Nothing. We have ordered a salute of five guns to celebrate the hundred and first birthday of the President of the Board of Trade.

The siren screams again.

C.-IN-C. [singing drowsily]:

> 'Oh we dont want to lose you;
> But we think you ought to go.'

He collapses, apparently into a deep sleep.

SHOUTS WITHOUT. Shut the windows! Shut the windows! Gas! Gas!
    Another salvo.
    Oldhand rises and rushes toward the open window to shut it. He staggers, and can only clutch at the sill to steady himself.

OLDHAND. [with a vacant grin which develops into a smile of radiant happiness, sings] 'It's a long way to Tipperary–'
    He falls dead.

Third Fable

A pleasant spot in the Isle of Wight. A building of steel and glass is inscribed ANTHROPOMETRIC LABORATORY. *On the terrace before it a bench and chairs. Seated in conference are a middle-aged gentleman in a gay pullover and broadly striped nylon trousers, and two women: a comely matron in a purple academic gown, and a junior in short-skirted overall and blue slacks.*

A tourist comes along. His embroidered smock and trimmed beard proclaim the would-be artist. He stops on seeing the three, and produces a camera.

THE GIRL. Hello! What are you doing here?

THE TOURIST. Only hiking round the island. May I take a snapshot?

THE GIRL. You have no business to be here. You have no business to be on the Isle of Wight at all. Who let you land?

THE TOURIST. I came in my own boat. I landed on the beach. What harm am I doing?

THE GIRL. This is a colony of the Upper Ten. Anybodies are not allowed here.

THE TOURIST. I'm not an Anybody: I'm classed as a Mediocrity.

THE GIRL. Neither Mediocrities nor Anybodies are admitted. Go back to your boat; and clear out.

THE MATRON. Stop. You say you are classed as a Mediocrity. Did you pass with honors?

THE TOURIST. No. They were grossly unfair to me. I'm not a Mediocrity: I'm a genius.

THE MATRON. Indeed! Have you a job of any sort?

THE TOURIST. No. They offered me a job as hospital porter because I'm physically strong. How utterly beneath me! When I told them I am a genius and shewed them my drawings, they offered to make me a housepainter. I dont want to paint houses: my destiny is to paint temples in fresco.

THE GENTLEMAN [*amused*] Like Michael Angelo, eh?

THE TOURIST. Oh, I can do better work than Michael Angelo. He is out of date. I am ultra-modern.

THE GENTLEMAN [*to the Matron*] The very man for us.

THE MATRON [*to the Tourist*] You are quite sure that you are a genius, are you?

THE TOURIST. Quite. I dont look like a bank clerk, do I?

THE MATRON. Well, we have no temples here for you to paint; but we can offer you a job that will enable you to support yourself and have enough leisure to paint what you like until the world recognizes your genius.

THE TOURIST. What sort of work will I have to do? I warn you I cant pass examinations; and I hate being regulated and disciplined. I must have perfect freedom.

THE MATRON. Anthropometric work is what we do here. Classifying men and women according to their abilities. Filling up their qualification certificates. Analyzing their secretions and reactions and so on. Quite easy laboratory work.

THE TOURIST. That will suit me down to the ground. I'm a first-rate judge of character.

THE MATRON. Splendid. Take this in to the office at the end of the passage on the right. You can have tea in the canteen when they have settled with you. [*She hands him a ticket*].

THE TOURIST [*hungrily*] Thank you.

He takes the ticket and goes into the laboratory.

THE GENTLEMAN. He will be a heaven-sent treasure.

THE GIRL. I dont agree. He seems to me to be a conceited fool who thinks himself a genius.

THE GENTLEMAN. Exactly. We shall go by his secretions and reactions: not by his own notions.

A young man in rags, unshaven, and disreputable looking, comes along.

THE GIRL. Who is this awful looking tramp? [*To him*] Hello! Who are you; and what are you doing here?

HE. I'm doing nothing here because nobody will give me anything to do. I'm devilishly hungry. Have you by any chance a crust of bread to spare?

THE MATRON. How did you get into this island? Why were you allowed to land?

HE. I was a stowaway, madam. They wanted to send me back; but the captain of the return boat would not take me: he said I was too dirty and probably infectious and verminous. The medical officer quarantined me; but I convinced him that I am only a harmless tramp, fit for nothing better; so he let me go. And here I am.

THE MATRON. Do you do nothing to earn your bread?

THE TRAMP. I ask for it. People mostly give it to me. If not, I sing for it. Then they give me a penny or two to stop singing and go away. It's a way of life like any other. It suits me. I'm good for nothing else.

THE GENTLEMAN. How do you know you are good for nothing else?

THE TRAMP. Well, what else am I good for? You can take me into your laboratory and try if you like. There is a canteen there, isnt there?

THE GENTLEMAN. I see you are not unintelligent. You are not uneducated. You could surely work for your living.

THE TRAMP. No. Anything but that. Working is not living. If you are on that tack you wont give me anything: I know your sort. Good morning. [He starts to go].

THE GIRL. Stop. You are hungry. I'll get you some bread. [She goes into the laboratory].

THE TRAMP. Look at that, now! Ask; and it shall be given to you.

THE GENTLEMAN. Listen to me. I'll give you five guineas if youll submit to a test of your capacity in our laboratory.

THE TRAMP. It would be robbing you. I tell you I have no capacity. I'm an out-and-out Goodfornothing. And five guineas is too much to give a tramp. I must live from hand to mouth. All the joy of life goes when you have five guineas in your pocket.

THE GENTLEMAN. You need not keep it in your pocket. You can buy a decent suit of clothes with it. You need one badly. You are in rags.

THE TRAMP. Of course I'm in rags. Who would give alms to a well-dressed man? It's my business to be in rags.

THE GENTLEMAN. Very well, I'll have you arrested and put through the laboratory and classified. That is the law, compulsory for everybody. If you refuse you may be classed as irresponsible. That means that youll be enlisted in the military police or kept under tutelage in a Labor Brigade. Or you may be classed as dangerous and incorrigible, in which case youll be liquidated.

THE TRAMP. I know all that. What good will it do you? Why are you offering me five guineas when you have only to call the police and put me through the mill for nothing?

THE GENTLEMAN. You have ability enough to cross-examine me. You may have administrative ability, and be cunning enough to shirk its responsibilities. You may be one of the Artful Dodgers who know that begging is easier and happier than bossing.

THE TRAMP. Ha! ha! ha! You suspect me of being a heaven-born genius! Very well: test me til you are black in the face. Youll only be wasting your time; but that wont hurt me, because time is of no value to me: it's my profession to waste it. Youll find I can do nothing. Mind: I'm not a fool: youre quite right there; but I'm a duffer, a hopeless duffer. I can always see what the other fellows ought to do; but I cant do it. Ive tried my hand at everything: no use: Ive failed every time. Ive tastes but no talents. I'd like to be a Shakespear; but I cant write plays. I'd like to be a Michael Angelo or a Raphael; but I can neither draw nor paint. I'd love to be a Mozart or a Beethoven; but I can neither compose a symphony nor play a concerto. I envy Einstein his mathematical genius; but beyond the pence table I cant add two and two together. I know a lot, and can do nothing. When I tell the clever chaps what to do, they wont do it, and tell me I'm ignorant and crazy. And so I am: I know it only too well. Youd better give me a meal or the price of one, and let me jog on the footpath way. My name's not Prospero: it's Autolycus.

THE GENTLEMAN. If you know what other people ought to do, youll be too busy telling them, and making laws for them, to do any of it yourself. In with you into the canteen; and get your bread there.

THE TRAMP. I fly for the bread. You are the boss here: the archpriest, chooser of rulers, lord of human destiny. And your choice is a government of tramps! Ha! ha! ha! ha! ha! ha! ha! [*He goes into the laboratory roaring with laughter*].

THE GENTLEMAN. Two big catches for today. A nincompoop who thinks he's a genius; and a genius who thinks he's a nincompoop.

THE MATRON. I prefer nincompoops. I can always depend on them to do what was done last time. But I never know what a genius will be up to next, except that it will be something upsetting.

Fourth Fable

The same place in the Isle of Wight: but the building is now inscribed DIET
COMMISSIONERS. *A Commissioner in cap and gown sits at a writing
table talking into a dictaphone. He has earphones hanging from his ears.*

COMMISSIONER. What I am going to dictate is for the printer; so keep a
carbon copy. It is for the new edition of my book on Human Diet. Are
you ready? . . . Right. The heading is Chapter four. Living on Air. Now
for the text. Ahem!

In the twentieth century the tribes of New Zealand had, under the
influence of British colonists, left off eating their prisoners of war. The
British themselves, influenced by a prophet whose name has come
down to us in various forms as Shelley, Shakespear, and Shavius, had
already, after some centuries of restricted cannibalism in which only
fishes, frogs, birds, sheep, cows, pigs, rabbits, and whales were eaten,
been gradually persuaded to abstain from these also, and to live on
plants and fruits, and even on grass, honey, and nuts: a diet which
they called vegetarian. Full stop. New paragraph. Ahem!

As this change saved the labor of breeding animals for food, and
supported human health and longevity quite as well, if not better, than
the eating of dead animals, it was for some time unchallenged as a step
forward in civilization. But some unforeseen consequences followed.
When cattle were no longer bred and slaughtered for food, milk and
butter, cheese and eggs, were no longer to be had. Grass, leaves, and
nettles became the staple diet. This was sufficient for rude physical
health. At the Olympic Games grass eating athletes broke all the records. This was not surprising, as it had long been known that bulls
and elephants, fed on grass and leaves, were the strongest, most fertile,
most passionate animals known. But they were also the most ferocious,
being so dangerous that nobody dared cross a field in which a bull was
loose, and every elephant had to have an armed keeper to restrain it. It
had also been noticed that human vegetarians were restless, pugnaci-
ous, and savagely abusive in their continual controversies with the
remaining meat eaters, who found it easy and pleasant to lead sed-
entary lives in stuffy rooms whilst the vegetarians could not live
without much exercise in the fresh air. When grass eating became

general men became more ferocious and dangerous than bulls. Happily they also became less capable of organized action of any kind. They could not or would not make political alliances, nor engage in industrial mass production or wage world wars. Atomic bombs and poison gases and the like were quite beyond their powers of co-operation: their ferocities and animosities, like those of the bull, did not go beyond trespassers within sight and reach. With the ending of wars their numbers increased enormously; but to the few born thinkers who still cropped up among them and ruled them as far as they were capable of being ruled, it was apparent that they were changing into supergorillas through eating grass and leaves. And though they lived longer than the meat eaters they still suffered from certain deadly diseases and from decay of teeth, failure of eyesight, and decrepitude in old age. Their ablest biologists had to agree that the human race, having tried eating everything on earth that was eatable, had found no food that did not sooner or later poison them. This was challenged by a Russian woman, a noted vegetarian athlete. She pointed out that there was a diet that had not been tried: namely, living on air and water. The supergorillas ridiculed her, alleging that air is not food: it is nothing; and mankind cannot live on nothing in empty space. But a famous mathematician shewed just then that there is no such thing as nothing, and that space is not emptiness and in fact does not exist. There is substance, called matter, everywhere: in fact, the universe consists of nothing else; but whether we can perceive it, or eat and drink it, depends on temperature, rate of radiation, and the sensitiveness of the instruments for detecting and measuring it. As temperature rises, water changes from solid ice to liquid fluid, from liquid fluid to steam, from steam to gas; but it is none the less substantial even at temperatures that are quite immeasureable and hardly conceviable. It followed logically that living on air is as possible as living on flesh or on grass and chopped carrots, though as men cannot live under water, nor fishes out of it, each phase of substance has its appropriate form of life and diet and set of habits. Such creatures as angels are as possible as whales and minnows, elephants and microbes.

The Russian woman claimed that she had lived for months on air and water, but on condition that the air was fresh and that she took the hardest physical exercise daily. It was already known that the vigils and fasts of saints did not weaken them when their spiritual activity was intense enough to produce a state of ecstasy. Full stop: new paragraph.

This briefly is the history of the epoch-making change in social organization produced by the ending of the food problem which had through all recorded history made men the slaves of nature, and defeated all their aspirations to be free to do what they like instead of what they must. The world became a world of athletes, artists, craftsmen, physicists, and mathematicians, instead of farmers, millers, bakers, butchers, bar tenders, brewers, and distillers. Hunger and thirst, which had for centuries meant the need for bread and onions, cheese and beer, beef and mutton, became a search for knowledge of nature and power over it, and a desire for truth and righteousness. The supergorilla became the soldier and servant of Creative Evolution. Full stop. Postscript.

Stop typing and listen to instructions. What I have just dictated is for the tenth edition of my primer for infant schools in the rudimentary biology series. I have dictated only the full stops at the end of the paragraphs. I will fill in the commas and colons and semicolons on the typescript. Leave the type and the format and the illustrations to the printer: he is a better artist in books than I am. He will need paper for two hundred million copies. Goodbye.

He takes off his headphones; puts the cover on the dictaphone; sighs with relief at having done a tedious job; and goes into the building.

Fifth Fable

The scene is unchanged; but the building is now labelled GENETIC INSTIT-
UTE. *On the terrace, seated round a table loaded with old books, are four
persons of uncertain age, apparently in the prime of life. Two of them are male,
one female, the fourth a hermaphrodite. They wear white sleeveless tunics like
heralds' tabards on which are embroidered different flower designs, the two
men being distinguished by a thistle and a shamrock respectively, the woman
by a rose, and the hermaphrodite by an elm with a vine round its trunk. The
sleeves of the men are red, of the woman green, of the hermaphrodite the two
colors in a chequered harlequin pattern. The men are close-cropped and clean-
shaven: the woman's hair is dressed like that of the Milo Venus. They are in
animated discussion, each with an open book on which they occasionally
thump to emphasize their points*

SHAMROCK. I cannot make head or tail of this nineteenth century stuff.
They seem to have considered our business unmentionable, and tried
to write books about it in which it was not mentioned. [*He shuts the
book impatiently*].

ROSE. That seems hardly possible. Our business is the very first business
of any human society: the reproduction of the human race, the most
mentionable subject in the world and the most important.

SHAMROCK. Well, Ive been through every scrap of nineteenth century
writing that remains; and I tell you that their textbooks on physiology
dont mention the reproductive organs nor hint at such a thing as sex.
You would not guess from them that it existed.

HERM. To say nothing of hermaphrodites. Being myself a hermaphrodite
I have looked myself up in the nineteenth century books; and I simply
wasnt there.

THISTLE. Oh, they were the damnedest fools: it is impossible to understand how they kept going for a week, much less for years. They had
not brains enough to make an alphabet capable of spelling their language. They counted their goods in twelves but could not count their
money in more than tens because they had only ten fingers and could
not invent the two missing figures. They could not change their working hours by the sun oftener than twice a year; and it took one of the
worst of the killing matches they called wars to make them go even

that far. Their calendar is incomprehensible: they could not fix their festivals nor make their months tally with the moon. In music their keyboards had only twelve notes in the octave instead of our sixty-four. One would think they might at least have managed nineteen to play their babyish thirds and sixths bearably in tune. They wasted millions of hours every day because they could not or would not do the simplest things; and when their five per cent of geniuses made wonderful machines for them: big machines that could rise from the ground and fly, and little ones that could think and calculate, they accepted them as gifts from some imaginary paradise they called heaven. When one of their bodily organs went wrong they did not set it right: they just cut it out, and left the patient to recover from the shock or die. When the patient was ill all over and could not be cut to pieces they dosed him with poisons: I hunted out a case of a well-known woman who was given nine different poisons for some trouble they called typhoid. The amazing thing is that she survived it. She must have had the constitution of a bear. It was in the nineteenth century that they gave up believing in idols and priests, and took to believing in medicine men and surgeons. Let us drop digging into this past that is unconceivable, and start from what we really know of the present.

He shuts his book and throws it away.

SHAMROCK [*shutting his book*] Agreed. But why did they consider sex unmentionable?

ROSE. Simply because their methods were so disgusting that they had no decent language for them. You think their methods were like ours, and their passions like ours. You could not make a greater mistake. The seminal fluids which our chemists make in the laboratory, and which it is our business to experiment with, were unknown to them: they had to use glandular excretions from the living body to perpetuate the race. To initiate births they had to practice personal contacts which I would rather not describe. Strangest of all, they seem to have experienced in such contacts the ecstasies which are normal with us in our pursuit of knowledge and power, and culminate in our explorations and discoveries. The religions they believed in were so wildly absurd that one would suppose they could believe anything.

SHAMROCK. Oh, come! They must have had some common sense or they couldnt have lived.

ROSE. They had gleams of it. In spite of their sensual ecstasies, they had decency enough to reserve their highest veneration for persons who abstained from them, exalting them under the special titles of saints, nuns, priests, angels, gods and the like.

HERM. Not always. There were people called Greeks who had dozens of gods whose adventures were scandalously sensual. They poisoned an old man for trying to teach their young men to reason. Serve him right, too; for some of his reasonings were sheer logomachies: in England called puns.

ROSE. True. Another set of them, called Jews or Israelites, tortured a young man to death for trying to persuade them that the divinity they worshipped was in themselves, and promising that if they killed him he would rise from the dead and establish a kingdom of righteousness not among angels in the clouds but on earth among human men and women.

HERM. That was not why they killed him: they believed anyone who promised that much. They killed him because he made a riot in their temple and drove out the money changers, whom he mistook for thieves, being too young and not enough of a financier to know how useful and necessary they were to pilgrims. His name was Hitler, poor chap!

ROSE. All the same, utterly as we are unlike these primitive savages, we are descended from them; and though we manufacture ourselves scientifically, we are not yet agreed as to the sort of mankind we ought to make, nor how many at a time, nor how long they ought to last. We all want the Just Man Made Perfect; but when the chemists ask us for an exact prescription of the necessary protoplasms, hormones, vitamins, enzymes and the rest, we never agree on the last milligram of each ingredient: and it is that milligram that determines whether the resulting product will be a poet or a mathematician.

HERM. I'm against all this. It revolts me. I tell you again and again we shall never make decent human beings out of chemical salts. We must get rid of our physical bodies altogether, except for stuffed specimens in the Natural History Museum. I dont want to be a body: I want to be a mind and nothing but a mind. In the sixteenth century men made it their first article of religion to worship a god who had neither body, parts, nor passions: sensual passions. Even in the dark ages of the nineteenth and twentieth centuries there was a man who aspired to be a vortex in thought, and a woman who declared that the mind made the body and not the body the mind. Demolish all the laboratories. Build temples in which we can pray and pray and pray for deliverance from our bodies until the change occurs naturally as all real changes do.

ROSE. My child, how much farther would that take us? We should still be unable to agree on what sort of mind we needed. Prayer, we know, is a great creative power; but to pray effectively you must know what to pray for. In the sixteenth century there was a famous mathematician who declared that our utmost knowledge was no more than a grain of sand picked up on the margin of the ocean of our ignorance. He was a silly fellow who thought that the world was only forty centuries old and that straight lines were ethically right; but the utmost that we know is still no more than his grain of sand. I would like to be a mind without a body; but that has not happened to me yet; and meanwhile, as another sixteenth [century] sage said, the world must be peopled; and as we can no longer endure the old unmentionable methods we must make material citizens out of material substances in biochemical laboratories. I was manufactured that way myself; and so were you, my boy.

HERM. My body was, and my mind such as it is. But my desire to get rid of my body was not. Where did that come from? Can you tell me?

ROSE. No; but when we know even that, it will be only another grain of sand on the seashore. But it will be worth picking up; and so will all the other grains.

SHAMROCK. In the infinity of time, when the oceans dry up and make no more sand, we shall pick them all up. What then?

ROSE. The pursuit of knowledge and power will never end.

Sixth and Last Fable

As before, except that the building is now labelled

SIXTH FORM SCHOOL
SCHEDULED HISTORIC MONUMENT

On the terrace are five students in class, wearing uniforms with six sleeve stripes. Their individual numbers are on their caps. Numbers 1, 2, 3, are youths. 4 and 5 are maidens. Number 1 is older than number 2, number 4 than number 5.

The teacher, a matron, in cap and gown, enters from the building and takes her place.

TEACHER. Let me introduce myself. You have just been promoted to the sixth form. I am your teacher. Explain to me how and why the sixth form differs from the fifth.

YOUTH 1. We shall explain nothing to you. If you are our teacher it is for us to question you: not for you to question us.

MAIDEN 5. Do not be prehistoric. Savages thousands of years ago schooled their children by asking them conundrums and beating them if they could not answer them. You are not going to start that game on us, are you?

YOUTH 3. If you do, Mother Hubbard, youll not have a happy time with us.

TEACHER. You are quite right. It is what I expected you to say. My question was a test. Three of you have shewn that you understand the relation between us as teacher and pupils in the sixth form. The rest of you, if you also agree, will signify the same in the usual manner.

All the students raise their hands in assent.

TEACHER. Good. Now fire away. Ask your questions.

YOUTH 3. What questions shall we ask?

TEACHER. Aha! You see it is not so easy to ask questions. Is there nothing you want to know? If not, the sixth form is not for you: it is out of your mental range; and you can go back to the fifth form and take your leaving certificate.

YOUTH 3. Oh I say! Give me time to think of something.

TEACHER. Two minutes; or back to the fifth you go.

YOUTH 2 [*prompting*] Ask her whether when a pine cone disappears

174

into the ground it is the ground that wraps the pine cone up or the cone that buries itself into the clay.

TEACHER. Good, Number Two. I dont know; and neither does anyone else. And you, Number Three, do you really want to know?

YOUTH 3. No. I didnt know that cones bury themselves; and I dont care a dump whether they do or not.

TEACHER. Dont care a dump is vulgar. You should say dont care a dam.

YOUTH 3. Oh, I'm not literary. What does dam mean?

TEACHER. It means a negligible trifle.

YOUTH 2. Wrong, Teacher. My Dark Ages dictionary defines it as a form of profanity in use among clergymen.

TEACHER. In the sixth form, the teacher is always wrong.

YOUTH 1. You are both wrong. It means an animal's mother.

MAIDEN 5. No it doesnt. It means a wall across a river valley to pen it up as a lake.

YOUTH 3. All I meant is what the teacher says.

TEACHER. And so the teacher is always right. For announcing this, Number Three, I'll give you another minute to ask me a question that you do really care about.

YOUTH 3. Why are you so down on me? I am not the only one who hasnt a question ready for you.

TEACHER. The sixth form should be bursting with questions. I'll come to the others presently. I pick on you because your looks do not suggest more than fifth form brains.

YOUTH 1. Dont look at his face. Look at his fingers.

TEACHER. Fingers are not brains.

YOUTH 3. Yes they are. My brains are in my fingers: yours are only in your head. Have you ever invented a machine and constructed it?

TEACHER. No. Have you?

YOUTH 3. Yes.

TEACHER. How?

YOUTH 3. I dont know. I cant find words for it: I'm no talker. But I can do things. And I wont go down to the fifth. Here I am and here I stick, whatever you say.

TEACHER. So you shall. You know your own mind, though you cannot speak it.

YOUTH 3. I have no mind. I can only do things.

MAIDEN 4. I have a question, Teacher.

TEACHER. Out with it.

MAIDEN 4. How is it that the things that come into Number Three's head never come into mine? Why can he do things that I cant do?

Why can I do things that he cant do? I can write an essay: he cant write even a specification of the machines he invents. If you ask him to, he can only twiddle his fingers as if they were wheels and levers? He has to employ a Third Form patent agent to describe it for him.

TEACHER. Ah, now we are coming to the riddle of the universe. You young things always ask it, and will not take 'I don't know' for an answer. Can any of you tell me the story of the Sphinx?

MAIDEN 5. I can. The Spinx was a quadruped with a woman's head and breasts, who put conundrums to everyone who came along, and devoured them if they could not answer them.

TEACHER. Yes: that is the story. But where is the interest of it for you?

MAIDEN 5. Well, a story is a story. I like stories.

MAIDEN 4. She does, Teacher: she is always reading them. And she tells stories about herself. All lies.

YOUTH 2. Why does she tell lies? That is what I want to know.

YOUTH 3. The Sphinx story is rot. Why should the Sphinx eat everybody who couldnt answer its riddles?

YOUTH 1. Why should it kill itself if anyone did answer them? Tell me that.

TEACHER. Never ask why. Ask what, when, where, how, who, which; but never why. Only first form children, who think their parents know everything, ask why. In the sixth form you are supposed to know that why is unanswerable.

YOUTH 3. Nonsense. Why is not unanswerable. Why does water boil? Because its temperature has been raised to 100 Centigrade. What is wrong with that?

TEACHER. That is not why: it is how. Why was it boiled?

YOUTH 2. Because some fellow wanted to boil an egg and eat it. That is why.

TEACHER. Why did he want to eat it?

YOUTH 2. Because he wanted to live and not starve.

TEACHER. That is a fact, not a reason. Why did he want to live?

YOUTH 2. Like everybody else, I suppose.

TEACHER. Why does everybody want to live, however unhappily? Why does anybody want to live?

YOUTH 3. How the devil does anybody know? You dont know. I dont know.

TEACHER. Why dont we know?

YOUTH 2. Because we dont. Thats why.

TEACHER. No. Why is beyond knowledge. All the whys lead to the great interrogation mark that shines for ever across the sky like a rainbow. Why do we exist? Why does the universe exist?

YOUTH I. If you ask me I should say the universe is a big joke.

MAIDEN 4. I do not see any fun in it. I should say it is a big mistake.

YOUTH 2. A joke must have a joker. A mistake must have a blunderer. If the world exists it must have a creator.

TEACHER. Must it? How do you know? One of the ancient gods, named Napoleon, pointed to the sky full of stars and said 'Who made all that?' His soothsayer replied 'Whoever it was, who made Him?'

MAIDEN 4. Or Her? Why –

TEACHER. Order, order! Let us have no more whys. They only set you chasing your own tails, like cats. Let us get to work. I call for questions beginning with how.

MAIDEN 5. How do thoughts come into our heads? I dont have a lot of thoughts like Number Four here. She is a highbrow; but I was born quite emptyheaded. Yet I get thoughts that nobody ever suggested to me. Where did they come from?

TEACHER. As to that, there are many theories. Have you none of your own, any of you?

YOUTH 2. My grandfather lectured about the theory of the Disembodied Races. I picked it up from him when I was a kid. Of course the old man is now out-of-date: I dont take him seriously; but the theory sticks in my head because Ive never thought of anything better.

YOUTH I. Our biology professor in the fifth swore by it. But I cannot quite stomach it.

TEACHER. Can you give me a reason for that?

YOUTH I. Well, I was brought up to consider that we are the vanguard of civilization, the last step in creative evolution. But according to the theory we are only a survival of the sort of mankind that existed in the twentieth century, no better than black beetles compared to the supermen who evolved into the disembodied. I am not a black beetle.

YOUTH 3. Rot! If we were black beetles, the supermen would have tramped on us and killed us, or poisoned us with phosphorus.

YOUTH I. They may be keeping us for their amusement, as we keep our pets. I told you the universe is a joke. That is my theory.

MAIDEN 5. But where do our thoughts come from? They must be flying about in the air. My father never said 'I think.' He always said 'It strikes me.' When I was a child I thought that something in the air had hit him.

YOUTH I. What is the use of talking such utter nonsense? How could people get rid of their bodies?

TEACHER. People actually did get rid of their bodies. They got rid of their tails, of their fur, of their teeth. They acquired thumbs and enlarged their brains. They seem to have done what they liked with their bodies.

YOUTH 2. Anyhow, they had to eat and drink. They couldnt have done so without stomachs and bowels.

TEACHER. Yes they could: at least so the histories say. They found they could live on air, and that eating and drinking caused diseases of which their bodies died.

YOUTH 2. You believe that!!!

TEACHER. I believe nothing. But there is the same evidence for it as for anything else that happened millions of years before we were born. It is so written and recorded. As I can neither witness the past nor foresee the future I must take such history as there is as part of my framework of thought. Without such a framework I cannot think any more than a carpenter can cut wood without a saw.

YOUTH 2. Now you are getting beyond me, Teacher. I dont understand.

TEACHER. Do not try to understand. You must be content with such brains as you have until more understanding comes to you. Your question is where our thoughts come from and how they strike us, as Number Five's father put it. The theory is that the Disembodied Races still exist as Thought Vortexes, and are penetrating our thick skulls in their continual pursuit of knowledge and power, since they need our hands and brains as tools in that pursuit.

MAIDEN 4. Some of our thoughts are damnably mischievous. We slaughter one another and destroy the cities we build. What puts that into our heads? Not the pursuit of knowledge and power.

TEACHER. Yes; for the pursuit of knowledge and power involves the slaughter and destruction of everything that opposes it. The disembodied must inspire the soldier and the hunter as well as the pacifist and philanthropist.

YOUTH 1. But why should anybody oppose it if all thoughts come from well meaning vortexes?

TEACHER. Because even the vortexes have to do their work by trial and error. They have to learn by mistakes as well as by successes. We have to destroy the locust and the hook worm and the Colorado beetle because, if we did not, they would destroy us. We have to execute criminals who have no conscience and are incorrigible. They are old experiments of the Life Force. They were well intentioned and perhaps necessary at the time. But they are no longer either useful or necessary, and must now be exterminated. They cannot be exterminated by disembodied thought. The mongoose must be inspired to kill the cobra, the chemist to distil poisons, the physicist to make nuclear bombs, others to be big game hunters, judges, executioners, and killers of all sorts, often the most amiable of mortals outside their specific functions as destroyers of vermin. The ruthless foxhunter loves dogs: the physicist and chemists adore their children and keep animals as pets.

YOUTH 2. Look here, Teacher. Talk sense. Do these disembodied thoughts die when their number is up, as we do? If not, there can hardly be room for them in the universe after all these millions of centuries.

MAIDEN 5. Yes: that is what I want to know. How old is the world?

TEACHER. We do not know. We lost count in the dark ages that followed the twentieth century. There are traces of many civilizations that followed; and we may yet discover traces of many more. Some of them were atavistic.

MAIDEN 5. At a what?

TEACHER. Atavistic. Not an advance on the civilization before it, but a throw-back to an earlier one. Like those children of ours who cannot get beyond the First Form, and grow up to be idiots or savages. We kill them. But we are ourselves a throw-back to the twentieth century, and may be killed as idiots and savages if we meet a later and higher civilization.

YOUTH I. I dont believe it. We are the highest form of life and the most advanced civilization yet evolved.

YOUTH 2. Same here. Who can believe this fairy tale about disembodied thoughts? There is not a scrap of evidence for it. Nobody can believe it.

MAIDEN 4. Steady, Number Two: steady. Lots of us can believe it and do believe it. Our schoolfellows who have never got beyond the third or fourth form believe in what they call the immortality of the soul.

YOUTH I [*contemptuously*] Yes, because they are afraid to die.

TEACHER. That makes no difference. What is an immortal soul but a disembodied thought? I have received this morning a letter from a man who tells me he was for nineteen years a chain smoker of cigarets. He had no religious faith; but one day he chanced on a religious meeting in the park, and heard the preacher exhorting his flock to listen to the voice of God. He said it would surely come to them and guide them. The smoker tried the experiment of listening just for fun; and soon his head was filled with the words 'Quit smoking. Quit smoking.' He quitted without the least difficulty, and has never smoked since, though he had tried before and always failed. What was that but the prompting of a disembodied thought? Millions of our third and fourth form people believe it.

YOUTH 2. Well, I am sixth form; and I dont believe it. Your correspondent is just a liar.

MAIDEN 4. What rubbish you talk, Number Two! Do fourth form people let themselves be eaten by lions in the circus, burnt at the stake, or live lives of unselfish charity rather than stop telling lies? It is much more likely that you are a fool.

YOUTH 2. May be; but that does not answer the question.

MAIDEN 5. Hear hear! The smoker may be a liar or Number Two a fool; but where did the thoughts come from? What puts them into our heads? The preachers say they are whispered by God. Anyhow they are whispered; and I want to know exactly how.

TEACHER. Like all young things you want to begin by knowing everything. I can give you only the advice of the preachers: listen until you are told.

A youth, clothed in feathers like a bird, appears suddenly.

TEACHER. Hullo! Who are you? What are you doing here?

THE FEATHERED ONE. I am an embodied thought. I am what you call the word made flesh.

YOUTH 3. Rats! How did you get here? Not by your wings: you havnt got any. You are a Cockyolly Bird.

THE FEATHERED ONE. I do not fly: I levitate. Call me Cockyolly if you like. But it would be more respectful to call me Raphael.

MAIDEN 4. Why should we respect you in that ridiculous costume?

THE TEACHER. Do you seriously wish us to believe that you are one of the disembodied, again incarnate?

RAPHAEL. Why not? Evolution can go backwards as well as forwards. If the body can become a vortex, the vortex can also become a body.

THE TEACHER. And you are such a body?

RAPHAEL. I am curious to know what it is like to be a body. Curiosity never dies.

MAIDEN 4. How do you like it so far?

RAPHAEL. I do not like nor dislike. I experience.

YOUTH 3. That nonsense will not go down here, Cocky. It sounds smart enough; but it means nothing. Why should we respect you?

RAPHAEL. You had better. I am restraining my magnetic field. If I turned it on it would kill you.

MAIDEN 5. Dont provoke him, Number Three. I feel awful.

MAIDEN 4. You cannot experience bodied life unless you have a girl, and marry, and have children, as we do. Have you brought a girl with you?

RAPHAEL. No. I stop short of your eating and drinking and so forth, and of your reproductive methods. They revolt me.

MAIDEN 4. No passions, then?

RAPHAEL. On the contrary: intellectual passion, mathematical passion, passion for discovery and exploration: the mightiest of all the passions.

THE TEACHER. But none of our passions?

RAPHAEL. Yes. Your passion for teaching.

YOUTH 2. Then you have come to teach us?

RAPHAEL. No. I am here to learn, not to teach. I pass on. [*He vanishes*].

ALL [*screaming*] Hi! Stop! Come back! We have a lot to ask you. Dont go yet. Wait a bit, Raphael.

YOUTH 3. No use. He has invented some trick of vanishing before he is found out. He is only a Confidence Trick man.

THE TEACHER. Nonsense! He did not ask us for anything.

MAIDEN 4. He was just sampling us.

YOUTH 1. He told us nothing. We know nothing.

YOUTH 3. Rot! You want to know too much. We know how to make cyclotrons and hundred inch telescopes. We have harnessed atomic energy. He couldnt make a safety pin or a wheelbarrow to save his life.

THE TEACHER. Enough. We can never want to know too much. Attention! [*All rise*]. You will get at the schoolbook counter copies of an old poem called The Book of Job. You will read it through; and –

YOUTH 2. I read it through when I was thirteen. It was an argument between an old josser named Job and one of the old gods, who pretended he had made the universe. Job said if so he had made it very unfairly. But what use is all that to me? I dont believe the old god made the universe.

TEACHER. You will read the book over again from the point of view that the old god made no such pretence, and crushed Job by shewing that he could put ten times as many unanswerable questions to Job as Job could put to him. It will teach you that I can do the same to you. All will read the book and ask questions or write essays before next Friday.

A jubilant march is heard.

TEACHER. Lunch. March. [*Beating time*] Left-right, left-right, left-right. *They tramp out rhythmically.*

Shakes Versus Shav:

A Puppet Play

with

Preface

Preface

This in all actuarial probability is my last play and the climax of my eminence, such as it is. I thought my career as a playwright was finished when Waldo Lanchester of the Malvern Marionette Theatre, our chief living puppet master, sent me figures of two puppets, Shakespear and myself, with a request that I should supply one of my famous dramas for them, not to last longer than ten minutes or thereabouts. I accomplished this feat, and was gratified by Mr Lanchester's immediate approval.

I have learnt part of my craft as conductor of rehearsals (producer, they call it) from puppets. Their unvarying intensity of facial expression, impossible for living actors, keeps the imagination of the spectators continuously stimulated. When one of them is speaking or tumbling and the rest left aside, these, though in full view, are invisible, as they should be. Living actors have to learn that they too must be invisible while the protagonists are conversing, and therefore must not move a muscle nor change their expression, instead of, as beginners mostly do, playing to them and robbing them of the audience's undivided attention.

Puppets have also a fascination of their own, because there is nothing wonderful in a living actor moving and speaking, but that wooden headed dolls should do so is a marvel that never palls.

And they can survive treatment that would kill live actors. When I first saw them in my boyhood nothing delighted me more than when all the puppets went up in a balloon and presently dropped from the skies with an appalling crash on the floor.

Nowadays the development of stagecraft into filmcraft may destroy the idiosyncratic puppet charm. Televised puppets could enjoy the scenic backgrounds of the cinema. Sound recording could enable the puppet master to give all his attention to the strings he is manipulating, the dialogue being spoken by a company of first-rate speakers as in the theatre. The old puppet master spoke all the parts himself in accents which he differentiated by Punch-and-Judy squeaks and the like. I can imagine the puppets simulating living performers so perfectly that the spectators will be completely illuded. The result would be the death of puppetry; for it would lose its charm with its magic. So let reformers beware.

Nothing can extinguish my interest in Shakespear. It began when I was a small boy, and extends to Stratford-upon-Avon, where I have attended so many bardic festivals that I have come to regard it almost as a supplementary birthplace of my own.

No year passes without the arrival of a batch of books contending that Shakespear was somebody else. The argument is always the same. Such early works as Venus and Adonis, Lucrece, and Love's Labour's Lost, could not possibly have been written by an illiterate clown and poacher who could hardly write his own name. This is unquestionably true. But the inference that Shakespear did not write them does not follow. What does follow is that Shakespear was not an illiterate clown but a well read grammar-schooled son in a family of good middle-class standing, cultured enough to be habitual playgoers and private entertainers of the players.

This, on investigation, proves to be exactly what Shakespear was. His father, John Shakespear, Gent, was an alderman who demanded a coat of arms which was finally granted. His mother was of equal rank and social pretension. John finally failed commercially, having no doubt let his artist turn get the better of his mercantile occupation, and leave him unable to afford a university education for William, had he ever wanted to make a professional scholar of him.

These circumstances interest me because they are just like my own. They were a considerable cut above those of Bunyan and Cobbett, both great masters of language, who nevertheless could not have written Venus and Adonis nor Love's Labour's Lost. One does not forget Bunyan's 'The Latin I Borrow.' Shakespear's standing was nearer to Ruskin's, whose splendid style owes much more to his mother's insistence on his learning the Bible by heart than to his Oxford degree.

So much for Bacon-Shakespear and all the other fables founded on that entirely fictitious figure Shaxper or Shasper the illiterate bumpkin.

Enough too for my feeling that the real Shakespear might have been myself, and for the shallow mistaking of it for mere professional jealousy.

Ayot Saint Lawrence, 1949

Shakes enters and salutes the audience with a flourish of his hat.

SHAKES. Now is the winter of our discontent
  Made glorious summer by the Malvern sun.
  I, William Shakes, was born in Stratford town,
  Where every year a festival is held
  To honour my renown not for an age
  But for all time. Hither I raging come
  An infamous impostor to chastize,
  Who in an ecstasy of self-conceit
  Shortens my name to Shav, and dares pretend
  Here to reincarnate my very self,
  And in your stately playhouse to set up
  A festival, and plant a mulberry
  In most presumptuous mockery of mine.
  Tell me, ye citizens of Malvern,
  Where I may find this caitiff. Face to face
  Set but this fiend of Ireland and myself;
  And leave the rest to me. [*Shav enters*]. Who art thou?
  That rearst a forehead almost rivalling mine?
SHAV. Nay, who art thou, that knowest not these features
  Pictured throughout the globe? Who should I be
  But G. B. S.?
SHAKES. What! Stand, thou shameless fraud.
  For one or both of us the hour is come.
  Put up your hands.
SHAV. Come on.
    *They spar. Shakes knocks Shav down with a straight left and begins
    counting him out, stooping over him and beating the seconds with his finger.*
SHAKES. Hackerty-backerty one, Hackerty-backerty two.
Hackerty-backerty three . . . Hackerty-backerty nine –
    *At the count of nine Shav springs up and knocks Shakes down with a right
    to the chin.*
SHAV [*counting*] Hackerty-backerty one, . . . Hackerty-backerty ten. Out.
SHAKES. Out! And by thee! Never. [*He rises*]. Younger you are
  By full three hundred years, and therefore carry
  A heavier punch than mine; but what of that?

187

Death will soon finish you; but as for me,
Not marble nor the gilded monuments
Of princes –
SHAV. – shall outlive your powerful rhymes.
So you have told us: I have read your sonnets.
SHAKES. Couldst write Macbeth?
SHAV. No need. He has been bettered
  By Walter Scott's Rob Roy. Behold, and blush.
    *Rob Roy and Macbeth appear, Rob in Highland tartan and kilt with
    claymore, Macbeth in kingly costume.*
MACBETH. Thus far into the bowels of the land
  Have we marched on without impediment.
  Shall I still call you Campbell?
ROB [*in a strong Scotch accent*] Caumill me no Caumills.
  Ma fet is on ma native heath: ma name's Macgregor.
MACBETH. I have no words. My voice is in my sword. Lay on, Rob Roy;
  And damned be he that proves the smaller boy.
    *He draws and stands on guard. Rob draws; spins round several times like
    a man throwing a hammer; and finally cuts off Macbeth's head at one
    stroke.*
ROB. Whaur's your Wullie Shaxper the noo?
    Bagpipe and drum music, to which Rob dances off.
MACBETH [*headless*] I will return to Stratford: the hotels
  Are cheaper there. [*He picks up his head, and goes off with it under his
  arm to the tune of British Grenadiers*].
SHAKES. Call you this cateran
  Better than my Macbeth, one line from whom
  Is worth a thousand of your piffling plays.
SHAV. Quote one. Just one. I challenge thee. One line.
SHAKES. 'The shardborne beetle with his drowsy hum.'
SHAV. Hast never heard of Adam Lindsay Gordon?
SHAKES. A name that sings. What of him?
SHAV.   He eclipsed
  Thy shardborne beetle. Hear his mighty lines.
    [*Reciting*]
  'The beetle booms adown the glooms
  And bumps among the clumps.'
SHAKES [*roaring with laughter*] Ha ha! Ho ho! My lungs like chanticleer
  Must crow their fill. This fellow hath an ear.
  How does it run? 'The beetle booms –
SHAV. Adown the glooms –

SHAKES. And bumps –

SHAV. Among the clumps.' Well done, Australia!
  Shav laughs.

SHAKES. Laughest thou at thyself? Pullst thou my leg?

SHAV. There is more fun in heaven and earth, sweet William,
  Than is dreamt of in your philosophy.

SHAKES. Where is thy Hamlet? Couldst thou write King Lear?

SHAV. Aye, with his daughters all complete. Couldst thou
  Have written Heartbreak House? Behold my Lear.
  *A transparency is suddenly lit up, shewing Captain Shotover seated, as in
  Millais' picture called North-West Passage, with a young woman of virginal
  beauty.*

SHOTOVER [*raising his hand and intoning*] I built a house for my daugh-
  ters and opened the doors thereof
  That men might come for their choosing, and their betters spring from
    their love;
  But one of them married a numskull: the other a liar wed;
  And now she must lie beside him even as she made her bed.

THE VIRGIN. 'Yes: this silly house, this strangely happy house, this
  agonizing house, this house without foundations. I shall call it Heartbreak House.'

SHOTOVER. Enough. Enough. Let the heart break in silence.
  The picture vanishes.

SHAKES. You stole that word from me: did I not write
  'The heartache and the thousand natural woes
  That flesh is heir to'?

SHAV.   You were not the first
  To sing of broken hearts. I was the first
  That taught your faithless Timons how to mend them.

SHAKES. Taught what you could not know. Sing if you can
  My cloud capped towers, my gorgeous palaces,
  My solemn temples. The great globe itself,
  Yea, all which it inherit, shall dissolve –

SHAV.   – and like this foolish little show of ours
  Leave not a wrack behind. So you have said.
  I say the world will long outlast our day.
  Tomorrow and tomorrow and tomorrow
  We puppets shall replay our scene. Meanwhile,
  Immortal William dead and turned to clay
  May stop a hole to keep the wind away.
  Oh that that earth which kept the world in awe

Should patch a wall t' expel the winter's flaw!

SHAKES. These words are mine, not thine.

SHAV.   Peace, jealous Bard:

We both are mortal. For a moment suffer
My glimmering light to shine.

A light appears between them.

SHAKES. Out, out, brief candle! [*He puffs it out*].

Darkness. The play ends.

THE END

Why She Would Not:

A Little Comedy

Scene I

A path through a wood. A fine summer afternoon. A lady, goodlooking, well dressed, and not over thirty, is being conducted along the path by a burly and rather dangerous looking man, middle aged, ugly, dressed in a braided coat and mutton pie cap which give him the air of being a hotel porter or commissionaire of some sort.

THE LADY [*stopping*] Where are we now? I should hardly call this a short cut.

THE MAN [*truculently*] I'm damned if I know. Two miles from anywhere.

THE LADY. But you must know. You are a forest guide.

THE MAN. Guide my foot! I'm no bloody guide. How much money have you got on you?

THE LADY. Why?

THE MAN. Because I mean to have it off you, see? Hand over.

THE LADY. Do you mean to rob me? You said you were a guide; and we agreed for seven-and-sixpence. I meant to give you ten shillings if you were civil; but now I will give you your seven-and-sixpence and not a penny more. If you dare try to rob me I'll call the police.

THE MAN. Call away. There isnt a copper within five miles. Are them pearls round your neck real? Whether or no I mean to have them. You have three pounds in notes in your handbag: I saw them when you paid your taxi. Are you going to hand over quietly or shall I have to take them? It'll hurt a bit.

A YOUNG MALE VOICE [*very affable*] Is there anything amiss? Can I help?

The Man and the Lady start violently, not having noticed the newcomer until he arrives between them. He is a likeable looking juvenile in a workman's cap, but otherwise might by his clothes be an artisan off duty or a gentleman. His accent is that of a wellbred man.

THE MAN [*ferociously*] Who the hell are you?

THE NEWCOMER. Nobody but a tramp looking for a job.

THE MAN. Well, dont you come interfering with me. Get out of here, double quick.

THE NEWCOMER [*sunnily*] I'm in no hurry. The lady might like me to stay. If she wants a witness I'm on the job.

THE LADY. Oh yes: please stay. This man is trying to rob me.

THE NEWCOMER. Oh dear! That wont do, you know, matey. Thou shalt not steal.

THE MAN [*with exaggerated fierceness*] Who are you calling matey? Listen here. Are you going to get out or have I to sling you out?

THE NEWCOMER [*gaily*] You can try. I'm game for a scrap. Fists, catch as catch can, up and down wrestling, or all three together? Be quick. The mounted police patrol will pass at six. Take off your coat; and come on.

THE MAN [*he is an abject coward*] Easy, governor, easy. I dont want no fighting. All I asked of the lady was my money for guiding her.

THE NEWCOMER [*to the Lady*] Give it to him and get rid of him.

THE LADY. I never refused to give it to him. Here it is. [*She gives the Man five shillings*].

THE MAN [*humbly*] Thank you, lady. [*He hurries away, almost running*].

THE LADY. How brave of you to offer to fight that big man!

THE NEWCOMER. Bluff, dear lady, pure bluff. A bully is not always a coward; but a big coward is almost always a bully. I took his measure; that is all. Where do you want to go to?

THE LADY. To Timbertown. I live there. I am Miss White of Four Towers: a very famous old house. I can reward you handsomely for rescuing me when I get home.

THE NEWCOMER. I know the way. A mile and a half. Can you walk it?

THE LADY. Yes of course. I can walk ten miles.

THE NEWCOMER. Right O! Follow me.

They go off together.

Scene II

At the gates of a pretentious country house surrounded by a high stone wall and overshadowed by heavy elm trees. The wall is broken by four sham towers with battlemented tops.

The Newcomer and the Lady arrive. She opens her bag and takes out a key to unlock the wicket.

THE LADY. Here we are. This is my house.

THE NEWCOMER [*looking at it*] Oh. Is it?

He is not as much impressed as she expected. She fingers the cash pocket in her bag, and is obviously embarrassed.

THE NEWCOMER. You are safe at home now. I must hurry into the town to get a night's lodging. Goodnight, lady. [*He turns to go*].

THE LADY. O please wait a moment. I hardly know –

THE NEWCOMER. How much to tip me, eh?

THE LADY. Well, I must reward you. You have done me a great service. I promised –

THE NEWCOMER. You did. But rescuing ladies from robbers is not my profession: it is only my amusement as an amateur. But you can do something for me. You said your name was White. Your people are the greatest timber merchants and woodmen in the county. Well, I'm a carpenter of sorts. Could you get me a job in the timber yard at three pound ten a week? I cant live on less.

THE LADY. Oh, I'm sure I can. My grandfather is chairman of the Board. My brother is manager. What is your name? Where do you live?

THE NEWCOMER. My name is Henry Bossborn. I live nowhere, or where I can: I have no address. I'll call on Thursday at your kitchen door: you can leave word with your maid if there is any news for me. Good night.

THE LADY [*very graciously*] Au revoir.

BOSSBORN. Not necessarily. Adieu: remember me.

He goes decisively. She unlocks the wicket and goes home.

Scene III

The boardroom of White Sons and Bros Ltd. In the chair old Reginald White, still keen and attentive, but mostly silent. Jasper White, domineering but not quite up to his father's mark. Montgomery Smith, counting-house chief, and two clerks who make notes but say nothing, and three or four members of the Board, silent lookers-on. Bossborn, looking quite smart in a clean white collar and well brushed suit, is before them, bareheaded.

OLD REGINALD. Well, Bossborn, you have done a plucky service to my granddaughter, Miss Serafina White, who holds many shares in this concern.

BOSSBORN. Oh, nothing, sir. I could have killed the fellow.

OLD REGINALD. The lady says he was twice your size and weight. We must find you a job. You want one, dont you?

BOSSBORN. I want three pound ten a week, sir. I must live.

OLD REGINALD. You are a white collar case, I suppose. We shall have to make room for you in the counting house.

BOSSBORN. No, sir, manual worker, carpenter on the wages list. Three pound ten and the usual bonus, same as the rest in the carpenters' shop.

OLD REGINALD. Oh well, if you prefer it: that will be easy. [*To Jasper*] Tell him his duties.

JASPER [*much more distant and peremptory*] Youll be here at six on Monday morning, and clock in sharp to the minute. We dont allow unpunctuality here. The foreman will direct you to a place on the bench, where you will be expected to work – to work, mind you, not to dawdle – until eleven, when you can knock off for five minutes for a cup of tea. Half an hour off for a meal at one. Work again at the bench until four. Overtime wages one and a half. Five day week: nothing on Saturdays. A week's notice if you are a slacker. Thats all. You can go.

BOSSBORN. I'm very grateful to you gentlemen for offering me this job. But I'm afraid it will not suit me. I must take to the road again.

JASPER. Why? It is what you ask for.

BOSSBORN. I'm not that sort of man. I cant clock in, and work at regular hours at the bench. I cant do what you call work at all. It is not in my nature. I must come when I like and go when I like and stay away when I like. I get up at eight, breakfast at nine, and read the papers until ten. I've never in my life got up at five in the morning.

JASPER. In short, you are an unemployable walking gentleman. You expect to be paid three pound ten a week for doing nothing.

BOSSBORN. Three pound ten and the bonus. Not exactly for doing nothing. I ask to have the run of the works and just loaf round to see if there is anything I can do.

SMITH. Well, of all the –! Just to snoop round and find out all our trade secrets and sell them to the next timber yard.

OLD REGINALD. We have no secrets here. All the world is welcome to learn the ways of White Ltd. Straightforward work and first quality. Let those who can copy us and welcome.

SMITH. Yes, sir, we know that. But this young fellow can make a living by going from one firm to another, taking a job and being sacked as a slacker at a fortnight's notice; then going on to the next shop and doing it again.

BOSSBORN. I can meet you on that. Take me on for a fortnight on my own terms. If at the end of the fortnight you find me worth keeping for another week you pay me for the whole three weeks; but if you find me no use I get no wages at all. nothing but the sack.

OLD REGINALD. How is that, Mr Smith?

SMITH. Well, sir, if you want a sleeping partner, this is the man for you. That is all I can say.

OLD REGINALD [*rising*] We'll try him. Come with me, Bossborn: my granddaughter is waiting in my private room to hear how you have got on.

BOSSBORN. Good morning, gentlemen. [*He follows old Reginald out*].

SMITH. The old man is going dotty. You really ought to take over, Mr Jasper.

JASPER. Let him have his way. We shall soon be rid of this rotter.

Scene IV

The drawingroom of Four Towers, overcrowded with massive early Victorian furniture, thick curtains, small but heavy tables crowded with nicnacs, sea shells, stuffed birds in glass cases, carpets and wall paper with huge flower designs, movement obstructed and light excluded in every possible way.

Two years have elapsed since the incident in the wood.

Bossborn, now a very smart city man, matured and important looking, is being entertained by Serafina.

BOSSBORN. Twice round the world!

SERAFINA. Yes, twice. And a winter in Durban.

BOSSBORN. Why twice?

SERAFINA. Once for sightseeing. But life in a pleasure ship is so easy and comfortable and careless and social that at the end of the trip you just stick to the ship and start again for another round-the-world cruise, mostly with the same people. Quite a lot of them spend their lives going round and round. It costs only about a thousand a year; and everything is done for you.

BOSSBORN. Then why did you come back here?

SERAFINA. Homesick. For me there is no place like Four Towers. Besides, I had to come back after father's death to settle about his will and all that. I shall never leave dear Four Towers again. I was born here; and I shall die here.

BOSSBORN. Hmmm! There are better places.

SERAFINA. Not for me. Nowhere on earth. But never mind that now. What about yourself? I hear you have made terrible changes in the company, and that you and Jasper are on very bad terms. You have pensioned off poor old Smith and dismissed four clerks who had been with us for sixteen years and never had a word against them.

BOSSBORN. Their work is done by a girl with a calculating and invoicing typewriter as big as herself. Smith was twenty-five years out of date. The waste of labor all over the place was frightful.

SERAFINA. Before I went away Jasper said that either you or he would have to go when father retired. We Whites like to be masters in our own house. I like to be mistress in mine.

BOSSBORN. Oh, that is all over. Ive trained Jasper in my methods, and am now in business on my own.

SERAFINA. Have you set up in opposition to us?

BOSSBORN. Not at all. I'm still a director and shareholder. My own business is land agency, dealer in real estate, private banking, building, and so on. Anything there is money in and that I understand.

SERAFINA. How wonderful! And only two years ago you were a tramp looking for a job.

BOSSBORN. And you got one for me. What can I do for you in return?

SERAFINA. Well, there is something you could perhaps advise me on. My old nurse and housekeeper thinks there is something wrong with the drainage here; and the gardener thinks that two of the four towers are not quite safe. Would you greatly mind if I asked you to have a look round and tell me if there is really anything wrong, and if so what I ought to do about it?

BOSSBORN. I need not look round. I have had my eye on Four Towers for some time; and I know it inside and out. There is no drainage.

SERAFINA. No drainage! But there must be.

BOSSBORN. Absolutely none. The sewage has been simply soaking into the soil for heaven knows how many years. None of the towers are worth repairing. The one thing to be done is blow them up, get rid of that prison wall, cut down those trees that shut out the sunlight, and knock down this ugly, unhealthy, troublesome, costly house. It is not fit to live in. I'll build you a modern house with a beautiful view in a better situation. This neighborhood was fashionable fifty years ago: it is now east end. I'll build six prefabricated villas lettable at moderate rents to replace your four rotten old towers and bring you in a tidy addition to your income.

SERAFINA [*rising in boiling wrath*] Mr Bossborn: leave my house.

BOSSBORN. Oh! [*rising*] Why?

198

SERAFINA. I can hardly speak. My house! My house, the great house of Timbertown. My beautiful house, built by my people and never lived in by anyone else. I was born here. And you dare –! Go; or I will call my servants to shew you out. And never approach my door again: it will be shut in your face.

BOSSBORN [*quite unmoved*] Think it over! I'll call again in a month. [*He goes promptly*].

Serafina rings the bell and strides about the room, raging, then rings again violently three times. Her old nurse-housekeeper rushes in, alarmed.

NURSE. Whats the matter, dearie?

SERAFINA. If that man calls here again, shut the door in his face. Slam it. Set the dog on him if he wont go. Tell the maids.

NURSE. Oh, we couldnt do that. Hes such a gentleman. We'll say you are not at home.

SERAFINA. Youll obey my orders. Gentleman! Do you know what he has done?

NURSE. No, dearie. It must be something dreadful to put you into a state like this. What was it?

SERAFINA. He said that my house – Four Towers! – is ugly, unhealthy, troublesome, not fit to live in. My house! The house I was born in.

NURSE [*unimpressed*] Well, you know, dearie, it is troublesome. We cant do without seven housemaids, and they are always complaining and wont stay long. There are always one or two of them sick. Theres no lift in the house with all those stairs to drag scuttles of coal up and down because there is no proper heating, only the old open grates. And the place is so dark with all those trees, and nothing to look at but a stone wall. In the kitchen they are always wondering why you live here instead of moving into a nice new house with every convenience.

SERAFINA [*astounded*] So you – you! – agree with him!

NURSE. Oh no, dearie, I could never agree with anyone against you. I know you think the world of the old house. But you can hardly blame the gentleman for saying what everybody says. He is such a nice gentleman. Think it over, dearie.

Scene V

The lounge in an ultra modern country house dated 1950, contrasting strangely with Four Towers. As before, Serafina hostess and Bossborn visitor.

BOSSBORN. Well, what is the matter today? Why have you sent for me?

SERAFINA. I want to have it out with you about my Thursday at-homes. You have stopped coming to them. Why?

BOSSBORN. Have I? Well, you see, I am full up of business all day. I have my own business to attend to all the forenoon, and in the afternoon there are Board meetings of directors and the County Council, and appointments of all sorts. Much as I like to turn up at your at-homes for the pleasure of seeing you I simply cannot find time for society and small talk. I am, unfortunately, a very busy man.

SERAFINA. How charmingly you pay out that budget of lies! A busy man can always find time to do anything he really wants to do, and excuses for everything he doesnt.

BOSSBORN. That is true. Ive not thought about it. To be quite frank, I dislike the society of ladies and gentlemen. They bore me. I am not at home among them. You know I am only an upstart tramp.

SERAFINA. Very clever. But a much bigger lie. I dont know where you got your courtly manners and the way you speak and carry your London clothes; but I know you are a cut above me socially, and look down on us poor provincials and tradespeople.

BOSSBORN. Well, suppose it is so. Let us assume that I was brought up as a court page, and was so bored by it that I broke loose from it, threw myself on the streets penniless just as Kropotkin when he grew out of being Tsar Alexander's page, chose an infantry regiment in Siberia instead of the Imperial Guards at the top of the tree in Petersburg. Such things happen. You may pretend that it happened to me. But if so does not this prove that I am not a snob?

SERAFINA. At last you may be telling the truth. But if you are not a snob why have you stopped coming to my at-homes? Answer me that.

BOSSBORN. What's the use of answering you if you will not believe a word I say? You seem to know the truth, whatever it may be. It is for you to tell it to me.

SERAFINA. The reason you have stopped coming is that you think I want to marry you.

BOSSBORN. Oh, nonsense!

SERAFINA. It is not nonsense. Do stop lying. It would be a social promotion for me. My old nurse, with her talk about your being a very nice gentleman, selected you for my husband from the time she first saw you. Everybody thinks I ought to get married before I am too old. If you came always to my at-homes they would think you are the man. That is what you are afraid of. You need not be afraid. I have sent for you to tell you that nothing on earth could induce me to marry you. So there. You can come as often as you like. I have no designs on you.

BOSSBORN. But have I offended you in any way? Are my manners inconsiderate?

SERAFINA. No. Your manners are perfect.

BOSSBORN. You just dont like me. Simply natural antipathy, eh?

SERAFINA. Not in the least. I like you and admire you more than any man I have ever known. You are a wonder.

BOSSBORN. Then why?

SERAFINA. I am afraid of you.

BOSSBORN. Afraid of me!!! Impossible. How? Why? Are you serious?

SERAFINA. Yes: afraid of you. Everybody is afraid of you.

BOSSBORN. Is there any use in saying that you have no reason to be afraid of me?

SERAFINA. Yes I have. I like to be mistress in my own house, as I was in Four Towers.

BOSSBORN. But you would be mistress in my house if we married.

SERAFINA. No one will ever be mistress in any house that you are in. Only your slaves and your bedfellow.

BOSSBORN. This bewilders me. Have I ever forced you to do anything you did not want to do?

SERAFINA. No; for I always had to do what you wanted me to do. I was happy at Four Towers: I loved it: I was born there and mistress of it and of myself: it was sacred to me. I turned you out of it for daring to say a word against it. Where is it now? And where am I? Just where you put me: I might as well have been a piece of furniture. Here in this house of your choosing and your building I have heard my four towers being blown up, bang, bang, bang, bang, striking on my heart like an earthquake; and I never lifted my finger to stop you as I could have done if I had been my own mistress. At the works, where my grandfather always had the last word until he died, you came; and with Jasper and Smith and all the rest against you, you turned the whole place inside out: poor old Smith and his clerks had to retire; Jasper had to knuckle under; our splendid old craftsmen had to learn new machines or be sacked and replaced by American mechanics.

BOSSBORN. Yes yes yes; but they consented: they were willing. I doubled, trebled, quadrupled the product and the profit. You could not live in Four Towers now because you are so enormously more comfortable and civilized here. You can all do far more as you like with the leisure my reforms give you than you could before I came. Leisure is the only reality of freedom. I coerce nobody: I only point out the way.

SERAFINA. Yes: your way, not our way.

BOSSBORN. Neither my way nor yours. The way of the world. Some people call it God's way.

SERAFINA. Anyhow I will live my own life, not yours. If I marry, my choice will not be a Bossborn.

BOSSBORN. Is that final?

SERAFINA. Yes. Friendship only.

BOSSBORN. So be it. Good day to you.

He rises and goes out promptly, as before.

MORE ABOUT PENGUINS, PELICANS AND PUFFINS

For further information about books available from Penguins please write to Dept EP, Penguin Books Ltd, Harmondsworth, Middlesex UB7 ODA.

In the U.S.A.: For a complete list of books available from Penguins in the United States write to Dept DG, Penguin Books, 299 Murray Hill Parkway, East Rutherford, New Jersey 07073.

In Canada: For a complete list of books available from Penguins in Canada write to Penguin Books Canada Ltd, 2801 John Street, Markham, Ontario L3R 1B4.

In Australia: For a complete list of books available from Penguins in Australia write to the Marketing Department, Penguin Books Australia Ltd, P.O. Box 257, Ringwood, Victoria 3134.

In New Zealand: For a complete list of books available from Penguins in New Zealand write to the Marketing Department, Penguin Books (N.Z.) Ltd, Private Bag, Takapuna, Auckland 9.

In India: For a complete list of books available from Penguins in India write to Penguin Overseas Ltd, 706 Eros Apartments, 56 Nehru Place, New Delhi 110019.

THE PENGUIN SHAW

Bernard Shaw's *The Intelligent Woman's Guide to Socialism, Capitalism, Sovietism, and Fascism* was the first Pelican book to be published, in May 1937. Since then many of his plays have been published as Penguins. All of them are complete with Shaw's original prefaces, which put the argument of his play in strong and witty terms and serve as examples of Shaw's individual and assertive press style. The following are published:

GEORGE BERNARD SHAW

The Black Girl in Search of God and some Lesser Tales

The centrepiece of this colourful collection is *The Black Girl in Search of God*, a tale in the manner of Voltaire's *Candide*. In her search for the true God, the black girl encounters a series of old gentlemen, generally clothed in long white nightshirts. When she is tired of arguing and of laying about her with her knobkerry, she settles down with a red-haired Irish socialist, following Voltaire's advice that the wisest attitude to life is to cultivate one's own garden.

The *Lesser Tales* range from a satirical fairy story featuring a charwoman's entry into heaven, to an obituary of an old revolutionary hero; from an essay (in dramatic form) on the theatre, to an exposition of Don Giovanni's character. All these tales bear the true Shavian imprint; some unashamedly pack a message, others satirize outworn ideas and institutions. All are confident and incisive.

Cashel Byron's Profession

Bernard Shaw was obsessed with prize-fighting all his life – he entered the English Amateur Boxing Association Championship as middleweight – and his racy, romantic, adventure story superbly evokes the bruised knuckles and raw hopes of the ringside.

After pole-axing his mathematics master with a perfect right, Cashel Byron, the unloved son of a successful actress, runs away to Australia. He returns, and becomes the most famous fighter of his age, only to be floored by the lovely and impossible Lydia Carew.

'Genuine and remarkable narrative talent ... a talent of strength, spirit, capacity ... it is all mad, mad and deliriously delightful ... All I ask is more of it' – Robert Louis Stevenson

Also published:

THE INTELLIGENT WOMAN'S GUIDE TO
SOCIALISM, CAPITALISM, SOVIETISM AND FASCISM

TENNESSEE WILLIAMS

Sweet Bird of Youth
A Streetcar Named Desire
The Glass Menagerie

Writing in 1959, at about the time when Elia Kazan directed *Sweet Bird of Youth* on Broadway, Tennessee Williams described his first successful play as being 'about as violent as you can get on the stage. During the nineteen years since then I have only produced five plays that are *not* violent.' First among these he placed *The Glass Menagerie*, the 'memory' play which was first presented in London in 1948 and in which he employed every device of scenery, lighting, and music to evoke nostalgia. The following year, however, he scored one of his biggest successes with *A Streetcar Named Desire*, in which a woman's pathetic fantasies of primness and respectability are stripped down and violently exposed in New Orleans.

Baby Doll
Something Unspoken
Suddenly Last Summer

The film of *Baby Doll* was produced and directed by Elia Kazan in 1956 from the screen-play contained in this volume – the original one written by Tennessee Williams. The *Daily Telegraph* called it 'a work of art – an absorbing study in frustration and poverty and racial intolerance', and *The Times*: 'That rare thing, a film script which makes easy and vivid reading.' John Osborne said of it: 'Williams has hit off the American Girl–Woman of the last hundred years . . . Make no mistake about it – this Baby Doll kid is a killer.'

Something Unspoken and *Suddenly Last Summer* were staged together under the title *Garden District* in 1958. The former is a humorous little vignette of the social manoeuvres of a wealthy Southern spinster. The latter, which was later scripted and filmed, is an intense and moving study of madness, of a man's escape from a mother-fixation, and of the revenge planned by the mother for the girl who liberated him and witnessed the final drama of his death.

NEW PENGUIN SHAKESPEARE

General Editor: T. J. B. Spencer